AQA History

AS
Unit 1

The Development of Germany, 1871–1925

Exclusively endorsed by AQA

Sally Waller

Nelson Thornes

Published in 2009 by:
Nelson Thornes Ltd
Delta Place
27 Bath Road
CHELTENHAM
GL53 7TH
United Kingdom

09 10 11 12 13 / 10 9 8 7 6 5 4 3 2 1

A catalogue record for this book is available from the British Library

978-1-4085-0314-0

Illustrations by: Angela Knowles, David Russell Illustration

Page make-up by Thomson Digital

Printed in Croatia by Zrinski

Contents

AQA introduction

Nelson Thornes and AQA

Nelson Thornes has worked in collaboration with AQA to ensure that this book offers you the best support for your AS or A level course and helps you to prepare for your exams. The partnership means that you can be confident that the range of learning, teaching and assessment practice materials has been checked by the senior examining team at AQA before formal approval, and is closely matched to the requirements of your specification.

How to use this book

This book covers the specification for your course and is arranged in a sequence approved by AQA.

The features in this book include:

Timeline

Key events are outlined at the beginning of the book. The events are colour-coded so you can clearly see the categories of change.

Learning objectives

At the beginning of each section you will find a list of learning objectives that contain targets linked to the requirements of the specification.

Key chronology

A short list of dates usually with a focus on a specific event or legislation.

Key profile

The profile of a key person you should be aware of to fully understand the period in question.

Key term

A term that you will need to be able to define and understand.

Did you know?

Interesting information to bring the subject under discussion to life.

Exploring the detail

Information to put further context around the subject under discussion.

A closer look

An in-depth look at a theme, person or event to deepen your understanding. Activities around the extra information may be included.

Sources

Sources to reinforce topics or themes and may provide fact or opinion. They may be quotations from historical works, contemporaries of the period or photographs.

Cross-reference

Links to related content within the book which may offer more detail on the subject in question.

Activity

Various activity types to provide you with different challenges and opportunities to demonstrate both the content and skills you are learning. Some can be worked on individually, some as part of group work and some are designed to specifically 'stretch and challenge'.

▦ Question

Questions to prompt further discussion on the topic under consideration and are an aid to revision.

▦ Summary questions

Summary questions at the end of each chapter to test your knowledge and allow you to demonstrate your understanding.

AQA Examiner's tip

Hints from AQA examiners to help you with your study and to prepare for your exam.

AQA Examination-style questions

Questions at the end of each section in the style that you can expect in your exam.

Learning outcomes

Learning outcomes at the end of each section remind you what you should know having completed the chapters in that section.

▦ Web links in the book

Because Nelson Thornes is not responsible for third party content online, there may be some changes to this material that are beyond our control. In order for us to ensure that the links referred to in the book are as up-to-date and stable as possible, the web sites provided are usually homepages with supporting instructions on how to reach the relevant pages if necessary.

Please let us know at **webadmin@nelsonthornes. com** if you find a link that doesn't work and we will do our best to correct this at reprint, or to list an alternative site.

Introduction to the History series

When Bruce Bogtrotter in Roald Dahl's *Matilda* was challenged to eat a huge chocolate cake, he just opened his mouth and ploughed in, taking bite after bite and lump after lump until the cake was gone and he was feeling decidedly sick. The picture is not dissimilar to that of some A level history students. They are attracted to history because of its inherent appeal but, when faced with a bulging file and a forthcoming examination, their enjoyment evaporates. They try desperately to cram their brains with an assortment of random facts and subsequently prove unable to control the outpouring of their ill-digested material in the examination.

The books in this series are designed to help students and teachers avoid this feeling of overload and examination panic by breaking down the AQA history specification in such a way that it is easily absorbed. Above all, they are designed to retain and promote students' enthusiasm for history by avoiding a dreary rehash of dates and events. Each book is divided into sections, closely matched to those given in the specification, and the content is further broken down into chapters that present the historical material in a lively and attractive form, offering guidance on the key terms, events and issues, and blending thought-provoking activities and questions in a way designed to advance students' understanding. By encouraging students to think for themselves and to share their ideas with others, as well as helping them to develop the knowledge and skills they will need to pass their examination, this book should ensure that students' learning remains a pleasure rather than an endurance test.

To make the most of what this book provides, students will need to develop efficient study skills from the start and it is worth spending some time considering what these involve:

- Good organisation of material in a subject-specific file. Organised notes help develop an organised brain and sensible filing ensures time is not wasted hunting for misplaced material. This book uses cross-references to indicate where material in one chapter has relevance to material in another. Students are advised to adopt the same technique.

- A sensible approach to note-making. Students are often too ready to copy large chunks of material from printed books or to download sheaves of printouts from the internet. This series is designed to encourage students to think about the notes they collect and to undertake research with a particular purpose in mind. The activities encourage students to pick out information that is relevant to the issue being addressed and to avoid making notes on material that is not properly understood.

- Taking time to think, which is by far the most important component of study. By encouraging students to think before they write or speak, be it for a written answer, presentation or class debate, students should learn to form opinions and make judgements based on the accumulation of evidence. These are the skills that the examiner will be looking for in the final examination. The beauty of history is that there is rarely a right or wrong answer so, with sufficient evidence, one student's view will count for as much as the next.

Unit 1

The topics offered for study in Unit 1 are all based on 'change and consolidation'. They invite consideration of what changed and why, as well as posing the question of what remained the same. Through a study of a period of about 50 to 60 years, students are encouraged to analyse the interplay of long-term and short-term reasons for change and to consider not only how governments have responded to the need for change but also to evaluate the ensuing consequences. Such historical analyses are, of course, relevant to an understanding of the present and, through such historical study, students will be guided towards a greater appreciation of the world around them today, as well as developing their understanding of the past.

Unit 1 is tested by a 1 hour 15 minute paper containing three questions, from which students need to select two. Details relating to the style of questions, with additional hints, are given in Table 1 and links to the examination requirements are provided throughout this book. Students should familiarise themselves with these and the marking criteria given below before attempting any of the practice examination questions at the end of each section.

Answers will be marked according to a scheme based on 'levels of response'. This means that the answer will be assessed according to which level best matches the historical skills displayed, taking both knowledge and understanding into account. All students should have a copy of these criteria and need to use them wisely.

Marking criteria

Question 1(a), 2(a) and 3(a)

Level 1 Answers will contain either some descriptive material that is only loosely linked to the focus of

Table 1 *Unit 1: style of questions and marks available*

Unit 1	Question	Marks	Question type	Question stem	Hints for students
Question 1, 2 and 3	(a)	12	This question is focused on a narrow issue within the period studied and requires an explanation	Why did… Explain why… In what ways… (was X important)	Make sure you explain 'why', not 'how', and try to order your answer in a way that shows you understand the inter-linkage of factors and which were the more important. You should try to reach an overall judgement/conclusion
Question 1, 2 and 3	(b)	24	This question links the narrow issue to a wider context and requires an awareness that issues and events can have different interpretations	How far… How important was… How successful…	This answer needs to be planned as you will need to develop an argument in your answer and show balanced judgement. Try to set out your argument in the introduction and, as you develop your ideas through your paragraphs, support your opinions with detailed evidence. Your conclusion should flow naturally and provide supported judgement

the question or some explicit comment with little, if any, appropriate support. Answers are likely to be generalised and assertive. The response will be limited in development and skills of written communication will be weak. *(0–2 marks)*

Level 2 Answers will demonstrate some knowledge and understanding of the demands of the question. They will **either** be almost entirely descriptive with few explicit links to the question **or** they will provide some explanations backed by evidence that is limited in range and/or depth. Answers will be coherent but weakly expressed and/or poorly structured. *(3–6 marks)*

Level 3 Answers will demonstrate good understanding of the demands of the question providing relevant explanations backed by appropriately selected information, although this may not be full or comprehensive. Answers will, for the most part, be clearly expressed and show some organisation in the presentation of material. *(7–9 marks)*

Level 4 Answers will be well focused, identifying a range of specific explanations backed by precise evidence and demonstrating good understanding of the connections and links between events/issues. Answers will, for the most part, be well written and organised. *(10–12 marks)*

Question 1(b), 2(b) and 3(b)

Level 1 Answers may **either** contain some descriptive material which is only loosely linked to the focus of the question **or** they may address only a part of the question. Alternatively, there may be some explicit comment with little, if any, appropriate support. Answers are likely to be generalised and assertive. There will be little, if any, awareness of differing

historical interpretations. The response will be limited in development and skills of written communication will be weak. *(0–6 marks)*

Level 2 Answers will show some understanding of the focus of the question. They will **either** be almost entirely descriptive with few explicit links to the question **or** they may contain some explicit comment with relevant but limited support. They will display limited understanding of differing historical interpretations. Answers will be coherent but weakly expressed and/or poorly structured. *(7–11 marks)*

Level 3 Answers will show a developed understanding of the demands of the question. They will provide some assessment, backed by relevant and appropriately selected evidence, but they will lack depth and/or balance. There will be some understanding of varying historical interpretations. Answers will, for the most part, be clearly expressed and show some organisation in the presentation of material. *(12–16 marks)*

Level 4 Answers will show explicit understanding of the demands of the question. They will develop a balanced argument backed by a good range of appropriately selected evidence and a good understanding of historical interpretations. Answers will, for the most part, show organisation and good skills of written communication. *(17–21 marks)*

Level 5 Answers will be well focused and closely argued. The arguments will be supported by precisely selected evidence leading to a relevant conclusion/judgement, incorporating well-developed understanding of historical interpretations and debate. Answers will, for the most part, be carefully organised and fluently written, using appropriate vocabulary. *(22–24 marks)*

Introduction to this book

Fig. 1 *The Frankfurt parliament of 1848*

There was no single state of Germany before 1871. The 39 states which, until 1866, filled the area between the Baltic to the north, the Rhine to the west and the Alps and Danube to the south and east had been created at the Congress of Vienna in 1815, following the defeat of the French emperor, Napoleon. Napoleon had been responsible for destroying the Holy Roman Empire, which had formerly comprised over 300 different German states, and French rule had given the German peoples their first taste of '**confederation**'. The states had come together in shared systems of administration and justice and this had helped create a greater sense of unity between them. However, it was also in combining to fight off the yoke of French domination that the states had found an even stronger feeling of common purpose. The reduction in their number in 1815 was, to some extent, a reflection of this 'coming together' that had already taken place.

Under the terms of the Vienna settlement, each Germanic state had its own ruler, but a new type of confederation called the 'Bund' was established, with a permanent central *diet*, or ruling body, the 'Bundesrat', at Frankfurt. The German-speaking part of the Austrian Empire and the Kingdom of Bohemia were included in this Bund and the diet was given an Austrian president. Since Austria commanded a powerful European Empire and was one of the victors of the Napoleonic wars, this seemed a sensible arrangement to ensure the stability of the states.

Key term

Confederation: group of states having separate internal governments with control over domestic policies but working together in matters of common interest.

Cross-reference

For more information on the Holy Roman Empire, refer to the key term 'Second Reich' on page 5.

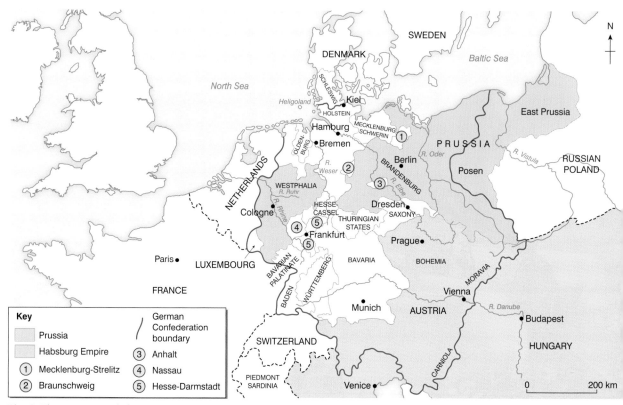

Fig. 3 *The German Confederation in 1815*

Fig. 2 *Kaiser Wilhelm I*

Prussia, the largest of the German states, had also played a significant part in the defeat of the French and consequently made some important gains at Vienna. Although some of its eastern territories were given to Russia and Poland, it acquired the Rhineland and Westphalia, half of Saxony and Pomerania. Such acquisitions were to have far-reaching consequences. Prussia had gained control of areas of huge economic and industrial potential, its population had been doubled and it had been transformed from an eastern European power into a central one. Although at the time Austria saw no rival in Prussia, with its split possessions, the history of the next 50 years concerns the struggle between these two powers to dominate the area of 'Germany'.

The Federal Act creating the Bund in 1815 had stipulated that individual states should establish constitutions with parliaments, but in practice this clause was obeyed or ignored at will. In Prussia, the ruler, Friedrich Wilhelm III, remained staunchly Conservative. He relied heavily on the Prussian Junker class of landowning aristocrats who provided his civil servants and army officers. They, like their ruler, were hostile to the forces of Liberalism, which had been stirred up by the French Revolution of the late 18th century.

However, in the years leading to 1848, economic development began to change the German Confederation. The Prussian Rhineland led the way in a frenzy of industrial expansion. The coal, iron and textile industries boomed and turned villages into cities, steam engines transformed production and by 1838 Prussia had built its first railway line from Berlin to Potsdam. Furthermore, by 1834, Prussia had developed an internal customs union, or 'Zollverein', whereby 18 of the German states had agreed to abandon customs barriers and to create a free trade zone for their goods, whilst maintaining tariffs on goods entering the zone from elsewhere. To their economic and political loss, Austria (and Bohemia) remained outside this union. Within it, greater economic integration bred not only prosperity and social change, but a stronger sense of unity.

It was in these 'Vormärz' years between 1815 and 1848 that Liberal and nationalist ideas gained a firm root in Germany. The expanding, urbanised working class developed a greater political awareness, although it was less among this class than among the ranks of the university professors, students and more forward-thinking members of the middle and upper classes that Liberal ideas found their most receptive audience. Amongst such intellectuals, the desire for greater political liberty became entwined with nationalist principles. A sense of a common heritage and a pride in contemporary Germanic achievement created a commitment to the unity of German-speaking peoples, and, thanks to the impact of the Zollverein under Prussian leadership, these Liberals and nationalists increasingly looked to Prussia as the potential leader of a united Germany.

However, the eruption of revolutions in many German states in 1848–9, as elsewhere in Europe, did not bring unity any nearer. Although there was an initial outburst of enthusiasm and a sense of expectation as Liberals in Vienna, Berlin, Cologne, Prague, Dresden, Baden and elsewhere sought concessions from autocratic regimes and many German states were forced into granting constitutions and Liberal promises, in many cases, the changes barely lasted a year. The rulers of Prussia, Bavaria, Baden and Württemberg at first agreed to participate in a *Vorparlament* or German parliament to draw up a constitution and bring about the unification of Germany. However, this middle-class-dominated Frankfurt parliament of 1848–9 became bogged down in debates about the new constitutional framework and whether Germany should become a 'Grossdeutschland' including German-speaking Austria, or a 'Kleindeutschland' excluding it. As it deliberated, the Conservative forces regrouped and Friedrich Wilhelm of Prussia recovered his nerve. When in March 1849, the Frankfurt parliament offered him the throne of a united Germany, he refused to 'pick up a crown from the gutter'.

1848–9 taught German Liberals a lesson. They could not impose a new future on Germany without an army or support from the princes. Some may have felt their cause was lost, but help was to come from an unexpected direction, although initially the appointment of Otto von Bismarck as Minister-President of Prussia in 1862 looked far from promising. Bismarck was 47 and of Junker background and interests, although a great intellect, like his mother who came from the middle classes. He was loyal to his Prussian heritage, rather than to Germany as a whole, and devoted to serving the new Prussian monarch, Wilhelm I, who had come to power in January 1861. Bismarck fully embraced Prussia's traditional authoritarian structure. He welcomed the military reforms of Albrecht von Roon, the Prussian Minister of War since 1859, who had expanded and strengthened the Prussian army. He was not interested in the arguments of the Liberal majority that had emerged in the Prussian *Landtag* and which had caused a crisis by refusing to sanction the national budget. He simply adjourned the assembly and continued to exact taxes without its sanction. He arrogantly told that body, 'The great questions of the day will not be decided by speeches and the resolutions of majorities – that was the great mistake of 1848 and 1849 – but by iron and blood', by which he meant industry and war. He hardly seemed the most likely candidate to fulfil the Liberals' hopes.

Whether Bismarck planned the unification of Germany, or merely reacted to events, remains an unanswered question amongst historians. It is probably fair to say that he came to power with ambitions to expel Austrian influence from Germany and increase Prussian control, but

Key term

'Vormärz': literally means 'before March' and refers to the years before the outbreak of revolution in Germany in March 1848.

the unfolding of events lends weight to the view that he was essentially a pragmatist – a man who seized opportunities, rather than one who followed a pre-conceived plan. The way he exploited the Schleswig-Holstein crisis is a prime example of his pragmatic action.

In 1863, the Danes challenged the Bund over the government of Schleswig and Holstein, the two northernmost German states. Bismarck persuaded Wilhelm I to participate in a joint Austro-Prussian military action against Denmark. The intervention succeeded and led to the 1865 Convention of Gastein by which these two duchies were formally divided between Prussia, which took responsibility for Schleswig, and Austria, which did the same for Holstein. This position provided Bismarck with potential to forge a war against Austria and so force them to cede their influence over 'Germany'. He secured the neutrality of the French and the support of the Italians, who were anxious to obtain Venetia from the Austrians, and engineered a war with Austria over the administration of the duchies in June 1866. Austria was defeated in just six weeks, culminating in a monumental Prussian victory at Sadowa in July. By the Peace of Prague, signed in August 1866, the old 'Bund' was abolished and the first stage of German unity accomplished. Prussia annexed the German states north of the river Main and a new 'North German Confederation' came into being, with Prussia in control of more than 4.5 million German people; two-thirds of all Germans, excluding Austrian Germans. Most of the Liberals in the Prussian Landtag promptly forgave Bismarck's illegal collecting of the budget for the past four years and passed an act of indemnity in his favour. A few objected but the majority rebranded themselves as 'National Liberals', committed to sharing Bismarck's enthusiasm for the unity of German people.

In return, Bismarck made a number of Liberal concessions. The North German Confederation was bound together by the principles of free trade and the rule of law and was to be ruled through a parliament with universal manhood suffrage, a secret ballot and parliamentary control of the budget. Such terms were to form the basis for the later 'Reich' constitution of 1871. However, there is no proof that Bismarck intended unification to go any further. The southern German states – Bavaria, Württemberg, Baden and Hesse-Darmstadt – had a stronger separatist tradition, partially enforced by a Catholic rather than a Protestant heritage, and closer ties to Austria. However, they were members of the Zollverein, which had its own 'Zollparlament' too, and, with the loss of reliable Austrian protection, were persuaded to make a series of defensive military treaties with the new Confederation, promising to fight with the Confederation in the event of war.

In 1867, Bismarck outwitted Napoleon III of France in the French emperor's bid to buy Luxemburg from the Dutch and, in 1869, Bismarck seized another opportunity when revolution in Spain left the Spanish throne vacant. The Prussians, probably on Bismarck's goading, put forward a candidate from their own royal house, Prince Leopold of Hohenzollern, but Napoleon III of France demanded that this candidature be withdrawn and, furthermore, that Wilhelm I should promise never to make such a claim again. Napoleon's stance provided Bismarck with an ideal opportunity to stir up feeling against the French. The Kaiser, who was staying at the health spa of Bad Ems, sent a reply to the emperor, which he communicated, by telegram, to Bismarck. Bismarck released an edited version to the press which made it appear that Wilhelm's words were insulting and mocking towards the French. When this 'Ems Telegram' appeared in the French press, there were immediate clamours for war with Prussia and, with his Ministers' encouragement, Napoleon III declared war on 19 July 1870.

Faced with a threat from France, the southern German states were persuaded to throw in their lot with the Prussians. The French, without

Cross-reference

The concept of 'Reich' is further explained in the key term box for 'Second Reich' on page 5. The Reich constitution of 1871 is described on page 14.

llies, were resoundingly beaten at Sedan in September 1870 and went on to suffer a humiliating siege of Paris until January 1871. At the resultant Treaty of Frankfurt in May 1871, they were forced to cede Alsace and Lorraine to Germany as well as paying £200,000 in reparations. Not only had Prussia proved its strength, but the glory of victory brought Wilhelm I the offer of the crown of a united Germany from the southern princes. By January 1871, the unification of Germany (excluding Austria) was complete and, what is more, it had been accomplished by Prussian military power, backed by the princely courts and the Conservative elites. The German national state was imposed 'from above'.

This book traces the development of this new Germany, with its Conservative roots yet modern dynamic economy, from the founding of the **'Second Reich'** in 1871 to its collapse in 1918. It also explores the early years of the Weimar Republic, set up in the wake of Germany's disastrous defeat in the First World War, through a period of political and economic upheaval to an era of greater confidence by 1925. It will examine the contradictions of the period: authoritarian rule challenged by modern democratic trends; the rise of Socialism and the influence of the German elites; the revolution of 1918–19 and the continuity between Reich and Republic. It is hoped that it will enable you to offer an answer to the question of why Germany was never able to develop as a stable Liberal parliamentary democracy in this period. Such are the themes and issues that you need to keep in mind as you read this book and, by examining the interplay of contrasting trends, you should acquire a full and rich understanding of the forces that created and shaped 20th century Germany.

Key term

Second Reich: Reich means German state (or empire) and that founded in 1871 was known as the Second Reich to distinguish it from the First Reich of the Holy Roman Empire, which covered the lands originally ruled by Charlemagne from the 9th to the 19th century. The Third Reich (1933–45) was the period of Nazi rule in Germany.

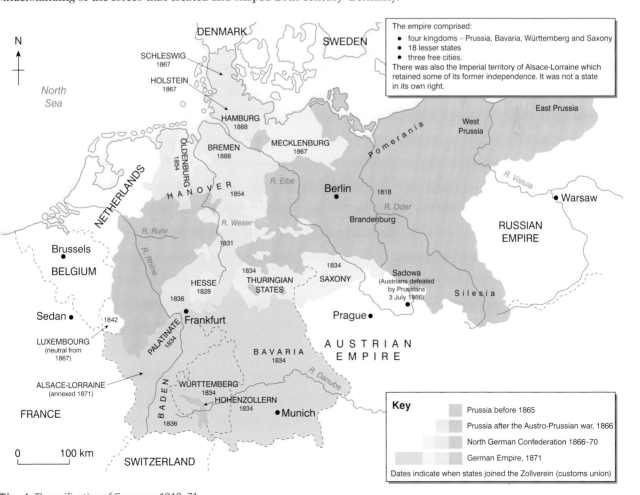

The empire comprised:
- four kingdoms – Prussia, Bavaria, Württemberg and Saxony
- 18 lesser states
- three free cities.

There was also the Imperial territory of Alsace-Lorraine which retained some of its former independence. It was not a state in its own right.

Key
- Prussia before 1865
- Prussia after the Austro-Prussian war, 1866
- North German Confederation 1866–70
- German Empire, 1871

Dates indicate when states joined the Zollverein (customs union)

Fig. 4 *The unification of Germany, 1818–71*

Timeline

The colours represent different types of event as follows: Economic and social, Political, International (including German foreign policy), Religious

1848	1848	1849	1850	1850	1859	1863
February Publication of *Communist Manifesto*	27 February to 13 March Outbreak of revolutions in German states leads to the setting up of the Frankfurt parliament which agrees basic civil rights	3 April Friedrich Wilhelm IV of Prussia rejects Imperial crown	1 September Reopening of the traditional federal *diet* of the German Confederation in Frankfurt	29 November Treaty of Olmütz	Prussian army reforms are instituted by war minister Albrecht von Roon	Lasalle founds the General German Workers' Association (ADAV)

1866	1867	1867	1867	1867	1869
14 September Prussian Indemnity Law settles the conflict between the crown and the diet	12 June National Liberal Party publishes its founding programme	14 June Constitution of the North German Confederation established	Bismarck becomes federal chancellor and foreign minister	First volume of *Das Kapital* is published by Karl Marx	Founding of the Social Democratic Workers' Party (SDAP) by August Bebel and Wilhelm Liebknecht

1872	1873	1875	1876	1876	1878
Jesuit activity is forbidden in Germany	'May Laws' directed against the influence of the Catholic Church in Prussia	Founding of the SAPD (Socialist Workers' Party of Germany) at Gotha by a merger of the SDAP and ADAV	15 February Founding of the Central Union of German Industrialists	Founding of Reichbank	11 May to 2 June Assassination attempt on Kaiser Wilhelm I

1884	1884	1888	1889	1890	1890
Germany annexes south-west Africa, Togoland and Cameroon	Accident Insurance Law is passed	9 March to 15 June Reign of Kaiser Friedrich III; he is succeeded by Kaiser Wilhelm II	Old Age and Invalidity Insurance Law is passed	20 February Reichstag elections: Conservative and National Liberal losses: the SPD and Centre Party both gain and the SPD becomes the single most popular party	20 March Bismarck is dismissed by Wilhelm II; Leo von Caprivi becomes Reich chancellor

1864	1864	1865	1866	1866	1866
German-Danish war over Schleswig-Holstein	**30 October** Peace of Vienna between Austria, Prussia and Denmark: Schleswig is ceded to Prussia and Holstein to Austria	**14 August** Gastein agreement regulates the occupation of Schleswig and Holstein	**June to July** Austro-Prussian war	**3 July** Battle of Sadowa (Königgrätz): Austria is defeated by Prussia	**23 August** Peace of Prague, dissolution of the German Confederation: Schleswig and Holstein become Prussian

1870	1870	1870	1871	1871	1871	1871
13 July Ems Telegram sent, Franco-Prussian war follows	**1 to 2 September** Battle of Sedan	**December** Founding of the Centre Party	**January** Prussian occupation of Paris leads to French capitulation	**18 January** German Empire is proclaimed at Versailles; Wilhelm I becomes Kaiser	**10 May** Treaty of Frankfurt: Germany annexes Alsace and half of Lorraine and France is compelled to pay occupation costs	Catholic section of Prussian culture ministry is closed

1878	1878	1879	1880	1880	1883
19 October Anti-Socialist Law passed by the Reichstag	Reichstag elections: Conservative parties gain seats	**12 July** Passing of protectionist legislation by the Reichstag	Legislation is passed to moderate the anti-Catholic laws of 1870s *Kulturkampf*	*Deutscher Kolonialverein* (German Colonial Association) formed	Sickness Insurance Law is passed

1891	1891	1894	1894	1894	1896
21 October Erfurt Programme of the SPD	Founding of the General German League (the future Pan-German League)	*Ostmarkenverein* (Eastern Marches Association) formed	General German League changes its name to Pan-German League	Prince Chlodwig zu Hohenlohe-Schillingsfürst becomes Reich chancellor	Unified legal code (*Bürgerliches Gesetzbuch*) is established for the German Empire

1897	1898	1900	1907	1908	1908	1909
Bernhard von Bülow becomes foreign minister	Founding of the Navy League and naval laws authorise massive expansion of the navy (1898–1900)	**10 October** Hohenlohe-Schillingsfürst resigns; his successor as chancellor is Bülow	**25 January** 'Hottentot Election': despite the nationalistic tenor of the election campaign, SPD gains a quarter of a million extra votes; but loses almost half its seats	**7 October** Women are allowed to study in Prussian universities	**28 October** Interview with the Kaiser published in the British *Daily Telegraph* leading to the *Daily Telegraph* Affair	**24 June** The Conservatives vote against the government on the issue of inheritance tax; this marks the end of the Bülow block

1917	1917	1917	1917	1917	1918
April USPD is founded by dissident members of the SPD	**3 July** Bethmann-Hollweg resigns as chancellor under pressure from generals Hindenburg and Ludendorff	**19 July** Peace Resolution is proposed in the Reichstag	**2 September** Founding of the extreme right-wing *Vaterlandspartei* (Fatherland Party) wanting victory with annexations	**7 November** Bolshevik revolution in Russia	**January** Strikes break out in Germany

1918	1918	1918	1918	1918	1918
6 November Revolution spreads to Hamburg, Bremen and Lübeck	**7 November** Revolution in Munich: Bavaria is declared a republic	**8 November** Government of Workers', Peasants' and Soldiers' Councils set up in Bavaria under Kurt Eisner	**9 November** Declaration of the German republic by Philipp Scheidemann; Kaiser Wilhelm II abdicates; Prince Max von Baden resigns and Friedrich Ebert becomes chancellor	**10 November** Formation of the Council of People's Representatives; Wilhelm II flees to the Netherlands	**11 November** Armistice is concluded at Compiègne

1919	1919	1919	1919	1919	1919
15 January Murder of Spartacist League leaders Karl Liebknecht and Rosa Luxemburg	**6 February** Opening of the National Assembly in Weimar	**11 February** Friedrich Ebert is elected Reich president	**21 February** Kurt Eisner is assassinated by right wingers	**6 April** Councils' republic (Räterepublik) is established in Bavaria	**2 May** Bavarian republic is suppressed by the army and *Freikorps* units

1909	1910	1912	1913	1914	1914	1914
14 July Bethmann-Hollweg replaces Bülow as chancellor	**6 March** Founding of the *Fortschrittliche Volkspartei* (Progressive People's Party) through the merger of left Liberal groups	**12 January** Reichstag elections: SPD becomes the largest party	**6 November** Protests against the German military by Alsatian civilians in the 'Zabern Affair'	**28 June** Archduke Franz Ferdinand assassinated at Sarajevo	**1 August** Germany declares war on Russia	**3 August** Germany declares war on France

1918	1918	1918	1918	1918	1918	1918
8 January US President Woodrow Wilson delivers 'Fourteen Points' speech proposing an end to the war	**3 March** Treaty of Brest-Litovsk with Russia	**21 March** German Spring Offensive on the Somme	**29 September** German military leaders request armistice negotiations	**3 October** Prince Max von Baden becomes Reich chancellor	**26 October** Reform of constitution: Ludendorff is effectively dismissed; Groener is appointed as his successor	**3 November** Kiel Mutiny is suppressed and escalates to armed revolt; workers and sailors' councils (soviets) are established

1918	1918	1918	1918	1919	1919
15 November Stinnes-Legien Agreement: establishment of *Zentralarbeitgemeinschaft* (ZAG), a cooperative forum for workers and employers	**16 to 20 December** Congress of Workers' and Soldiers' Councils meets in Berlin	**25 December** Stahlhelm veterans' association is formed	**30 December** Opening of the founding conference of the German Communist Party (KPD)	**5 January** Founding of the radical right-wing *Deutsche Arbeiterpartei* (German Workers' Party which subsequently became the Nazi Party (NSDAP))	**5 to 11 January** General strike and Communist Spartacist uprising in Berlin

1919	1919	1919	1919	1920	1920
28 June Signing of the Treaty of Versailles	**11 August** Weimar constitution comes into force	**September** Beginning of financial reforms of Matthias Erzberger	**8 October** Hugo Haase, leader of the USPD, is shot; he dies on 17 November	**10 January** Treaty of Versailles comes into force	**12 to 17 March** Kapp Putsch in Berlin

1920	1920	1920	1921	1921	1921	1921
15 March to 20 May Communist insurrection in the Ruhr valley	**27 March** Formation of Müller government ('Weimar coalition')	**16 October** USPD splits; the left wing (majority) later joins KPD	**24 January to 14 March** Paris/London conferences on reparations	**27 April** Allied Reparations Commission sets the total reparations bill at 132bn gold marks	**10 May** Formation of new Weimar coalition government led by Joseph Wirth	**11 May** Reichstag accepts London reparations plan unconditionally by 220 votes to 172

1923	1923	1924	1924	1924	1924	1924
15 November New currency (*Rentenmark*) is introduced (at 4.2 marks to the dollar)	**30 November** Stresemann government resigns	**26 February** Beer Hall Putsch leaders are tried for high treason	**1 April** Hitler is sentenced to five years in the Landsberg prison in Bavaria	**9 April** Dawes Plan issued	**11 October** Introduction of Reichsmark	**20 December** Hitler is released from Landsberg prison

1921	1922	1922	1922	1923	1923	1923
26 August Assassination of Matthias Erzberger by right-wing naval officers	**16 April** Treaty of Rapallo establishes economic cooperation between Germany and the Soviet Union	**24 June** Murder of foreign minister Walter Rathenau by members of the radical right wing	**18 July** Law for the Protection of the Republic, banning anti-republican associations, is passed by the Reichstag against opposition from KPD, DNVP and BVP	**September to November** Disturbances in Bavaria, Saxony, Thuringia, Hamburg and Aachen	**8 November** Beer Hall Putsch by Nazis in Munich	**11 November** US dollar is worth 631bn marks

1925	1925	1925	1925	1925	1925	1926
27 February NSDAP refounded	**28 February** Death of President Ebert	**25 April** Hindenburg is elected president	**14 July to 1 August** Evacuation of Ruhr	**16 October** Locarno Treaties are agreed, regulating German relations with the rest of western Europe; DNVP ministers resign in protest on 25 October	**8 December** Official publication of the first part of Hitler's *Mein Kampf*	**8 September** Germany joins the League of Nations

1 The new Germany, 1871–8

In this chapter you will learn about:

- the new German political structure established in 1871

- the further unification of Germany to 1878 and Bismarck's treatment of minority groups

- the reasons for, and success of, Bismarck's struggle against the Catholic Church in the *Kulturkampf*

- Bismarck's relationship with the Reichstag and the reasons for the political changes of 1878–9.

Activity

Research exercise

In pairs, undertake some research into Bismarck's background and personality. Draw up a character profile and present your findings to the rest of the class.

Activity

Thinking point

Bismarck's reputation is mixed. He has been accused of being an old-fashioned, conservative bully, concerned only with his personal power. However, he has also been praised as a superb 'manipulator' who knew what was best for Germany and ensured that he remained in control in order to achieve his aims. As you read this section, you should reflect on the kind of man that you feel Bismarck was and decide what you think would be a fair assessment of his career.

Fig. 1 *Otto von Bismarck, first chancellor of Imperial Germany, 1871–90*

In 1871, 56-year-old Otto von Bismarck was an overweight insomniac and hypochondriac. He weighed 112 kg and, although balding, had luxuriant eyebrows and an impressive 'walrus' moustache which virtually obscured his mouth. However, despite his imposing physical presence, he constantly complained of ill-health and his wife referred to him as her 'poor sick chicken'. Throughout his adult life, he suffered recurring bouts of rheumatism, chest and leg pains, facial spasms, headaches, toothache, shingles, ulcers, sickness and indigestion. In 1861, he nearly died from a leg injury and inflammation of the lungs. Of course, his liking for hearty meals, cigars and drink did not help and by 1880, he weighed 114 kg. Although he lost some weight after his doctors prescribed a special diet of herrings in 1883, his pains never disappeared. In January 1876 he had written to a friend:

> I have been suffering twelve months during the year. For the past year, my doctors have threatened me with the penalty of death if I do not give up my responsibilities. I sleep only in the daytime from eight to noon or one and am bad-tempered with all.

Bismarck was a 'loner' who, when not engaged in public duties, preferred a simple lifestyle. He had few friends and constantly feared that 'enemies' were ganging up on him. He relied on his long-suffering wife, Johanna, and his hunting dogs for company and yet Johanna hated Berlin and the city life which was necessary for her husband's work and often spent long periods in the country, leaving Bismarck to his own devices.

Such was the man who occupied one of the most powerful political positions in Europe in the years 1871–90. As Imperial chancellor, Bismarck served Kaiser Wilhelm I of Germany, dominating, manipulating and influencing the political and diplomatic scene so greatly that the history of Germany between 1871 and 1890 is usually seen as the history of Bismarck.

Did you know?

The new German constitution was virtually the same as the system which Bismarck had devised for the North German Confederation of 1867 – when only the northern states of Germany had been unified. Some alterations were made in November 1870 when Prussia made treaties with the southern German states and the new constitution was finally made law on 20 April 1871.

The German political structure in 1871

Influences

Having united Germany by war, Bismarck faced the task of drawing up a new German constitution, or system of government, which would define the way in which the Reich would be ruled. The German Empire

Activity

Pairs activity

In pairs, examine the details of the German constitution as given on pages 14 and 15.

Use this information to fill in the following chart, which provides some details of the British constitution in 1871 and invites you to compare this with the German one.

Britain	Germany
British monarch:	**German Kaiser:**
▨ Hereditary monarch. ▨ Officially appointed the Prime Minister and other ministers but choice restricted to those with a Commons majority. ▨ Ministers took responsibility for the command of the army on the monarch's behalf. ▨ Ministers directed foreign policy. ▨ Gave royal assent to laws (but had not exercised power of veto since 1707). ▨ Had to be informed of policy but showed complete impartiality.	
Prime minister:	**German chancellor:**
▨ Leader of the party with the biggest majority in the elections. ▨ Chose his own ministers. ▨ Could be questioned by and was answerable to parliament which could force his dismissal. ▨ Was dependent on his party's majority in parliament to carry through policies and make laws.	
Members of parliament:	**Reichstag deputies:**
▨ Elected by wealthier males with a votes. ▨ Could debate and vote on laws. ▨ Had right of free speech. ▨ Could criticise ministers and force them to resign.	

had 'officially' been formed by the voluntary agreement of its component states and cities, so there was no question that it would remain anything other than a confederation, in which these states retained considerable control over their own domestic government. Nevertheless, there also had to be a central administration and the powers of Wilhelm I – who had taken on the role of 'emperor of Germany' – needed to be made clear.

Since the early 19th century, the German Liberals, like those elsewhere in Europe, had been clamouring for a 'democratic constitution'. By this, they meant a system in which the power of the ruler and his ministers would be limited and which would give the people of Germany some control over their own government. They wanted Germany to have an elected parliament, chosen by 'the people' – or at least the wealthiest citizens of the country. The Liberals believed that this was the only way to guard the people's freedom. An elected parliament would represent the people's views, question ministers' policies and ensure that taxes were properly spent. Indeed, the Liberals had supported unification on the understanding that such a constitution would be the result.

However, Bismarck was no Liberal. He was already the Minister-President of Prussia and a representative of the traditional aristocratic 'Junker' class there. His basic views were conservative and his commitment to the authoritarian Prussian tradition was strong. He was deeply suspicious of 'people power' and Liebknecht, a socialist, was later to describe the constitution which he drew up as a sham. Liebknecht referred to it as 'a fig leaf to cover the nakedness of **absolutism**'. Although Bismarck claimed to support 'constitutions' and appeared to pander to the Liberals' ideas in order to harness their energies in pursuit of his aims for a strong united Germany, his view of what a constitution should be turned out to be very different from theirs.

Cross-reference

The German Liberals are outlined on pages 3–5.

Liebknecht is profiled on page 88, and his activities are described on pages 87 and 96–7.

Key term

Absolutism: a form of government in which all power resides with the ruler.

The new constitution

Kaiser	Government (chancellor and ministers)
■ Was the hereditary monarch (and always the King of Prussia too).	■ Was appointed and dismissed by the Kaiser (and responsible only to him, not to the Reichstag).
■ Appointed/dismissed chancellor and other ministers (Secretaries of State).	■ Decided outlines of policy with the Kaiser/Bundesrat. (Were not required to take account of the Reichstag's views/resolutions.)
■ Could call/dissolve the Reichstag.	■ Chancellor (and Kaiser) gave assent to all laws.
■ Commanded the army directly.	
■ Controlled foreign policy, including the right to make treaties and alliances and declare war if attacked.	
■ Gave assent to all laws (with the chancellor).	
■ Devised policies and laws in consultation with his chosen chancellor, ministers and the Bundesrat.	
■ Had the final say in any dispute over the constitution.	

Reichstag (parliament, also known as the Lower House)	Bundesrat (also known as the Upper House)
<ul><li>Members (deputies) elected by males over 25 years.</li><li>Deputies had the right of free speech.</li><li>Elections held every three years by an indirect voting system which varied in different regions.</li><li>Gave consent to all laws (including the annual budget which assessed the raising and spending of taxes).</li><li>Could question, debate, agree to or reject a law proposed by the chancellor.</li><li>Could not amend a law.</li><li>Could not demand the dismissal of the chancellor or any other ministers.</li></ul>	<ul><li>58 representatives from the 25 state governments in proportion to size of state (Prussia, as the largest state, had 17 members).</li><li>Presided over by the chancellor.</li><li>Could initiate legislation.</li><li>Decisions decided by majority vote except for any proposal to alter the constitution, which needed a majority of 14.</li><li>Had to approve new laws (along with the Reichstag, Kaiser and chancellor).</li><li>Could veto all legislation except a budget approved by the Reichstag.</li><li>Had to give approval to the Kaiser for a declaration of war (in cases where Germany was not under attack).</li></ul>

Questions

1 What do you think were Bismarck's main guiding principles in drawing up the German constitution of 1871?

2 To what extent was the German constitution a 'Prussian-dominated' constitution?

3 What are the strengths and weaknesses of this constitution?

Political features

Through the activity on page 13 and questions above you will have seen how, in many respects, the German constitution was undemocratic, authoritarian and Prussian-dominated. However, some aspects of it were quite Liberal. You may, for example, have been surprised to discover that Bismarck gave the vote to all men over the age of 25 years. In this respect the constitution may appear even more democratic than the British one! One explanation is that Bismarck was simply trying to win support by appearing to be forward-thinking. He seems to have believed that the ordinary German peasants and workers had traditional views similar to his own and that their support could help him keep the demands of the more radical, middle-class Liberals at bay.

Nevertheless, this opportunity for the broad mass of the people to express their views was a modern concept. The constitution guaranteed freedom of speech and the law was held in high regard. There were certainly signs of emergent democracy in Germany, and the political framework laid down by Bismarck produced some flourishing political parties and lively debates.

Fig. 2 *Bismarck sweeps Germany clean. Why do you think Bismarck is portrayed in this way?*

Cross-reference

Within Prussia itself, the system of voting for its own state government was different; the Prussian situation is described on page 59.

So, despite its limitations, it would be wrong to describe the 1871 constitution as wholly illiberal. If political groups were anxious to fight for a place in the Reichstag, they must have felt the prize worth having!

However, in 1871 the German political 'parties', as outlined below, were not quite like British political parties. They were not competing for the right to rule the country and preparing manifestos which offered broad policy proposals. They were actually more like pressure groups representing the interests of different sections of the community and wanting to be in a position to be able to advance the concerns of their followers.

Table 1 below indicates the main political groupings of the Bismarckian era.

Table 1 *The main political groupings from 1871*

Party	Key features
National Liberals (NL)	Formed in 1867 by those who supported Bismarck's policy of German unification. This was the party of the Protestant middle classes. It was supported by wealthy, well-educated men such as bankers, merchants and civil servants. It favoured free trade, a strong Germany and a constitutional Liberal state. After 1875, it grew more Conservative as its members felt threatened by the growing strength of the Social Democratic Party.
Centre Party (Zentrum)	Founded in 1870, this party represented the German Catholics and the minorities opposed to Bismarck. The party was strong in the southern German states, particularly Bavaria and also in the Rhineland. It was determined to preserve the position of the Catholic Church, especially in education. It was Conservative regarding the constitution and favoured greater decentralisation, but it was quite Liberal in its attitude to social reform.
The Social Democratic Party (SPD)	There was already a socialist grouping in 1871 but the SPD itself was not founded until 1875. This party represented the working classes and worked with the trade unions. It supported a reduction in the power of the elites and the extension of welfare reforms. Its most extreme members wanted a total overthrow of the constitution, but the majority were prepared to work within it in order to bring about better conditions for the masses.
German Conservative Party (DKP)	Conservative elements adopted the DKP name in 1876. This group mainly represented the Protestant and aristocratic Prussian Junker landowners. It was the most right wing of the political groups and detested the Reichstag because it was elected by universal suffrage. It was dominant in the Prussian Landtag (state government).
Free Conservatives or *Reichspartei* (FKP)	Formed in 1871, the FKP represented landowners, industrialists and businessmen. Its members were strong supporters of Bismarck and its geographic base was wider than the DKP.
The Progressives or *Fortschrittpartei* (DFP)	A party which believed in a Liberal, constitutional state but disliked centralism and militarism so was not very supportive of Bismarck. This group wanted to extend the powers of the Reichstag.

■ Cross-reference

For details of the socialist grouping in 1871, see page 31.

Bismarck's new constitution ensured that he held a pivotal position at the centre of government. He controlled the governments of Prussia and the German Empire and he was at the centre of policy making. He lectured the Reichstag to get them to accept his proposals and if they failed to comply, he sought the Kaiser's permission to dissolve the Lower House and hold new elections – with the intention of getting more supporters there. Although Bismarck was supposed, by law, to discuss proposed legislation with the Kaiser, Wilhelm I came to be so totally dependent on his chancellor that he more or less allowed him to go his own way. Since the Kaiser was so desperate to keep his services, whenever there were differences of opinion (as did happen on a number of occasions), Bismarck could usually get what he wanted by threatening to resign! Indeed Lady Emily Russell, wife of the British ambassador, was to write in 1880:

> The initiated know that the Kaiser has allowed Prince Bismarck to have his own way in everything and the great Chancellor revels in the absolute power he has acquired and does as he pleases. He lives in the country and governs the German Empire without ever taking the trouble to consult the Kaiser about his plans. Wilhelm only learns what is being done from the documents to which his signature is necessary and which his Majesty signs without questions or hesitation. Never has a subject been granted so much power from his sovereign and never has a minister inspired a nation with more terror. No wonder, then, that the Crown Prince (heir to the throne) should be so worried about this state of things, which he has not more personal power or influence to remedy than anyone else in Prussia. Prince Bismarck terrorises Germany with the Emperor's silent and cheerful consent.

 2

Fig. 3 *Bismarck and Kaiser Wilhelm I*

A closer look

Bismarck's power

There is much debate over the extent of power influenced by Bismarck. On the one hand, he seemed to have had almost dictatorial powers. As a result of the constitution, he was Prussian prime minister, foreign minister, Reich chancellor and he also presided over the Bundesrat. He manipulated Wilhelm I and interfered in the appointment of ministers (giving them little power beyond the carrying out of his instructions). He did not consult with others and he did not use a cabinet system (whereby ministers jointly decide policy). Indeed, it would seem that the government was more Bismarck's than the Kaiser's.

However, there were limitations to his power. He was ultimately answerable to the Kaiser. If he lost the support of the Kaiser, as did in fact happen after 1888, when Wilhelm I died, he had no power in his own right. In addition, the new Germany was a federal state and the individual states which made up the Confederation retained a great deal of independence. Bismarck could not ignore the Reichstag either, since he needed to ensure that he had majority support there, especially when the army budget was up for renewal. He found it increasingly difficult to keep the Reichstag 'on side' as his rule progressed and there were sometimes some quite ugly scenes. Finally, Bismarck's control of day-to-day decision making was limited by his frequent absences from Berlin because of his ill-health, which caused him to retreat to his country estates.

How far did the new German constitution of 1871 establish a democratic form of government in Germany?

A closer look

Prussia

Prussia controlled two-thirds of the territory of the new German Empire, commanded three-fifths of its population and possessed many of its industrial and mineral resources. The King of Prussia was the emperor, and the Minister-President of Prussia, the chancellor. Prussia also dominated the Bundesrat, with 17 of the 58 votes there (Bavaria was next highest with six) and the civil service and bureaucracy of the empire followed the pattern already established in Prussia. The Imperial army was modelled on the Prussian army and law codes were based on the Prussian ones. Yet, Prussia was a strongly authoritarian state. It had its own 'three class' franchise system which led to a Prussian parliament dominated by aristocratic Junkers. Consequently, Prussian influence acted as a brake on democratic change, while at the same time providing a source of strength, since Prussia's traditions of military prowess and administrative efficiency gave the German people something to be proud of and served as a patriotic focus. It is perhaps no coincidence that Bismarck chose to wear a Prussian military uniform, whenever possible, throughout his time as chancellor.

Domestic politics of the 'Liberal' era, 1871–8

Moves to further unification

After the proclamation of a united German Empire in 1871, Bismarck was still faced with the task of creating a nation from peoples who had different ways of life, different backgrounds and different religions. Broadly speaking, whilst northern Germany was mainly Protestant and in the throes of industrial development, the south was more rural and Catholic. Those with authority within the separate states, some of which had ruled themselves for hundreds of years, were jealous of their customs and anxious to protect their power and rights. Furthermore, the new empire included substantial minority groups who had never wanted to be part of Germany, for example the 2,300,000 Poles and the large numbers of Jews who lived in the east of Prussia. There were also Danes, who had been incorporated into the empire after the seizure of Schleswig in war, and French, particularly in Alsace-Lorraine, which had been taken in 1871 and which had added another one and a half million people to the Imperial population. Bismarck was consequently well aware of the importance of establishing central government control and removing any minority interest which might threaten the national state. He was later proud to say: 'In 1871, I had an empire, but by 1879, I had a nation.'

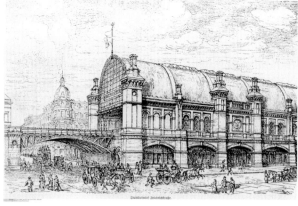

Fig. 4 *Symbol of the new Germany: the Friedrichstrasse railway station in Berlin. Seven large Berlin railway stations were built between 1866 and 1880*

The National Liberals had won 125 of 397 seats in the 1871 elections, making them the largest single party in the Reichstag. Their leader, von Bennigsen, was more than willing to cooperate with Bismarck to complete the process of German unification and, in particular, to promote measures which would help economic development and bring healthy competition in trade. In the first Reichstag session, over 100 acts were agreed to try to bring administrative and economic unity to the new state. Laws were passed which:

- turned the Prussian state bank into the Reichsbank (with a currency based on the Gold Standard)
- established a single currency throughout the Reich. From January 1876, the mark became the only legal tender
- abolished tariffs on all internal trade
- harmonised weights and measures
- extended and joined the railway network across the whole empire
- harmonised the postal system
- established a uniform law of commerce
- began the process of standardising law based on Prussian law codes. A national penal code was introduced in 1872 (although some lesser laws and control of the police remained state concerns). The full codification of civil law was not completed until January 1900.
- established a single court system (although full uniformity of legal practice was not achieved until 1877). A central supreme court (for appeals) was established at Leipzig in 1879.

However, despite the steps towards greater unification, Germany still retained the flag of the North German Confederation and there was no 'official' National Anthem.

Bismarck's political position

Many of Bismarck's Junker supporters were concerned about Bismarck's apparent 'alliance' with the National Liberals. They were jealous of the growing power of the merchants, businessmen and factory owners and feared the effects such change might have on the power of the landowners of Prussia. However, such fears were largely unjustified. Bismarck always retained the upper hand when working with the National Liberals. His concerns were for German unity and he recognised the need to 'balance interests', keeping both the Liberals and Conservatives on board as he went about his work. By cooperating with the National Liberals, he gained the support of the Reichstag, which made life easier for him, but he never felt bound to this group. Indeed, he was to say, in a speech of 1879:

> Since I have been a Minister I have never belonged to any party and have not been able to belong to any party. From the beginning of my career, I have had only one guiding star: that is, by what means and in what direction I could bring about German unity and how I can consolidate this unity; how I can promote it and shape it in such a manner that it will be maintained permanently. I cannot, and the government cannot, be at the beck and call of particular parties. It must go its own way; the way that it regards as correct. The government will require the support of the parties but it can never submit itself to the domination of any single party.

3

Bismarck showed his determination not to become beholden to the National Liberals when he pushed through the Press Law of

1874, allowing the government to prosecute editors who published material that they did not approve of and so undermining the Liberal principle of freedom of the press. He also thwarted the Reichstag's attempts to reduce Junker influence in the Prussian government. Most importantly of all, when the army budget, which had last been agreed in 1867, was requiring renewal in 1874, he tried to persuade the Reichstag that they should grant money for the army on a permanent basis so that military matters could be completely taken out of the Reichstag's control. Not surprisingly, the National Liberals were horrified at such a proposal.

Ultimately, a compromise was reached. In the Septennial Law, it was agreed that the Reichstag would vote on the military budget every seven years. This was essentially a defeat for Bismarck, but it was hardly a success for the Reichstag or for the National Liberals. By conceding to a seven yearly review, the Reichstag had lost a means with which to bargain with the chancellor. Given that much of the Reich's income came from indirect taxation and the contributions of the constituent states, losing this right of regular approval of military spending was yet another limitation to the Reichstag's power.

The national minorities

Bismarck adopted a mixed policy towards the minority racial groups. In the east, he favoured enforced Germanisation. In 1872–3, German was made the only language to be used in schools in the Polish-speaking areas and, in 1876, it was made the sole language of commerce. Only German could be used in the law courts too and the minority Poles were forced to accept German ways and customs. Bismarck's attack on the Catholic Church further weakened the cultural tradition of the Poles. Their Catholic leader, Cardinal Ledochowski, was imprisoned and the people left without a religious leader for 12 years. Germans were encouraged to buy up Polish farms in East Prussia, with the help of state loans, so as to ensure Germanic control there. In 1885–6, Bismarck even expelled 34,000 Poles and Jews whom he claimed had crossed into Germany from Russia and Austria, despite protestations by the Reichstag.

Bismarck was not personally anti-Semitic and he appreciated the contribution of Jewish financiers and businessmen to German industrial development. However, he was prepared to exploit anti-Semitism when it suited his purpose. Anti-Semitism made some headway in Germany at the time of the economic depression from the mid-1870s, when Jews were blamed as scapegoats. In 1878, Adolf Stoeker founded the Christian Socialist Workers' Party as an anti-Semitic party. This found some appeal with the lower middle classes and Bismarck briefly sought its support. However, he soon came to regard Stoeker with disfavour and forced him to withdraw from public affairs in 1889, although he returned on the accession of Wilhelm II.

From 1878, German became the only language permitted in the schools in Danish North Schleswig too. In 1879, when Austria was keen to make an alliance with Germany, Bismarck took the opportunity to abandon a promise made to Austria in 1866, that a plebiscite (direct vote) would be held in North Schleswig to decide the area's future.

Bismarck was reasonably conciliatory towards the French in Alsace-Lorraine, although they also suffered from the persecution of the Catholic Church. In 1874, Bismarck allotted 15 Reichstag deputies to represent the area. He also promoted the revival of Strasbourg University in 1880 and

■ **Question**

Explain why the Septennial Law was passed in 1874.

■ **Cross-reference**

Bismarck's attack on the Catholic Church, known as the *Kulturkampf*, is discussed later in this chapter on pages 21–5.

■ **Exploring the detail**

Governor-Generals of Alsace-Lorraine

The first Governor-General was Edwin Freiherr von Manteuffel, who was reputedly chosen because Bismarck considered him a rival and wanted him out of the way. Manteuffel immediately announced that he wanted Alsace-Lorraine to find a place as the 'core-land' of the German Reich, although he never achieved this. He was a cultivated and generous man and highly regarded by the inhabitants of the area. In 1885, Prince Chlodwig von Hohenlohe was chosen to succeed him. Although he had to carry out some coercive measures introduced by Bismarck in 1887 and 1888, despite his own disapproval of them, his conciliatory manner helped reconcile the Alsace-Lorrainers to German rule.

ppointed humane and conscientious governors – Edwin von Manteuffel o 1885 and Prince Chlodwig von Hohenlohe, who was himself a Catholic. However, Prussian civil servants ran the lower levels of government and German was the language of education and administration. Furthermore, ny strongly pro-French citizens were encouraged to leave the area, with he result that 400,000 people did so between 1870 and 1914. Alsace epeatedly elected deputies committed to the separation of the area from Germany, which must be an indication that Bismarck never succeeded in ruly integrating the peoples of these provinces.

Activity

Thinking point

Can you think of any reasons why Bismarck treated the people of Alsace-Lorraine differently from the Poles?

The Kulturkampf

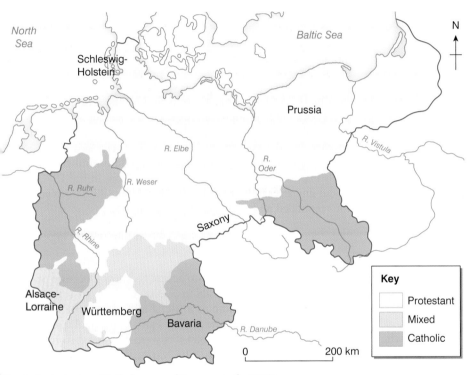

Fig. 5 *Protestant and Catholic areas of Germany in the 1870s*

Reasons

Bismarck's most determined stand against 'minorities' in his first seven years as chancellor was that taken against the Catholics. Since he believed that Germans should put their loyalty to the state above all else, this is, perhaps, unsurprising. 39 per cent of Germans were Catholics, compared to 61 per cent Protestants. Prussia and the Prussian Junker class were staunchly Protestant and Bismarck himself came from this background. Catholicism, on the other hand, was strong in the southern German states. These southern states were inclined to look for guidance from Austria (whom they had supported in 1866) and had been the last, and most reluctant, of the states to join the German Empire.

Bismarck's anti-Catholicism was also a reaction to the development of the Catholic Centre (*Zentrum*) Party, which had been set up to protect Catholic interests in 1870 and which gained 58 Reichstag deputies in 1871. The Centre was supported not only by the southern Catholics, but also by the Poles in the east and the French of Alsace-Lorraine.

In the 1864 *Syllabus of Errors*, the Pope had declared the Catholic Church to be opposed to Liberalism, Nationalism and 'recent' civilisation. In 1870,

Key term

Kulturkampf: literally meaning a struggle for culture or civilisation, in practice this was an attack on the Catholic Church and its political influence in Germany, particularly through the Centre Party.

Cross-reference

For the events of 1866, re-read the Introduction.

■ Exploring the detail

The Pope

The Pope is the head of the Catholic Church and resides in the Vatican in Rome. All Catholics look to the Pope as their spiritual leader.

■ Cross-reference

The Centre Party is outlined on page 16.

Fig. 6 *Bismarck as a bullfighter subduing the Catholic Church. Notice that the bull is wearing a papal crown*

■ Did you know?

The Catholic Church was traditionally conservative and the momentous changes that were affecting Europe in the 19th century caused it considerable alarm. Industrialisation was producing a more vociferous 'working class' and new theories were challenging the teaching of the Catholic Church. In 1859, Charles Darwin had published *Origin of the Species*, suggesting a non-biblical explanation of the creation of species, while between 1867 and 1894, Karl Marx was to publish the three-volumed *Das Kapital*, encouraging workers to rise against their masters and create a classless society. The Pope's own temporal (earthly) power had been challenged by the unification of Italy. The new doctrinal statements were, in part, an attempt to reinforce control.

■ Activity

Source analysis

Study Source 4. What arguments does Bismarck use to try to justify his Kulturkampf and dispel criticism?

he went on to proclaim the Doctrine of Papal Infallibility, which stated that on matters of morality and faith the Pope could not be wrong. This placed Catholics in a difficult position and meant that they could face difficult choices between the demands of their Church and their country.

Bismarck feared that the Centre Party would encourage civil disobedience among Catholics whenever the policies of the state conflicted with those of the Pope. These fears grew even more acute when, in 1874, the Centre Party under a new leader, the able politician Ludwig Windhorst, won 91 Reichstag seats, becoming the second largest party in the Reichstag and threatening Bismarck's ability to control the majority. Such a development confirmed Bismarck's determination to crush Catholic influence in Germany.

■ Key profile

Ludwig Windhorst

Ludwig Windhorst (1812–91) was born into a Catholic family in Hanover in 1812. He became a deputy and Minister of the Interior there and opposed Bismarck's annexation of his state. In 1874, he became leader of the Centre Party. It was chiefly owing to his skill and courage as a parliamentary debater, and his tact as a leader, that the party held its own and constantly increased in numbers. He was especially exposed to the attacks of Bismarck who, in the 1870s, attempted unsuccessfully to discredit him. After 1879, however, he became reconciled and even friendly to Bismarck.

Campaign

Some German Catholics had refused to accept the new Doctrine of Papal Infallibility. There were only about 50,000 of these so-called 'Old Catholics', but Bismarck saw them as a useful ally against the rest of the Catholic Church in general, and the Centre Party in particular, especially when 'Old Catholic' teachers and professors were dismissed from schools and universities by Catholic bishops. The National Liberals, who wanted to replace religious control of education with state control, also offered support and the campaign cemented the 'alliance' of 1871–8.

Claiming to be acting in the interests of the Old Catholics, in 1873, Bismarck launched the *Kulturkampf* with these words:

> The question before us, is, in my opinion, not a religious, ecclesiastical question. It is a political question. It is not, as our Catholic citizens are being persuaded, a matter of a struggle between a Protestant dynasty and a Catholic Church. It is not a matter of a struggle between belief and unbelief. It is a matter of conflict, which is as old as the human race, between monarchy and priesthood. What is at stake is the defence of the state.

4

Since 1871, a climate hostile to the Catholics and Centre Party had already started to develop in government. For example, there had been a series of newspaper articles against the Centre Party, and the Catholic section of the Prussian Ministry of Religion and Education had been abolished. Clergy had also been ordered to avoid any mention of politics while preaching. In May 1872, diplomatic relations with the Vatican had been broken off and the Jesuits, a religious order pledged to the spread of Catholicism and strong supporters of Papal authority, were forbidden from preaching or entering schools. This had led to the expulsion of almost all Jesuits from Prussia and an anti-Jesuit campaign had gradually begun to spread through the rest of Germany.

It was in a series of laws passed in Prussia between 1873 and 1875 that Bismarck intensified this Kulturkampf. In May 1873, the 'May' or 'Falk' laws were introduced by the Prussian Minister of Religion and Education, Adalbert Falk. These laws brought the Catholic Church more closely under government control. Catholic education came under state supervision, including the education of priests themselves. Only those who had studied in Germany and passed a state exam could become priests and existing priests were required to retrain and prove their loyalty to the state. The appointment of clergy was to be made by the state (rather than the Pope), and a civil marriage ceremony was made compulsory in Prussia and, subsequently, the rest of the empire. All other religious orders were dissolved, state financial aid to the Catholic Church was ended, and Prussian Catholics were deprived of legal and civil rights.

In 1874, the registration of births, marriages and deaths in Prussia was removed from the Church and taken over by the state. All states were given the right to restrict the freedom of movement of the clergy and any banned priest caught preaching could be placed under house arrest or even expelled from Germany. Finally, in 1875, the Prussian government was given the power to suspend state subsidies to **dioceses** where the clergy were resisting the new laws, and every religious order, except for nursing orders, was abolished.

At first, Wilhelm I was lukewarm in his support for the Kulturkampf. However, when Pius IX wrote to him in 1873 complaining about the Kulturkampf and adding that anyone who had been baptised belonged to the Pope, Wilhelm was much offended and showed some support. Nevertheless, many members of the royal family, including the Crown Prince Friedrich and his English wife, Victoria, regarded the campaign with disfavour.

Activity

Revision exercise

As you read through this section, make a timeline of the key events of the Kulturkampf.

Key term

Diocese: a unit of Church administration which was part of an ecclesiastical area headed by a bishop or archbishop.

Fig. 7 *Bismarck plays chess with Pope Pius IX. What is this cartoon trying to say about the Kulturkampf?*

Results and end of the Kulturkampf

The Pope sent a letter to all German bishops instructing them to disobey the anti-Catholic laws. Although Bismarck forbade the bishops to print the letter, by 1876 all the Catholic bishops of Prussia and all Polish bishops had been either imprisoned or exiled and 1,400 out of 4,600 Catholic parishes were without priests.

However, despite this repression, the Catholic Church continued to thrive. Bismarck had underestimated the strength of Catholicism and the extent of popular support which it enjoyed. Persecution created martyrs and encouraged even greater resistance. Many ordinary Catholics rallied to the cause of their Church and became more convinced than ever that they should support the Centre Party in order to defend their interests. The Centre Party's leader, Windhorst, rose to the challenge, organising meetings and 'national resistance tours' to attack the Kulturkampf and unite the Catholic voters. The party was extremely successful in whipping up support which cut across both class and regional divisions. By 1874, it had increased its number of Reichstag seats to 91 – fewer than the Liberals who held 155, but nearly twice as many as the next largest party, the Progressives.

Far from unifying the newly-created empire, Bismarck had intensified its divisions. In 1874, a Catholic barrel-maker tried to assassinate Bismarck. Furthermore, there were growing problems in the minority areas, among the Poles and peoples of Alsace-Lorraine. German Protestants were even expressing unease with Bismarck's attack on religious freedoms, while within the dominant National Liberal Party there were those, of Jewish blood, who disliked the way the campaign was also provoking more anti-Semitism in Germany.

By the late-1870s, Bismarck must have realised that the campaign had been a mistake. His frequent absences from Berlin, occasioned by his own poor health, made it difficult for him to keep control of the situation, and he seemed keen to find an excuse to bring this destructive campaign to an end.

Other factors also favoured the ending of the Kulturkampf. Bismarck:

- wanted a closer alliance with Catholic Austria and he feared that his anti-Catholic policies would stand in the way
- suspected that the Centre Party was giving support to those in France seeking revenge for Germany's seizure of Alsace-Lorraine in 1871
- wanted to change his economic policy and abandon free trade, after the agricultural and industrial depressions of the 1870s. Since this would lose him the support of the National Liberals, he could not afford to have the Centre Party (which favoured protection) as an 'enemy'
- wanted to build up the support of the Protestant Conservatives, who had grown increasingly hostile to the Kulturkampf because it was promoting anti-clericalism in Germany
- felt that increasing working-class support for Socialism posed an even greater threat to German unity and his own position than the Catholic Church. He could not hope to wage a war successfully against both Catholicism and Socialism and since the Catholic Church had declared against Socialism, Bismarck felt that he might be able to utilise the Centre Party and Catholicism against this new 'enemy'.

Cross-reference

Bismarck's economic policy, including the issues of free trade and protectionism, and the political changes of 1878–9, are discussed on pages 26–9. His policies against Socialism can be found on pages 32–3.

The death of Pius IX in 1878 and the election of a new and more liberal pope, Leo XIII, provided Bismarck with the excuse he needed to change to a policy of conciliation. One of Leo XIII's first acts was to write to Bismarck, expressing his wish for a reconciliation and an end to the struggle. Bismarck began long and difficult negotiations with the Pope's envoy. He put all the blame for the May Laws on Dr Falk, who was forced to resign. In 1880, the repeal of the May Laws began, together with the removal of the ban on foreign-trained priests within Germany. Catholic clergy gradually returned to their parishes. However, not all the laws were repealed. Civil marriages continued and the Jesuits were not allowed in Germany.

The struggle had several consequences:

- Bismarck's subsequent relations with the Papacy were good and in 1885 he even proposed the Pope as a mediator in Germany's colonial dispute with Spain.
- The Centre Party, which gained 93 seats in 1877, 94 in 1878 and 100 in 1881, transformed itself into a purely religious party and was no longer seen as the refuge of Bismarck's 'enemies' (*Reichsfeinde*). Leo XIII encouraged the Centre Party to support the existence of the German Empire and thus, in the long term, unity was strengthened.
- Closer relations with the Papacy and the support of the Centre Party facilitated an alliance with Austria, signed in 1879.
- The change of policy in 1878–9 enabled Bismarck to make himself independent from the National Liberals (whose prestige fell).
- The Kulturkampf highlighted Bismarck's qualities as a politician. His actions showed him to be the supreme opportunist who was able to move from persecution to conciliation to strengthen his position in the Reichstag and facilitate the policy changes he desired.

Activity

Revision exercise

The points given above provide some positive outcomes of the Kulturkampf. In pairs, prepare a balance sheet which shows both the positive and negative aspects of the Kulturkampf, and provides some comment on both.

Activity

Class debate

Divide your class into two groups. One group prepares speeches arguing that the Kulturkampf was a mistake and the other group that it was not. After presenting your speeches, take a vote to establish the overall view of the class.

Question

How successful was Bismarck in bringing about the full unification of Germany in the years 1871–8?

Political changes 1878–9

Bismarck's political realignment in 1878–9 has been described as a turning point in his domestic policy. It included the:

- abandonment of the Kulturkampf
- re-introduction of tariffs on the imports of foreign goods
- ending of the political alliance with the National Liberals
- creation of a Conservative/Centre support base in the Reichstag
- beginning of a new political struggle against Socialism.

Fig. 8 *The port of Hamburg. Sometimes known as the 'city of free trade', Hamburg had flourished in the economic boom, but by 1878 German manufacturers were anxious to reduce foreign imports*

Key terms

Free trade: having few or no duties or tariffs on imports or exports. Those who supported this, such as the National Liberals, believed it encouraged economic growth because it kept the price of imported raw materials low which, in turn, reduced the cost of manufactured goods. Consequently, these could be sold abroad at a more competitive price. It was also hoped that free trade would encourage other countries to reduce or remove duties.

Protection: introducing duties (tariffs) especially on imports. This would increase the price of imported goods, especially manufactured goods, and encourage consumers to buy home-produced goods. However, it could lead to retaliation, with other countries introducing similar tariffs, and so have an adverse effect on exports.

Economic concerns

The first area of change was in economic policy. In the 1870s, in order to keep the support of the National Liberals, Bismarck had followed a policy of **free trade**. The German economy had experienced a rapid boom in the early 1870s and had appeared strong enough to withstand foreign competition. However, in 1873, it suffered a serious financial crisis, when prices started falling throughout the world, and this was followed by several years of much slower growth. German manufacturers were alarmed and blamed the strong opposition which they faced from foreign competitors. Consequently, they started to demand **protection**.

Most European countries, with the exception of Britain, had moved towards protection by the late-1870s and, in 1878, some of the leading German manufacturers formed the 'Central Association of German Manufacturers' to campaign for the introduction of tariffs on imports in Germany. Agriculture was also suffering from a depression due to a series of bad harvests at the end of the 1870s and increased foreign competition from cheap American and Russian wheat. Peasant farmers and landowners alike feared for their incomes and survival. Like the manufacturers and industrialists, they began to campaign for protective tariffs against cheap foreign grain.

The views of these two groups are summed up in this declaration from industrialists and farmers in the Westphalia district in February 1877:

> In view of the depression which has lasted for many years and for the promotion of general economic interests it is necessary to preserve and develop home production as the first condition of general welfare. The main factors for the attainment of this aim are low freight rates, well-considered commercial treaties and tariffs and a rational system of taxation.

5

Table 2 *The price of wheat and rye in Berlin between 1871 and 1879*

Year	Wheat (marks per tonne)	Rye (marks per tonne)
1871	216	159
1872	238	163
1873	251	175
1874	233	170
1875	193	151
1876	206	154
1877	227	153
1878	194	132
1879	198	133

Williamson, D., **Bismarck and Germany 1862–90***, 1986*

Activity

Source analysis

Using Source 5, Table 2 and your own knowledge, explain why farmers and manufacturers both favoured the introduction of tariffs in the late-1870s.

It is difficult to know when Bismarck was converted to the idea of protection, although in 1876 he discreetly began to encourage the campaign, whilst carefully avoiding any definite commitment. Certainly, by 1878, he had become a supporter. There were a number of reasons for this:

- As a Junker landowner himself, Bismarck was sympathetic to the demands of the agriculturalists. A threat to agricultural incomes would undermine the economic position of the Junker aristocracy (who supplied the officers for the army and on whom the Imperial state rested).

- Bismarck favoured German self-sufficiency, especially in wheat. He did not want Germany to become dependent on foreign imports and felt it essential that the country should be able to feed itself, in case of war.

- Tariffs could provide the government with much needed revenue. The Reich government could not tax its citizens directly but was dependent on contributions from individual states. Since all other taxes had to have Reichstag approval, Bismarck favoured any means of gaining income which did not require dependency on an annual Reichstag vote.

- Bismarck was keen to work more closely with the German Conservative Party and the Centre Party (which included Junkers and factory owners). He needed their support against the growing threat of Socialism.

- Russia, which supplied Germany with wheat, had adopted a policy of protection. However, relations with Russia had become strained over issues in the Balkans in the years 1877–8 and protection could act as a form of retaliation.

Bismarck declared to the Reichstag in May 1879:

> The only country which persists in a policy of free trade is England and that will not last long. France and America have departed completely from this line; Austria instead of lowering her tariffs has made them higher; Russia has done the same. By opening the doors of our state to the imports of foreign countries, we have become the dumping ground for the production of those countries. Since we have become swamped by the surplus production of foreign nations, our prices have been depressed. The development of our industries and our entire economic position has suffered as a consequence.
>
> Let us finally close our doors and erect barriers, as we have proposed to you, in order to reserve for German industries at least the home market, which because of German good nature, has been exploited by foreigners. I see that those countries that have adopted protection are prospering and those countries which have free trade are deteriorating.

6

Questions

1 Summarise Bismarck's arguments as given in Source 6.

2 What arguments might the National Liberals and other supporters of free trade have used against those of Bismarck?

Cross-reference

For further details on the army budget and the Septennial Law, refer to page 20.

Political realignments

By the late-1870s, Bismarck had grown increasingly irritated by the National Liberals. They had forced him to agree to give the Reichstag the power to vote for the army budget every seven years and constantly demanded greater parliamentary powers. Their support for free trade, when others were clamouring for change, proved the final straw.

In the elections of 1877, the National Liberals had lost seats whilst the pro-protection Conservative parties did rather better. Bismarck did try to carry the National Liberals with him, proposing a programme of financial and constitutional reforms and offering their leader, R. V. Benningsen, the post of Prussian Minister of the Interior in 1877. However, negotiations broke down when the Liberals then insisted that two further colleagues, who belonged to the left wing of the party, should also join the Prussian government.

Table 3 *Number of Reichstag seats won by the political parties in the elections of 1871–8*

Party	1871	1874	1877	1878
German Conservatives	57	22	40	59
Free Conservatives	37	33	38	57
National Liberals	125	155	141	109
Progress Party	46	49	35	26
Centre Party	61	91	93	94
Social Democrats	2	9	12	9
Minorities, e.g. Poles, Danes, Alsatians	23	34	40	34

*Adapted from Murphy, D., Morris, T. and Fulbrook, M., **Germany 1848–1991**, 2008*

The economic changes of 1878–9 and their impact

In February 1878 Bismarck announced to the Reichstag the first stage of a comprehensive financial reform that would almost certainly involve the introduction of tariffs. However, the National Liberals led a campaign against these proposals and, in June 1878, an exasperated Bismarck called an election aimed to deprive the National Liberals of still more seats. His gamble paid off when they lost 29 seats and the Conservatives and Centre Party emerged with the overall majority.

Consequently, in 1879 Bismarck introduced legislation for levying tariffs on iron, iron goods and grain and for increasing indirect taxation on selected luxury goods. The bill was passed by a majority made up from the Conservatives, Free Conservatives, Centre and 15 so-called 'tariff rebels' from the National Liberal Party, who were forced to resign from that party as a result. The unity of the National Liberal Party was thus destroyed and important economic and political changes resulted.

Table 4 *Results of the changes of 1878–9*

Political	Economic
The National Liberal Party was seriously weakened by the crisis of 1878–9. There were already divisions before 1878 but these became permanent in 1879. The right wing of the party supported Bismarck over tariff reform and the Anti-Socialist Law. The supporters of free trade broke away and joined the more extreme Progressive Party.	Although agricultural prices continued to fall, the tariff on grain protected farmers and landowners from the worst effects of the agricultural depression. Landowners became strong supporters of Bismarck.
The main party of Liberalism lost support. There was less pressure on Bismarck to move towards a more representative system of government. In the 1880s he relied for his majorities in the Reichstag on an alliance between the Conservative parties and the Centre, together with the right wing of the National Liberal Party. The forces of Conservatism were therefore dominant in the 1880s.	Industrialists and businessmen abandoned their support for free trade and the National Liberal Party. In the 1880s they increasingly supported the Conservative Party. This became known as the 'alliance of steel and rye'.
Bismarck had demonstrated his supreme political skill and opportunism, his control over the Reichstag and his ability to make and break alliances.	Consumers suffered from artificially high prices on basic food products such as bread. High tariffs had adverse effects on living standards, especially for the very poor. This, in turn, provided greater support for Socialism and the SPD.
The Reich became more united in its support of protection since Bismarck presented tariffs as a patriotic necessity, essential for the defence of the fatherland.	

Summary question

Why did Bismarck change to a policy of protection at the end of the 1870s?

AQA Examiner's tip

Make a short list of factors which influenced Bismarck's decision. Don't forget these can be political as well as economic. Arrange these in a way that emphasises which you consider to be the most important factors, and how the various reasons link together.

Politics and economics, 1878–90

In this chapter you will learn about:

- the political struggles after 1878 and the impact of the Anti-Socialist Law

- the introduction of State Socialism and its results

- the political impact of economic and social change in Germany

- Bismarck's relationship with the Kaiser and the Reichstag.

Exploring the detail

Reichsfeinde

Bismarck employed the tactic of labelling groups which he regarded as a threat to his view of the German state as *Reichsfeinde* or 'Enemies of the Reich'. This enabled him to create an alliance of parties which supported him in the Reichstag (and Prussian Landtag) in opposition to these 'outsiders'. The Reichsfeinde were, variously, the German Catholics (from 1871), the Social Democrats (after 1878), the progressive, left-wing Liberals (early/mid-1880s), and the Poles of Eastern Prussia (from c.1885). However, such policies were prone to backfire as they strengthened the common identity of members of the victimised groups, destabilising rather than strengthening the state.

In June 1878, Bismarck was peacefully exercising his great danes and admiring his landed estate at Friedrichsruh near Hamburg, when news was brought of a terrible tragedy. Eighty-one-year-old Kaiser Wilhelm I had been rushed back to the royal palace, streaming with blood, after an attempted assassination. Fortunately the emperor's life had been spared, but the news, coming just one month after a previous assassination attempt, stopped Bismarck in his tracks. In May, it had been a plumber and ex-member of the SPD, named Max Hödel, who had tried to assassinate his beloved Kaiser. Investigations rapidly taught him that the second would-be assassin was Dr Karl Nobiling, an unemployed academic.

Fig. 1 *A London magazine reports the attempted assassination of Wilhelm I*

Nobiling had no connection with the Socialist Party, although it was said that he had expressed sympathy for the socialists before committing suicide and this was just what Bismarck wanted to hear. Bismarck's attempt to pass anti-socialist legislation after the first assassination attempt had been defeated by the Reichstag, but the new attempt provided further evidence that the socialists were 'Reichsfeinde' – enemies of the state. He hurried to the Reichstag and declared:

> We now have here in Berlin between sixty and one hundred thousand well-organised men who openly avow their resolve to fight against the established order. I deem it necessary that the state should shatter the power of these agitators.
>
> 1

Political struggles after 1878

Socialism in Germany in 1878

Bismarck perceived the emergence of the Social Democratic Party (SPD) and the growing popularity of Socialism as yet another threat to the unity of the Reich, as well as to his own position as chancellor.

Socialism already had a long history in Germany. There had been workers' parties in the more industrially advanced states of Germany in the 1840s and 1850s, but not until 1863 had various groups combined to form the General German Workers' Association (ADAV). This group was led

Fig. 2 *Karl Marx, father of Communism*

by Ferdinand Lassalle, and was committed to a socialist programme which included the redistribution of wealth and the abolition of private property. It had 15,000 members by the middle of the 1870s.

Key profile

Ferdinand Lassalle

Ferdinand Lassalle (1825–64) was a Jewish lawyer. He had begun as a Liberal nationalist and had been imprisoned for his part in the 1848 revolution in Germany. However, he had become convinced that the working class needed their own political party and in 1863 founded the General German Workers' Association, Germany's first Labour Party. Although left wing, Lassalle did not believe in Marxist revolution and was prepared to work with the state for the benefit of working people. He led a flamboyant lifestyle and was killed in a duel.

Fig. 3 *Ferdinand Lassalle, founder of the General German Workers' Association (ADAV)*

The ADAV was followed, in 1869, by a more Marxist organisation, the Social Democratic Workers' Party (SDAP), set up by Karl Liebknecht. This group had a more overtly revolutionary programme, including the abolition of class rule. By 1875, it had 9,000 members.

In 1875, these two groups met at Gotha and united to form the SPD. A programme was drawn up stating aims such as:

There should be:

1 Universal, equal and direct suffrage, with secret, obligatory voting by all citizens at all elections.
2 Legislation by the people.
3 Universal, equal and compulsory state education.
4 A progressive income tax to replace indirect taxation.
5 The right to form trade unions.
6 A reduction in the working day.
7 The abolition of child labour.
8 Protective laws for the life and health of the workers.

2

Did you know?

SPD or SAPD?

In fact the Social Democratic Party was only known as the SPD after 1890. From 1875 it was called the SAPD, or Socialist Workers' Party of Germany. However, few books make this distinction and to avoid confusion this book refers to the party as the SPD throughout.

Cross-reference

Karl Liebknecht is profiled on page 88.

Activity

Talking point

Read Source 2.

1 How revolutionary do you feel the socialist programme of 1875 was?

2 Which of the points do you think would most alarm Bismarck? Why?

■ **Exploring the detail**

Socialism

Socialism is a belief in equality and the abolition of class privilege. The Germans, Karl Marx and Friedrich Engels, were the main figures in 19th century European Socialism. In 1848, they co-authored the *Communist Manifesto* which put forward the idea that all history was the history of class struggles and that the final stage would come when the workers overthrew their capitalist masters so that, after a transitional period, governments would wither away as society became classless. However, not all socialists were Marxist or Communist. Some socialists wanted to remove existing governments but by more peaceful means, while the most moderate socialists wanted to achieve greater equality by working within existing state systems, seeking to reduce private profit, extend opportunities for all and spread welfare reforms.

The SPD was committed to the overthrow of the monarchy and the establishment of a republic with nationalised industries and workers enjoying a share of the profits. These were Marxist ideas but the party's leaders appreciated that they were unlikely to be able to lead Germany in revolution in the immediate future. Consequently, they were content to campaign to win seats in the Reichstag and in 1877 the party won half a million votes and 12 seats. This was a negligible amount, but five times that which the separate workers' parties had polled in 1871, and Bismarck was understandably concerned by the threat the new party posed to the position of Germany's Junkers and factory owners – and indeed to himself!

The Anti-Socialist Law

Bismarck believed that Socialism, which was an international movement like Catholicism, was a social and political threat to the unity of the German Empire and a threat to traditional German society in which the majority of peasants showed respect and deference to the monarchy, army and Junker aristocracy. Bismarck also knew that an attack on Socialism would strengthen Germany's ties with Russia and Austria, his Conservative allies overseas, who were intent on suppressing international revolutionary movements.

The two assassination attempts on the emperor in 1878 provided the opportunity Bismarck needed and he took advantage of the public alarm they caused to whip up anti-socialist feeling. He persuaded the Reichstag that the SPD should be suppressed in order to remove a major source of disloyalty.

The Anti-Socialist Law, which was passed in October 1878, declared:

> Organisations which through Social Democratic activities aim to overthrow the established state or social order are hereby forbidden.
>
> All meetings in which Social Democratic activities appear to be dedicated to the overthrow of the existing state or social order shall be dissolved.
>
> All publications in which Social Democratic influence appears to be aimed at overthrowing the established state or social order by breaching the public peace are forbidden.
>
> Anyone who takes part as a member of a forbidden organisation shall be punished with a fine of up to 500 marks or with imprisonment of three months.

As can be seen, the law banned meetings and publications as well as laying down penalties for those considered a threat to the state. These penalties included fines, imprisonment and, at the worst, exile from Germany. Police powers were also increased with powers to search houses, arrest on suspicion, break up meetings, processions and festive gatherings, suppress books, pamphlets, newspapers and periodicals, and seize the property of organisations perceived as a danger to the state. Trade unions and cultural associations with socialist connections were also banned. However, because of the fierce Reichstag opposition, led by the National Liberals and supported by the Centre and Progressive parties, the law did not actually ban the SPD as such. Members could still take part in elections and sit in the Reichstag and federal governments.

Consequences of the Anti-Socialist Law

As with the Kulturkampf, repression had the opposite effect from that which Bismarck had intended. The law deprived many people of their livelihoods and around 15,000 were sentenced to imprisonment or hard labour and many others forced to leave the country.

Since industrial workers were made to feel that the state was unsympathetic and unlikely to right their grievances, after an initial decline in support for the SPD following the act, members and supporters returned in increasing numbers. The number of people voting for the SPD rose from 437,158 in 1878 to 1,427,928 in 1890, and the number of seats held by the SPD rose from 9 to 35 in the same period. The act also helped divorce the socialist deputies – who had to appeal to the broader electoral constituency – from the more militant and persecuted activists and this had the effect of broadening the SPD's appeal.

 Activity

Thinking point

Did the Anti-Socialist Law do more to help or harm Socialism in Germany?

Table 1 *The effects of repression, 1878–90, for the SDP Party in Germany*

Negative	Positive
▪ Membership of the SPD initially declined in the immediate aftermath of the legislation.	▪ Within a few years, trade unionism revived. There was a series of strikes in the industrial and mining areas and by 1890 membership had reached 278,000.
▪ Trade unions were crushed.	▪ The socialist vote nearly doubled between 1878 and 1887.
▪ The cabinet, civil service and Prussian diet were purged in 1880 to remove Liberal sympathisers.	▪ Strong leadership rallied the party and organised resistance. In 1880, the SPD rejected anarchism and terrorism.
▪ 1,350 publications and 45 out of 47 socialist newspapers were suppressed.	▪ A new party newspaper, the *Social Democrat*, was published in Zurich and smuggled into Germany by the 'Red postmaster' – Julius Motteller.
▪ Many were exiled or imprisoned with hard labour.	
▪ The Prussian police expelled 67 leading socialists from Berlin (1879) and prominent socialists were driven from Breslau (1879), Hamburg (1880), and Leipzig (1881).	▪ Groups met in secret to discuss policy developments and collect financial contributions.
▪ Many socialists chose to emigrate, especially to the USA.	▪ Secret conferences were organised on foreign soil including Switzerland in 1880 and Denmark in 1883.
▪ Before the election of 1881, 600 socialists were arrested. The SPD had such difficulty in finding sufficient candidates to contest the elections that one, Bebel, stood in 35 constituencies.	▪ The SPD encouraged great loyalty from its members by organising educational courses, libraries, sports clubs and choral societies.

State Socialism

Bismarck was aware that repression alone would not reduce support for the SPD as many of the workers' grievances were legitimate. He appreciated the need to show the workers that the state was not unconcerned for their welfare and had more to offer the working class than the socialists. This is often referred to as the 'Carrot and stick' approach. Can you explain why?

As Bismarck said to the Reichstag in 1881:

 Key term

State Socialism: providing for workers' welfare through state-run insurance schemes.

> A beginning must be made in reconciling the labouring classes to the state. A remedy cannot be sought only through the repression of socialist excesses. It is necessary to have a definite advancement in the welfare of the working classes. The matter of first importance is the care of those workers who are incapable of earning a living. Previous provision for guarding workers against the risk of falling into helplessness through incapacity caused by accident or age have not proved adequate, and the inadequacy of such provisions has been a main contributing cause driving the working classes to seek help by joining the Social Democratic movement.

4

Activity

Source analysis

What motives are suggested in Sources 4 and 5 for the introduction of State Socialism?

Did you know?

Britain did not adopt similar state insurance schemes until 1908 (Old Age Pensions) and 1911 (Health and Unemployment Insurance). Lloyd George, the chancellor of the exchequer in the Liberal government of this period, sent civil servants to Germany to study the German scheme. It thus became a model for that later adopted by Britain.

In a conversation with a minister, Bismarck added:

> Anyone who has before him the prospect of a pension, be it ever so small, in old age or infirmity, is much happier and more content with his lot, much more tractable and easy to manage, than those whose future is uncertain. As the least taxed people in Europe we can bear with a good deal in that direction. If the result enables us to secure the future of our workers, the money will be well invested, for by spending it thus we may avert a social revolution which may break out fifty years hence.

5

Fig. 4 Socialism proved a difficult force to control

The main measures providing for state social security were:

Table 2 State social security measures

Date	Measure
May 1883	Medical insurance. This scheme was paid for jointly by employers and employees. It allowed for the payment of medical bills for workers and their families and covered 3 million workers.
June 1884	Accident insurance. This was paid for entirely by employers. It provided benefits and funeral grants to people who had been injured at work. In 1886 this was extended to cover 7 million agricultural workers.
May 1889	Old Age Pensions. These were introduced for people over the age of 70.

Bismarck's scheme was the first of its kind in the world and much more extensive than might have been expected at the time. Some workers were enthusiastic about it whilst others believed it was a 'sham' since the government had consistently opposed trade unions and Socialism. The Marxist Friedrich Engels, then in retirement, urged opposition to the scheme, insisting that the workers did not want concessions from an autocratic government but the removal of that government. However, his voice represented only an extreme minority. Some Liberals were also against the scheme for rather different reasons. They believed it extended the role of the state and threatened individual freedom and laissez-faire.

Although Bismarck had hoped the scheme would attract workers away from the SPD, support for the socialists continued to grow and reached nearly 1.5 million by 1890. The SPD's seats in the Reichstag had fallen to 11 in 1887 but three years later they reached 35. At the same time, employers grumbled at the trouble and expense of 'sticking in eleven million stamps every Saturday morning', referring to the insurance stamps which had to be placed in an insurance book for each worker covered by the scheme.

Whilst there was no violent revolution in Germany before 1918, State Socialism certainly failed in winning the workers' full allegiance. The Anti-Socialist Law was renewed four times, effectively making the activities of the socialist labour movement illegal until 30 September 1890. In 1889, Bismarck was so concerned that he proposed that the Anti-Socialist Law be made permanent. However, the Reichstag refused to pass this amendment, and the arrival of a new Kaiser, Wilhelm II, who believed that the workers could be won over by more social insurance schemes, led to the lapsing of the act.

Economic and social change within Germany

Question

How successful were Bismarck's attempts to curb the socialists between 1878 and 1890?

Fig. 5 *A north German naval construction yard c.1889*

Industrial growth

In 1896, Ernest Edwin Williams drew attention to some important changes that were being felt in Britain in 'Made in Germany'.

> Some of your own clothes were probably woven in Germany. You are likely to find that the toys, and the dolls, and the fairy books which your children maltreat in the nursery are made in Germany: nay, the material of your favourite newspaper had the same birthplace as like as not. Roam the house over, and the fateful mark will greet you at every turn, from the piano in your drawing room, to the mug on your kitchen dresser, blazoned though it be with the legend, 'Present from Margate'. Descend to your domestic depths and you will find your very drain-pipes German made. You jot down your reflections with a pencil made in Germany. At midnight your wife comes home from an opera made in Germany, with the aid of instruments and sheets of music made in Germany. You go to bed, and glare wrathfully at a text on the wall; it is illuminated with an English village church and it was 'Printed in Germany'.

This extract, written six years after Bismarck's resignation, helps summarise the huge growth in industrial activity that had taken place in Germany since the achievement of unification in 1871. Consider the following statistics:

Table 3 *Output of coal and steel*

Year	Coal (millions of tonnes)	Steel (millions of tonnes)
1871	29	0.2
1880	45	1.5
1890	70	2.2

*Taken from Lee, S., **Imperial Germany**, 1999*

Table 4 *Length of railway line*

Year	German railway line in kilometres	UK railway line in kilometres for comparison
1871	21,471	21,558
1880	33,838	25,060
1890	42,869	27,827

Table 5 *Population growth in Germany in thousands*

Year	Population	% rural	% urban
1871	41,059	63.9	36.1
1880	45,234	58.6	41.4
1890	49,428	57.5	42.5

Fig. 6 *The economic development of Germany, 1879–90. Can you explain the distribution of economic growth in Germany?*

Clearly, the German economy was growing – and growing fast! This growth was the product of a number of inter-related factors.

- **A huge growth in the German population**. This provided both the market and the labour force for the expanding economy. Furthermore, the balance of the population was towards younger generations who were more mobile and willing to adapt to new skills.

- **The availability of raw materials within the newly united state**. There was coal from the Ruhr, Saar and Silesia, iron-ore from Alsace-Lorraine and the Ruhr and potash from Alsace-Lorraine.

- **Germany's geographical advantages**. These included navigable rivers like the Rhine and Elbe, and the broad flat northern plain which was well suited to the construction of railways. The railway system, essentially complete by 1880, proved invaluable for the transport of raw materials and manufactured goods. The canal and river system stimulated the shipbuilding industry which, in turn, facilitated the growth of overseas trade. By 1908 the total tonnage of the German merchant navy was to be second only to Britain.

- **A highly-developed education system**. German elementary education was deemed the best in the world, whilst higher education made increasing provision for the development of the technical skills necessary in industrial development. In 1870, for example, there were more science graduates at just one German university – Munich – than the total number of science graduates at all English universities.

- **Unification**. This, in itself, had given a boost to economic growth, whilst the tariffs on imports introduced by Bismarck in 1878 helped protect German industry from foreign competition and stimulated further development.

Exploring the detail
The development of cartels

Although Germany suffered from the worldwide depression from 1873, this helped German industry in some ways as it encouraged greater cooperation rather than rivalry between businesses. Some associations were established to encourage lobbying and to put pressure on the government to introduce protection. Some firms went even further in order to reduce internal competition – they formed cartels or associations of producers in similar trades or processes. These increased from 8 in 1875 to 70 by 1887.

Cartels are explained more fully on page 134.

Cross-reference

Bismarck's introduction of tariffs in 1878 is covered on page 29.

■ **The German banking system**. German banks were free from state control and they became heavily involved in industrial research and development. The number of banks increased and close links between banks and businesses developed. Their own representatives were often invited on to boards of directors of firms.

■ **The development of chemicals and electricals**. Germany became a world leader in the newer chemical and electrical industries. Germany had abundant reserves of coal and potash which became the basis for numerous chemical products which were discovered by German scientists in the last decade of the 19th century. By the 1890s Germany had established a virtual world monopoly in the production of synthetic dyes, artificial fibres, some photographic materials, some drugs, plastics and new explosives. In the electrical field German firms such as Siemens led the way in the production of such things as dynamos.

■ **The expansion of overseas trade**. This provided markets for expanding German industry. Food, raw materials and particular types of manufactured goods had to be imported. To pay for these Germany sold abroad chemicals, metal goods and machinery, textiles and coal. In 1890, Germany was buying nearly £200m worth of foreign goods and selling £153m.

Activity

Revision exercise

Working in pairs, draw a spider diagram of the main reasons for industrial development. Using different coloured lines, show links between some of these reasons. Explain briefly, on the coloured lines, how one factor encouraged another.

Agricultural change

As German industry grew, agriculture declined in comparison. However, the extent of this decline should not be exaggerated.

Table 6 *Assessing the extent of agricultural decline*

Evidence for decline	Evidence against decline
■ Decline in agricultural prices and, consequently, in the incomes of farmers and landowners.	■ The growth of towns and the protection given to German grain growers after 1879 created opportunities for the more enterprising farmers to supply food to a growing domestic market.
■ A series of bad harvests in the late-1870s compensated for by the import of grain from the USA.	
■ The building of new railways and roads which broke down the isolation of rural communities and exposed farmers to competition from outside.	■ Farm machinery and fertilisers were beginning to become available. Those farmers who had the money to invest in such innovations could and did greatly raise their yield.
■ The growing number of peasants who abandoned agriculture and moved to the industrial towns. (The percentage of the population employed in agriculture fell from 50% in 1871 to 35% in 1907.)	■ More than 4m acres of land were brought under cultivation between 1880 and 1900.
■ Landowners who failed to modernise production methods or did not adapt to changing market conditions were forced to sell up or mortgage farms.	■ Rootcrops, like potatoes and sugar beet, encouraged a revolution in German agriculture. They facilitated more rapid crop rotation, encouraged greater use of fertilisers and machinery and provided additional fodder for livestock.
■ In the 1880s the share of agriculture in the GNP (Gross National Product) was 35–40% while industry's share was 30–35%. By 1914, agriculture had fallen back to 25% with industry at 45%.	■ There grew a more business-like cultivation of the land, with heavy reliance on large numbers of cheap seasonal workers.

Social change

In simple terms, rapid industrial change meant that millions of ordinary people had to come to terms with fundamental changes in their way of life. Yet, surprisingly, German society seems to have remained divided along traditional class lines.

Part of the reason for this was that the very speed of Germany's industrialisation meant less social mobility than in Britain and Belgium, where the process had taken place over a much longer period of time. In Germany industrialisation reinforced the existing divisions. The Junker class remained as dominant as ever and was joined by the owners of big business, while the working class, which strengthened its identity and expanded in size, was firmly set apart from the social elites.

Industrialisation encouraged urbanisation as many peasants left their farms for the towns, even though they often only travelled a few miles. Some made longer journeys, travelling, for example, from the eastern provinces of Prussia to Berlin and the industrial towns of the Ruhr valley. Large factories, like those belonging to Krupps (see page 40) in Essen, attracted thousands of peasants' sons, forced to leave their family farms by the decline of peasant agriculture. By 1890, 47 per cent were city dwellers compared with 36 per cent in 1871.

Fig. 7 *Migration increased as economic change undermined some rural communities*

Activity

Challenge your thinking

What links might be expected between industrial and social change?

Table 7 *Growth of major cities, 1875–90 (thousands)*

City	1875	1890
Berlin	967	1,588
Cologne	135	282
Dresden	197	276
Dusseldorf	81	145
Essen	55	79
Hamburg	265	324
Kiel	37	69
Leipzig	127	295
Munich	193	349

*Quoted in Simpson, W., **The Second Reich – Germany 1871–1918**, 1995*

Activity

Research and analysis

Identify the towns in Table 7 on a map and try to discover specific reasons for the growth of each.

Krupp

Friedrich Krupp (1787–1826) launched the family's metal-based activities by building a small steel foundry in Essen in 1811. However, it was not until his son Alfred (1812–87), later known as 'the Cannon King', took control at the age of 14 that the business became a success. Alfred invested heavily in new technology and became a significant manufacturer of railway material and locomotives at a time when railway building was booming. In 1862, he was the first to use the new Bessemer steel process (imported from Britain) which made possible the mass production of steel. In 1869, he became the first manufacturer in Germany to use the Siemens-Martin process which superseded it.

The company began to make armaments *c.*1847 and at the Great Exhibition, held at the Crystal Palace in London in 1851, Alfred exhibited a six-pounder cannon made entirely from steel. This caused a sensation in the engineering world and the Essen works at once became famous. The unification of Germany provided the opportunities Alfred needed and once the quality of his breech-loading cannon of cast steel gained recognition, his factory developed very rapidly. Alfred acquired many mines and expanded production, providing subsidised housing for his workers and offering a programme of health and retirement benefits. By the time of his death in 1887, when the business passed to his son, the manufacture of armaments represented around 50 per cent of the total output and over 75,000 people were employed. Krupps was the world's largest industrial company.

Middle classes

The main beneficiaries of industrialisation were those of the middle class, especially the great industrialists such as the Krupps, Thyssens and Hugenbergs who became the elite or upper middle class. The middle ranks of the middle classes were also expanding. White collar workers in industry, education and the bureaucracy were in great demand for their scientific, technical or administrative skills. The numbers of lawyers, teachers and civil servants, for example, grew as business and its demands became more complex.

Fig. 8 *A Krupp 71-tonne gun of 1881*

The lower middle class or 'Mittelstand' embraced a wide variety of occupations and standards of living. This included small businessmen, shopkeepers, artisans (skilled workers or craftsmen) and minor officials. Their position was less secure than those above them. They could, for example, be squeezed by a down-turn in the economy, or challenged from below by the unionised working class and from above by the larger, more productive enterprises of big business.

Working classes

The growing working class in the industrial cities experienced some of the benefits deriving from the rapid creation of wealth. On the whole, employment rates were good and wages rose. Bismarck's State Socialism provided some benefits and there were opportunities for workers to advance themselves through education and job opportunities.

However, there were wide variations in wage levels. Coal miners, for example, tended to be better paid than many others and there remained

■ Cross-reference

Bismarck's measures to promote State Socialism are outlined earlier in this chapter on pages 33–5.

many families, especially in the big cities, whose standard of living fell below the poverty line. In Berlin in 1871, 10,000 people were classified as homeless. In industrial areas, it was not unusual for workers to toil through a 10 or 12-hour day, six days per week, often in unhealthy and dangerous conditions. There was no system of rigorous inspection and in the 1880s in Germany's larger cities the average life expectancy was below 40 years.

The Royal Commission on Labour, 1893, reported:

> In Berlin conditions are especially bad, and the average number of persons inhabiting one tenement has risen from 60.7 in 1880 to 66.0 in 1885. Subletting was shown by the 1880 census to be exceedingly frequent. One instance is given of a household taking 34 night lodgers. In another case there were eleven, including women. Thirty eight per cent of the families taking night lodgers lived in a single room; one instance is mentioned in which a man and his wife shared their room with seven men and one woman.

7

Landowners

Although the pace of change was much slower in the countryside than the cities, even the villages and small towns of rural Germany were undergoing change. The position of the Junker landowners was threatened by falling incomes from agriculture. The smaller the estate and the further east it was situated, the greater the levels of debt it was likely to experience. Some landowners were forced to sell their estates to the newly rich upper middle class families from the cities. Nevertheless, the political and social dominance of the Junker class in Prussia remained as strong as ever and local government remained in the hands of the landowning Junker class.

Peasants

Peasants and rural labourers suffered the most from the economic changes of this period. Many were reduced to dependence on seasonal labour and had to face increasing competition from cheap imported labour – often Polish, Russian or from Austria-Hungary. Some smallholders did well, for example dairy and vegetable producers near the towns. Except in Bavaria, where estates were handed down intact to the eldest son, those peasants who owned their land tended to divide it among their children, which made subsistence even more difficult. Overpopulation drove living standards down still further, forcing more and more peasants to seek work in the cities.

The political impact of economic and social change

Growing industrialisation and urbanisation encouraged workers' movements. Trade unions grew in number and membership and in 1890 the General Federation of Trade Unions was founded by Karl Legien. Trade unions campaigned for better working conditions, shorter hours and more pay and encouraged workers to strike to achieve their aims. The unions also supported the growth of Socialism, which flourished in the industrial cities. Socialists encouraged the German workers to question the workings of Capitalism, protesting that the factory hands were being exploited by the factory owners.

Fig. 9 *The breaking up of a meeting of the Social Democrats in 1881. Among the participants were Karl Liebknecht and August Bebel*

Activity

Group activity

Make a copy of the following table. Fill in some details in each column and then, as a group, decide which social group:

■ experienced the greatest change

■ benefited most from economic change.

Use a scale of 1–4, with 1 as the greatest change/most benefit.

This can be used for a class discussion on the effects of economic change.

Social class	Extent of change	Scale of change (1–4)	To what extent benefited?	Scale of benefit (1–4)
Middle class				
Working class				
Landowners				
Peasants				

Key profile

Karl Legien

Karl Legien (1860–1920) was a working man who began life as a turner – metal working with a lathe. He joined the turners' trade union in 1886 and soon became its chairman. When he founded and became president of the General Federation of Trade Unions in 1890, it had just 250,000 members but he built up its organisation as an effective working men's body. He also ensured it remained independent of the SPD. He never forgot his own craft and kept a workshop to the end of his life in the basement of his house where he enjoyed metal working as a leisure activity. In 1893, he became a socialist member of the Reichstag. One of his last acts was to organise a general strike in Berlin in 1920 which brought down the Kapp **Putsch**, a right-wing attempt to overthrow the Weimar Republic.

Key term

Putsch: an attempt to overthrow a government and seize control.

Cross-reference

Details of the Kapp Putsch can be found on pages 114–15.

Cross-reference

For further details of Bismarck's tariff reform refer to page 29.

Question

How important were the economic changes of the years 1871–90 for the political development of Germany?

Such developments frightened Bismarck and the traditional landed elites of Germany and encouraged an aggressive stance. However, Bismarck bore no hatred for the working classes as such and he genuinely tried to improve the workers' lot through his State Socialism schemes. Nevertheless, all socialist attempts to promote modest social and political reform were resisted and consequently, whilst Germany continued to grow as an 'economic giant', politically the country failed to evolve to meet the economic and social change, leaving it a 'political dwarf'.

Economic changes also had the effect of driving the right-wing Conservatives into an uncompromising defensive position. Both manufacturers and farmers banded together to preserve their status. Both campaigned for tariffs in 1879 and this alliance of the industrial and agrarian elites ensured that the empire developed as an increasingly authoritarian and anti-democratic state.

Bismarck's relationship with the Kaiser and Reichstag

The constitution of 1871 had created a Reichstag with limited powers. Bismarck hated having to pander to that Reichstag and if he disliked sharing power with other ministers, he resented even more having to take account of the views of the political parties in the Reichstag. According to the memoirs of Prince von Bülow:

> In my presence, Bismarck expressed some extreme opinions about his domestic enemies. He did not want, in the least, to govern autocratically, he said, although there are those who daily accuse him of this. He was perfectly well aware that, in Germany, in the second half of the nineteenth century, absolutism and autocracy would be impossible. But a parliamentary regime seemed to him just impossible. Our parties possessed neither the patriotism of the French nor the sound common sense of the English. Considering the political hopelessness of the average German, a full parliamentary system would lead to weakness and incompetence at the top and to over-confidence and ever new demands from below.

8　　　*Adapted from Prince von Bülow, **Memoirs: Early Years and Diplomatic Service 1849–1897**, 1932*

However, for all his misgivings, Bismarck appreciated that without Reichstag support he could not carry out his policies. It was in his interests to ensure he could command a majority there so that he could make new laws and obtain the taxes he needed for government and the army.

The relationship was never easy, even though Bismarck tried to ensure he had groups in the Reichstag 'on his side'. Bismarck's first major struggle over the issue of military spending took place despite his 'alliance' with the majority National Liberals and the resulting Septennial Law of 1874 was essentially a defeat for the chancellor. After the political changes of 1878–9, Bismarck turned to his more natural supporters – the Conservatives – and, less obviously, to the Centre Party and he tried to use their fears of socialist revolution to get their support for his measures.

In 1880, when the Reichstag was proving awkward, Bismarck considered setting up an alternative Reich Council which would 'bypass' the Reichstag. As an experiment, he tried this out in Prussia, where he launched a Prussian Council with representatives from commerce, industry and agriculture. Unsurprisingly, the scheme was rejected by the Reichstag and after the 1881 Reichstag election, three-quarters of the Reichstag were left hostile to the government.

In 1886–7, when the army budget was again due for renewal and Bismarck wanted a 10 per cent increase to finance army growth, he exploited the Boulanger Crisis of 1886 in France to create a war scare and in January 1887 he dissolved the Reichstag. The subsequent election was fought in an atmosphere of artificially contrived crisis and brought gains for those parties who supported Bismarck. Through his exploitation of the Boulanger Crisis, he had skilfully engineered a majority in the Reichstag which passed the army bill. This marked the high watermark of Bismarck's control of the Reichstag and illustrated his skill as an opportunist.

Three years later, however, Bismarck's position was less secure. In October 1890, Bismarck proposed a new anti-socialist bill which was not only intended to operate permanently but contained an extreme clause for the expulsion of socialist agitators. The National Liberals refused to support it,

Cross-reference

For further details of the constitution and the powers of the Reichstag refer to pages 14–15.

Cross-reference

Bismarck's alliance with the National Liberal Party is covered on pages 18–20.

The political changes of 1878–9 are discussed on pages 28–9.

Exploring the detail

The Boulanger Crisis

The Boulanger Crisis began with the appointment in France in 1886 of a little known general, Georges Boulanger, as Minister of War. In the succeeding months he was transformed into a national cult figure as the long-awaited military saviour of France. Boulanger was one of those who wanted revenge for the defeat of France in 1871 and the return of the lost provinces of Alsace-Lorraine. The arrest of a French official on the border of Alsace in April 1887 brought threats of war from the minister. Bismarck used this as evidence of the possibility of war with France.

since it contained a clause which gave the police powers to drive socialists from their homes. However, the Conservatives said they would no longer support it if this clause was abandoned! Bismarck did not know what to do and rashly suggested that perhaps it was best to allow the socialists to rise in rebellion so that the army could be called upon to crush them once and for all. The Reichstag rejected the bill and another general election was held. It was to be Bismarck's last as chancellor.

Activity

Thinking point

1 Make a copy of the table below. Give a rating and brief explanation for each of Bismarck's policies (1 = very successful; 5 = total failure).

	Rating 1–5	Explanation
German constitution		
Kulturkampf		
Socialism		
Relations with the Kaiser and Reichstag		

2 Have a class discussion about Bismarck's policies. Each member of the group could prepare a talk outlining the arguments and evidence for the success or failure of one of the policies shown in the table.

Bismarck's resignation

Bismarck's resignation in 1890 came about following a change of Kaiser. Kaiser Wilhelm I had died in 1888 and was succeeded by his son, Friedrich. The latter, however, died in the same year from cancer of the throat.

Friedrich's son, Wilhelm, became Kaiser in 1888 and had no intention of taking a back-seat role in policy making. A few weeks after becoming emperor he said, 'I shall let the old man snuffle on for six months, then I shall rule myself'. Bismarck, who had experienced little or no interference from Wilhelm II's predecessors, made no attempt to gain the friendship of the young Kaiser and either ignored him or poured scorn on his policy suggestions.

The two differed over several key issues:

- Bismarck wanted to control policy making and maintain his position as Minister-President of Prussia. The Kaiser believed in personal rule and wanted to reduce the powers of the Minister-President.
- Bismarck wanted to repress Socialism and workers' agitation, Wilhelm II was more sympathetic and believed he could win over the industrial workers where Bismarck had failed.
- Bismarck wanted to maintain close relations with Russia, the Kaiser favoured Austria.
- The chancellor cared nothing for popularity and was happy to fight the 'Reichsfeinde' and remain aloof in politics. Wilhelm wanted to be loved and honoured by all classes in society and perceived himself as the 'people's emperor'.

The first clash was over Socialism. The new Kaiser was sympathetic to the plight of German workers and, in 1889, intervened in a miners' strike in the Ruhr, lecturing the employers on their social responsibilities. He strongly opposed Bismarck's attempt to make the Anti-Socialist Law permanent. Wilhelm planned social reforms which were put before the Crown Council

Exploring the detail

In January 1887, Friedrich developed an inflammation of the throat and a persistent cough. He could only talk in a hoarse whisper. His doctors were convinced that he was suffering from cancer of the throat. A leading consultant examined him and said that there was no evidence of cancer but this was almost certainly a lie, to save Friedrich from an operation that would have almost certainly killed him. By February 1888, Friedrich had lost the power of speech and he died on 13 June 1888, having ruled for only 99 days.

in January 1890. Bismarck showed little interest in these and suggested that the proposals should be examined by a committee of ministers.

In the 1890 elections, which followed the defeat of Bismarck's permanent anti-socialist measure, the SPD and Progressives increased their seats, whilst the Conservative groupings, and in particular the number of Free Conservatives, who were favourable to Bismarck, decreased.

Table 8 *Number of Reichstag seats won by the political parties in the elections of 1881–90*

Party	1881	1884	1887	1890
Conservatives	50	78	80	73
Free Conservatives	28	28	41	20
National Liberals	47	51	99	42
Progress Party	60			
Centre Party	100	99	98	106
Social Democrats	12	24	11	35
Minorities, e.g. Poles, Danes, Alsatians	45	43	33	38

Murphy, D., Morris, T. and Fulbrook, M., **Germany 1848–1991***, 2008*

Bismarck did not consider resignation but produced two further bills. The first called for an increase in the army of 125,000 men and the other for a permanent and even more brutal anti-socialist law. He expected these to be rejected by the Reichstag but had plans to call on the Bundesrat to alter the constitution so that the Reichstag would lose most of its powers and voting rights. The chancellor seemed to have lost touch with reality. The measures he had proposed would have wrecked the empire that he had devoted his life to creating and Wilhelm rejected this scheme out of hand.

Two further incidents finally ended Bismarck's career. First, he discovered an out-of-date Prussian Cabinet order of 1852, which declared that ministers could only approach the Kaiser through the Minister-President (or, by 1890, chancellor) of Germany. Wilhelm demanded that this order be withdrawn. Secondly, Bismarck told the Kaiser that Wilhelm could not undertake a planned visit to Russia because he had received unfavourable reports from the German Ambassador there. Wilhelm was furious and demanded to see the reports. He liked what he read even less. In them the Tsar had described him as 'an ill-bred youngster of bad faith'.

His fury was turned on Bismarck. He demanded his resignation and Bismarck, using the emperor's 'meddling in foreign affairs' as an excuse, supplied it. He was, however, surprised when Wilhelm II accepted it. Thus, in March 1890, the 'grand old man' departed from the German chancellory.

Bismarck's letter of resignation said:

> I would have asked to be relieved of my offices to Your Majesty long ago if I had not had the impression that Your Majesty wished to make use of the experiences and abilities of a faithful servant of your ancestors. Since I am now certain that Your Majesty does not require them I may retire from political life without having to fear that my decision may be condemned as untimely by public opinion.

Bismarck's legacy

There is much debate over the legacy left by Bismarck. On the one hand, Bismarck was successful in meeting the challenges presented

Cross-reference

Measures taken by Wilhelm II's first chancellor, Caprivi, to help the German workers are covered in more detail on pages 51–2.

DROPPING THE PILOT.

Fig. 10 *'Dropping the pilot, 1890.' Can you think of some suitable thought bubbles to accompany this famous Punch cartoon?*

Activity

Talking point

In groups, examine Figure 10.

1. What message is the cartoonist trying to get across?

2. How does the cartoonist put across this message?

Activity

Revision exercise

Produce a spider diagram showing the reasons for Bismarck's resignation. Indicate the cause you consider to be the most important.

by the new German Reich in the years after 1871, especially from the Catholic Church, Socialism and the minority groups. On the other, by the 1880s, he found it difficult to maintain the political system he had forged in 1871. This left a number of problems for his successors. These included:

- the constitution. The authoritarian constitution had not proved adaptable to the changing economic and social situation in Germany and, more especially, the growth of Socialism. It had given a lot of power to the Kaiser, especially in appointing and dismissing the chancellor.

- the position of the Reichstag. Bismarck had denied the Reichstag a positive role in the making of laws and seemed to thrive on confrontation with the Lower House. This left a weakened Lower House to face an ambitious and interfering emperor.

- a tradition of confrontation. Bismarck had often intensified divisions within Germany by his policies of confrontation, especially against the Catholic Church and socialists. This pattern was set to continue in the years 1890 to 1914.

- the position of the army. Bismarck had given the army a prominent position in the German Reich so that the general staff had a lot of influence over the formulation of German foreign policy.

Learning outcomes

In this section you have learnt about the ways in which Germany developed under Bismarck. You have seen how Germany evolved as a single united country, growing economically into a strong European state. However, you have also seen how the political structure which Bismarck put in place in 1871 was strained by these economic and social developments and how, politically, Germany in 1890 was left in an unsatisfactory state.

You have learnt how government in this period was dominated by Bismarck's attempts to keep some sort of balance between the various political and social groups in Germany. In the next section you will discover what happened to that balance under the new, young and ambitious Kaiser.

AQA Examination-style questions

(a)   Explain why Bismarck resigned in 1890 as chancellor of Germany.   *(12 marks)*

Examiner's tip   You will find it helpful to use your spider diagram, prepared for the activity on page 45, to answer part (a). You will need to assess the personality and policy clashes between Bismarck and Wilhelm II and consider a range of factors, some long term and others more immediate. Try to show how these factors are interlinked and, if possible, identify a main factor, which you should stress in your conclusion.

(b)   How successful were Bismarck's domestic policies in the years 1871–90 in establishing a strong German state?   *(24 marks)*

Examiner's tip   For part (b), the activity on page 44 will help you to consider the main areas of Bismarck's domestic policy and to evaluate the ways in which Bismarck succeeded in establishing a strong German state and the ways in which he failed to do so. You will, of course, need to be clear about what is meant by a 'strong' state. Before you begin your answer, decide whether you will argue that he was primarily successful (with some reservations) or vice versa. Try to maintain a coherent line, but do include arguments on both sides for a balanced response.

3 Domestic politics under Kaiser Wilhelm II

In this chapter you will learn about:

- the personality and influence of Kaiser Wilhelm II

- the policies of Kaiser Wilhelm II's chancellors

- the relationship between the Kaiser and his chancellors

- the Kaiser's personal influence in government in the years 1907–13.

In 1894, the diplomat Ernst Jäckh was among those chosen to accompany Kaiser Wilhelm II as he cruised through the North Sea. He recorded in his diary:

> In the mornings we all do exercises together with the Kaiser. It is a curious sight: all those old military fogeys having to do their knee jerks with strained faces! The Kaiser sometimes laughs out loud and eggs them on with a dig in the ribs. The old boys then pretend that they are particularly delighted over such a favour, but in fact, they clench their fists in their pockets and afterwards grumble among themselves about the Kaiser, like a lot of old women.

1

Such was the man who had become the Kaiser of Germany in 1888.

Kaiser Wilhelm II and his Reich chancellors

The new Kaiser

Kaiser Wilhelm II was just 27 years of age when he took the Imperial throne of Germany. He was full of personal energy and ambition and appeared confident in his ability to make the right decisions. He wrote, in 1892:

> We, Hohenzollerns, are used to advancing slowly and painfully amidst troubles. How often have my ancestors had to battle for policies in direct opposition to the will of the ignorant people, which first opposed and in the end blessed them. What do I care for popularity? I am guided only by my duty and the responsibility of my clear conscience towards God.

2

Fig. 1 *The youthful Kaiser Wilhelm II*

However, his personality was not as straightforward as it might at first appear. Behind this apparent confidence lay a very uncertain character – nervous, moody, changeable and unpredictable. He was sensitive to criticism and demonstrated wild fluctuations in mood. He wanted to control the details of government, yet he could never bring himself to take time over state papers or to sit down to serious study. He appeared to be full of vigour, yet this energy was dissipated by frantic journeys around his empire and at sea on his yacht – so much so that he gained the nickname the 'Reisekaiser' or travelling emperor. In company, he could appear courteous and charming, yet he found it difficult to relate to others on anything more than a superficial level. He was obstinate and could easily become so obsessed by a single idea that any disagreement produced wild outbursts of rage. He was really only ever at ease when surrounded by military personnel. He adored public ceremony and his military uniforms – which he changed several times a day – and just like the Army Commander he was, he tended to expect automatic and unquestioning obedience from everyone around him.

His mother wrote in a letter to her mother, Queen Victoria, in 1887:

> Willy is chauvinistic and ultra Prussian to a degree and with a violence which is very painful to me.

Queen Victoria of Great Britain, in return, considered her grandson to be in a 'very unhealthy and unnatural state of mind' and that he might 'at any moment become impossible'.

As seen in Source 1, Wilhelm II's 'sense of humour' bordered on the sadistic. When shaking hands, he would sometimes turn the rings on his strong right hand inwards and clench the hand of his unwary guest so hard that it brought tears to their eyes. He loved childish pranks and games – chasing his elderly companions through the corridors of a ship, or, as reported on one occasion, cutting a general's braces with a penknife. In 1908, the 56-year-old General Hülsen, head of the military cabinet, was made to don a tutu for an impromptu post-supper ballet performance. Sadly, he collapsed and never revived.

Wilhelm upset King Ferdinand of Bulgaria by slapping him hard on his behind, in public, while the Grand Duke Vladimir of Russia was hit over the back with a field marshal's baton. The Duke of Saxe-Coburg-Gotha suffered a pinching and pummelling on one visit and, on another, was made to lie on his back whilst Wilhelm sat on his belly.

Much time has been spent trying to explain Wilhelm II's complex personality and mood swings (see page 49) but, whatever the cause, Wilhelm's unstable character was not well placed for him to be leading one of Europe's strongest states, with huge political powers at his disposal.

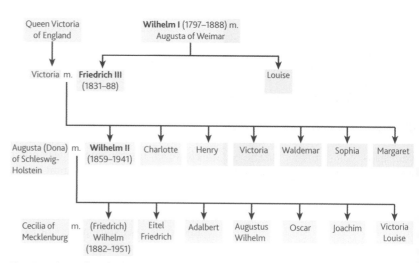

Fig. 2 *Hohenzollern family tree*

Key profile

Kaiser Wilhelm II

Wilhelm II (1859–1941) was the grandson of Wilhelm I. His parents were Friedrich of Prussia, who had become Kaiser for 99 days before his premature death, and Victoria, the eldest daughter of Queen Victoria of Great Britain. This posed a contradiction. Whilst his father inculcated in him a love of the Prussian military tradition, his mother encouraged a 'liberal' outlook on life. However, Wilhelm never liked his mother and her preference for all things English antagonised him. A difficult breech birth left him with a withered arm, defective hearing and paralysis on the left side of his body. Subconsciously or not, he blamed his mother – and England!

Wilhelm was subsequently subjected to a strict and painful upbringing in an attempt to force him to overcome these disabilities. Frightening medical treatments, unapproachable parents and the demands of a surly personal tutor, Hinzpeter, combined to create a child who was both introverted and emotionally ill at ease. Wilhelm was given no peace in the attempt to force him to master the military skills expected of a prince and he painfully learnt the art of horse-riding and, to his credit, became an able horseman and competent sailor. He was sent to Bonn University, but was much more influenced by his experience of military life, first with the Prussian Foot Guards and then as Colonel of the Guard Hussars where he developed his enthusiasm for uniforms and the externals of military life.

Fig. 3 *Kaiser Wilhelm II (right). This is one of very few pictures which shows the Kaiser's withered left arm. Can you think why?*

Explanations for Wilhelm's behaviour have suggested that he suffered from Attention Deficiency Disorder (a condition which can manifest itself in unpredictable and irrational behaviour) or was a repressed homosexual. Nevertheless, he married Princess Augusta Victoria of Schleswig-Holstein-Sonderburg-Augustenburg in 1881 and fathered six sons and a daughter.

The main reason why Wilhelm engineered Bismarck's downfall was because he wanted to play an active political role himself. Although Wilhelm I had been content to allow Bismarck to 'rule', Wilhelm II was not. The problem was that, although he wanted to be at the helm of the affairs, Wilhelm II had neither the concentration nor judgement to run the government effectively. Although he sought advice from courtiers such as Philipp zu Eulenburg, who also had to cover up criticism of Wilhelm's actions, Wilhelm ensured that he wielded ultimate power. This became even more marked after he dismissed his first choice of chancellor, General Leo Caprivi.

Activity

Research exercise

1. Wilhelm II's mother commented that he was 'ultra Prussian' (see page 48). What did she mean by this? Is this an unfair stereotype?

2. Undertake some further research in Wilhelm II's character and upbringing. Share your findings with your class and then write an answer to the following question:

   How far did Wilhelm II's upbringing and personality prepare him for the role of Kaiser?

Fig. 4 *Philipp Fürst zu Eulenburg, one of the Kaiser's favourites*

Philipp Fürst zu Eulenburg und Hertefeld

Philipp Fürst zu Eulenburg (1847–1921) had wanted to become a poet or painter, but was forced by his Prussian father into a military career. He trained as an officer, but joined the foreign office in 1877 and subsequently worked as a diplomat. He got to know the future Kaiser Wilhelm II in 1886, and became one of Wilhelm's favourites. The Eulenburg's landed estate in Liebenberg became a centre of power where a circle of friends, including Count von Moltke, met. The circle was referred to by jealous enemies as the 'camarillo' and its members possessed considerable influence. Philipp served as Prussian minister in several German states in the 1880s and as German ambassador in Vienna from 1894 to 1902. In 1892, Philipp's cousin, Count Botho zu Eulenburg, became Minister-President of Prussia, breaking Bismarck's tradition of the Imperial chancellor also holding this office and extending the influence of the Eulenburg family further. It was the camarillo's suggestion that led to Caprivi's removal as chancellor and his replacement with von Bülow. In 1908, Philipp Eulenburg, by then a happily married man and father of eight children, who had been accused by a German journalist of being homosexual, was charged with perjury during a libel case. Homosexual activity was illegal at that time in Germany and the accusations and trial which followed destroyed his public image and his health. In the end the trial was indefinitely adjourned, but it was noted that Wilhelm made no attempt to defend him and, after this, his influence over Wilhelm ceased.

German chancellors, 1890–1914

1890–4 General Leo Caprivi

1894–1900 Prince Chlodwig zu Hohenlohe-Schillingsfürst

1900–9 Count Bernhard von Bülow

1909–17 Bethmann-Hollweg

The Reich chancellors and their policies

Although Bismarck's 1871 constitution had failed to define the power of chancellor clearly, the need for the German chancellor to countersign all the Kaiser's decrees and orders (excepting those relating to foreign policy) ensured that whoever held this office was crucial for the workings of the political system. Under Wilhelm I, the Kaiser had been prepared to allow Bismarck, as chancellor, to develop policies that he was able to carry out with the support of the majority of the Reichstag. Under Wilhelm II this was to change. In May 1891, Wilhelm declared: 'There is only one man in charge of the Reich, and I will not tolerate any other.'

Policy decisions were therefore largely taken out of the chancellors' hands. Chancellors were merely expected to ensure that the Kaiser's wishes were carried out and that government ran smoothly. This, not surprisingly, is the one thing that did not happen! Their dependence on the emperor and lack of responsibility to the Reichstag meant that legislation often faltered and their 'leadership' was weak and ineffectual. The lynchpin which had held the Bismarckian system together had gone and they struggled to operate against a shifting political background which saw the stunning advance of the socialist labour movement (SDP) (see Table 1).

Table 1 *Election results, 1890–1912*

Party	1890	1893	1898	1903	1907	1912
Conservatives	93	100	79	75	84	57
Other right-wing parties	7	21	31	22	33	19
National Liberals	42	53	46	51	54	45
Centre Party	106	96	102	100	95	91
Progressives – left-wing Liberals	76	48	49	36	49	42
Social Democrats	35	44	56	81	43	110
Minorities, e.g. Poles, Danes, Alsatians	38	35	34	32	29	33

*Adapted from Farmer, A. and Stiles, A., **The Unification of Germany 1815–1919**, 2007*

General Georg Leo, Count von Caprivi, 1890–4

Key profile

General Leo Caprivi

Caprivi (1831–99) was of Italian and Slovenian origin. He had entered the Prussian army in 1849 and served in the Austro-Prussian and the Franco-Prussian wars. From 1883 to 1888 he was the chief of the Imperial Admiralty. He was an intelligent man and soon demonstrated his abilities as an administrator of mildly progressive views. He was briefly appointed commander of the Tenth Army Corps in Hanover (1888–90) before he was summoned by Wilhem II to succeed Bismarck as chancellor.

Activity

Statistical analysis

Compare Table 1 with Tables 3 and 8 on pages 28 and 45.

What trends and changes in voting behaviour can you detect?

Fig. 5 *General Georg Leo, Count von Caprivi, chancellor of Germany 1890–4*

Having quarrelled with Bismarck over the continuation of the anti-socialist bill, Wilhelm was looking for a chancellor who would adopt a more moderate, conciliatory approach to the problems raised by Socialism. Wilhelm favoured a military figure and personally selected Caprivi from a list of generals. In accepting office, Caprivi admitted publicly that he had merely obeyed his Kaiser's orders as a soldier and had no political programme. However, he had some administrative experience and was regarded as a moderniser, and the Kaiser told him bluntly, 'Don't worry. All statesmen cook with water, and it is I who take the responsibility.'

Caprivi set out a 'new course' for German politics which included:

- giving ministers more influence over policy making and developing greater cooperation with the Reichstag
- bringing about social reform to reconcile the working classes with the established order
- lowering tariffs to improve Germany's export trade and enable industry to expand.

As part of this new programme, Caprivi allowed the Anti-Socialist Law to lapse in 1890 and he introduced a series of reforms in an attempt to take support away from Socialism and reduce social tension:

- Industrial Tribunals (courts) were set up to arbitrate in wage disputes in July 1890. Caprivi invited trade union representatives to sit in on these tribunals.
- Hours of work for women were reduced to a maximum of 11.

Questions

1 Why do you think these proposals were described as a 'new course'?

2 Do they justify this description?

■ Activity

Pairs activity

In pairs, consider each of the various groups mentioned in turn. Try to explain why they approved or disapproved of these different reforms and which they particularly favoured or disliked.

■ Cross-reference

The Agrarian League is explained on page 74.

The camarillo is explained in Eulenburg's profile on page 50.

■ In 1891, Sunday working was forbidden and a guaranteed minimum wage established.

■ The employment of children under 13 years of age was forbidden and 13–18 year olds restricted to a maximum day of 10 hours.

■ A finance bill introduced progressive income tax whereby the more a person earned, the more he paid.

■ Duties on imported wheat, rye, cattle and timber were reduced under two trade treaties of 1891 and 1894. (Duties on industrial imports remained.)

These measures were generally welcomed by the working classes, the socialists, industrialists, Centre Party supporters and Liberals. However, the Conservative Junkers disapproved and, led by the Eulenburgs, Holstein, the Agrarian League and the camarillo, they did all they could to bring Caprivi down.

■ **Key profile**

Baron Friedrich von Holstein

Friedrich von Holstein (1837–1909) was a strong right-wing nationalist who took control of foreign affairs from 1890 when Bismarck resigned. Since Caprivi had little interest in this area, Holstein easily found a place for himself and, although he was officially only a political counsellor in the foreign office, he wielded a great deal of influence and advised the Kaiser directly. Although Wilhelm II relied heavily on him, he remained almost totally unknown outside government circles.

■ Exploring the detail

Military spending

The Kaiser was determined to increase military spending because he feared that, one day, Germany might have to face a war. France remained bitter about the loss of Alsace-Lorraine, and Russia, which had been allied to Germany in Bismarck's time, had developed closer relations with France since 1890. Von Schlieffen, the German Chief of Staff, had drawn up the 'Schlieffen Plan' in 1892 (see page 78) on the assumption that if a war broke out, Germany would need to defeat France before Russia could mobilise in order to win. If this plan was to be effective, it was necessary to expand the army reserve and, although its details were not disclosed to the Reichstag, Wilhelm demanded Caprivi win approval for higher taxes to support increased military expenditure.

The hostility of the Conservatives towards Caprivi was increased by the chancellor's compromise agreement with the Reichstag in 1893. This was made in order to get support for the Army Bill of 1892, drawn up at the Kaiser's demand, in order to increase the size of the army by 84,000. To gain the Reichstag's approval, Caprivi agreed to reduce military service from three to two years and to allow the Reichstag to discuss the military budget every five years instead of every seven. To the Conservatives this was a humiliating surrender.

Caprivi found it difficult to work with the Kaiser. When the chancellor tried to take the initiative and to follow his own policies, the Kaiser would often interfere. So, for example, Caprivi tried to reverse an aspect of the Kulturkampf and allow both Protestant and Catholic Church authorities more control over education. However, Wilhelm, who did not want to have to rely on the Centre Party to pass the bill, forced him to withdraw the proposed legislation. The historian, Layton, says that he was 'more astute and independent-minded than the Kaiser had bargained for', while Porter and Armour have referred to him as 'an intelligent man with a mind of his own'. This is not what the Kaiser had been wanting.

Socialism was also an issue on which the chancellor and Kaiser came to disagree, despite their initial consensus that Socialism could be killed by reforms and that repression was counter-productive. The SPD continued to grow. They made considerable gains in the 1893 election and this, in addition to a wave of attacks by anarchists throughout Europe, convinced Wilhelm that an Anti-Socialist Subversion Bill was needed once again. When Caprivi refused to introduce this legislation, Philipp zu Eulenburg encouraged Wilhelm to present the bill to the Reichstag anyway. He suggested that if the Reichstag refused it, Wilhelm should rule without a parliament. This was the end for Caprivi. He managed to talk the Kaiser out of taking such a course of action, but then resigned. He complained:

> My relations with the All Highest have become intolerable. You cannot imagine how relieved I will feel to get out of here.

Caprivi's departure was Germany's loss. Caprivi had genuinely tried to plot a new course and to change the confrontational political atmosphere left by Bismarck to one of compromise and advance. Had he succeeded in his aim of winning over the industrialists and integrating the working classes and their organisations into German political life, the future of that country might well have been different. Indeed, Stürmer has suggested that: 'Industrial Germany might have become, instead of an uncertain giant, the centrepiece of European stability.' Caprivi's sincere attempts at reform, however, had alienated the traditional forces of power and influence and it was clear that, without the support of the court favourites and the Kaiser, his position was impossible.

Caprivi's dismissal demonstrated the decline that had taken place in the role of chancellor since the days of Bismarck. Thereafter, Wilhelm avoided independent-minded chancellors and, instead, his own personal influence became even more marked.

Prince Chlodwig zu Hohenlohe-Schillingsfürst, 1894–1900

Wilhelm chose, as his new chancellor, Prince Chlodwig zu Hohenlohe-Schillingsfürst. He was 75 years of age and was selected, not for his personal abilities, but because he posed no political threat to those who surrounded the Kaiser.

Question

Explain why Caprivi resigned as chancellor of Germany in 1894.

Key profile

Prince Chlodwig zu Hohenlohe-Schillingsfürst

Prince Chlodwig zu Hohenlohe-Schillingsfürst (1819–1901) was a Bavarian aristocrat. He was a Catholic, but disliked the Centre Party and he had refused to oppose the Kulturkampf. Although he had limited political experience and no obvious policies of his own, he was regarded as mildly Liberal although happy to take up the Conservative demand for action against the 'socialist threat'.

Cross-reference

Election results are detailed in Table 1 on page 51.

He was seen as little more than a figurehead chancellor and the Kaiser described him as his 'straw doll'. Accordingly, Hohenlohe tried to do as the Kaiser asked and introduced bills to curb socialist 'subversion'. Two bills were attempted, in 1894 (Subversion Bill) and 1899 (Anti-Union Bill). These proposed stiffer penalties for subversion and trade union activity but both were thrown out by the Reichstag. The Conservatives, who in earlier years might have been relied upon to carry such measures, no longer commanded a majority in the Reichstag. Indeed, their representation fell by 21 per cent between 1893 and 1898. It seemed as though constitutional government had reached breaking point. The Kaiser was not prepared to bow to the wishes of the Reichstag majority, while the Reichstag was not prepared to accept the Kaiser and chancellor's proposed legislation.

Sammlungspolitik *and the policy of concentration*

The Kaiser's advisers led by Philipp zu Eulenburg pressed for a change of approach from 1897. They encouraged the Kaiser to by-pass the chancellor and choose his own ministers. Hohenlohe despaired in a letter of 1897:

Question

To what extent does Source 3 justify the view that:

- Hohenlohe was simply a figurehead chancellor?
- 1897 marks the beginning of a changed approach to government?

Without authority, government is impossible. If I cannot get the Kaiser's consent to measures I regard as necessary, then I have no authority. I cannot stay if H.M. removes ministers against my will. Likewise I cannot stay if the Kaiser appoints ministers without consulting me. I cannot govern against public opinion as well as against the Kaiser. To govern against the Kaiser and the public is to hang in mid-air. That is impossible.

3

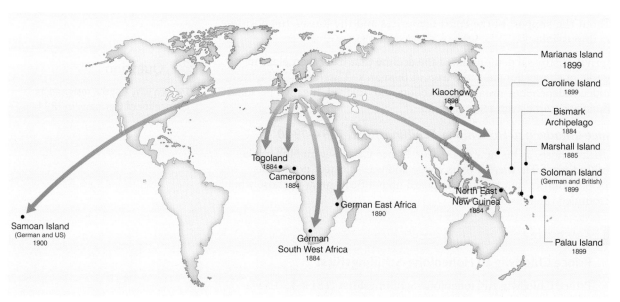

Fig. 6 *Germany's colonial acquisitions, 1884–1900*

Cross-reference

Weltpolitik is described in more detail on pages 78–80.

To review the alliance of steel and rye, refer back to Table 4 on page 29.

This change coincided with the Kaiser's developing interest in *Weltpolitik* – a drive to achieve world power status through the expansion of naval power and colonial annexations. Wilhelm's court circle believed that Weltpolitik had the power to unite peoples of different political and economic backgrounds and so overcome the difficulties government was facing in the Reichstag. Although Hohenlohe officially remained as chancellor, in practice the Kaiser began to act as his own chancellor and worked with his preferred ministers to determine Imperial policy. The main personnel to influence decisions in these years were:

- Dr Joannes von Miquel, Prussian finance minister made vice-president of the Prussian Ministry of State in 1897
- Ernst von Koller, former Prussian Minister of the Interior (who had been dismissed in 1895 by the Prussian Ministry of State, after it came to light that he was revealing cabinet discussions to the military)

- Bernhard von Bülow, foreign minister from 1897 (and chancellor from 1900)
- Admiral von Tirpitz, Navy secretary from 1897
- Count Arthur von Posadowsky-Wehner, Minister of Interior from 1897.

A new policy known as *Sammlungspolitik*, or the policy of concentration, emerged. *Sammlung* means 'rallying together' and it was a policy intended to rouse, or concentrate, nationalist sympathies, bringing the landowners and industrialists together in the face of the perceived threat from Socialism and anarchism and in support of the empire's ambitious foreign policy.

Caprivi's tariff reforms, which had hit at the farmers, had broken the alliance between landowners and industrialists while his social reforms had failed to win over the working class and had, instead, alienated the middle classes. The Kaiser's advisers believed that this damage could be undone by highlighting the threat from Socialism. They hoped to win back the middle classes in support of the Kaiser and to reunite landowners and industrialists in a new alliance of 'steel and rye'. This policy of 'concentration' deliberately polarised German society into two hostile camps – the forces of law, order and respectability on the one hand, and the forces of radicalism and Socialism on the other.

Fig. 7 *Admiral von Tirpitz, Secretary of State for Naval Affairs 1897–1916*

Consequently, Posadowsky-Wehner as Minister of Interior tried to highlight the dangers of Socialism and he introduced a bill in 1899 to impose prison sentences for strike action which could be deemed harmful to 'public security'. However, like Hohenlohe's bills before it, it was rejected by a large majority in the Reichstag.

When he faced opposition such as this, the Kaiser talked dangerously of abandoning the constitution and removing the workers' franchise. However, his preoccupation with foreign policy and the effects of the economic boom of the 1890s, quite apart from Hohenlohe's attempts at restraint, prevented any such wild action. The socialists carefully tried to avoid provoking confrontation, and were generally supportive of appeals to patriotism so, despite the ministers' talk, they remained an increasingly popular force in politics.

Bülow, at the foreign office, responded with enthusiasm to the Sammlungspolitik principle and declared in 1897:

> I am putting the main emphasis on foreign policy. Only a successful foreign policy can help to reconcile, pacify, rally, unite.

Part of this drive involved the construction of a new naval fleet. Admiral von Tirpitz took a personal interest in this and two naval bills were introduced in 1898 and 1900 which committed Germany to the construction of 38 battleships, 8 battle cruisers and 24 cruisers. Tirpitz and, from March 1898, the Navy League successfully launched a huge press campaign to win popular support for the programme, and its dangers were curiously ignored. Even if the naval policy was intended to rally support at home, rather than challenge Britain abroad, its implications were to lead Germany towards war.

Cross-reference

The Navy League and the construction of the new German navy are covered on pages 74–6 and 78.

It was over an issue concerning Germany's colonial policy towards China that a disagreement between the Kaiser and his chancellor gave Hohenlohe the excuse to resign. He was probably glad of the opportunity to escape his unpredictable master and he left just as a new quarrel was breaking in the Reichstag over tariffs.

Count Bernhard von Bülow, 1900–9

Fig. 8 *Count Bernhard von Bülow, chancellor of Germany 1900–9*

■ Key profile

Count Bernhard von Bülow

Count Bernhard von Bülow (1849–1929) was an aristocratic Junker who had served as a member of the Prussian civil service and had experience as a diplomat and at the foreign office. In 1887, he had advocated the ethnic cleansing of all Poles in the German Empire. He served as foreign secretary from 1897 to 1900 where he favoured an adventurous foreign policy and was responsible for the policy of colonial expansion.

Count Bernhard von Bülow had been groomed as Hohenlohe's replacement by Wilhelm's inner circle of courtiers, particularly Philipp zu Eulenburg. As early as 1895, Wilhelm had written:

> Bülow shall become my Bismarck and as he and my grandfather pounded Germany together externally, so we two will clean up the filth of parliamentary and party machinery internally.

Bülow had gone out of his way to flatter the emperor and win his backing, as seen in this letter, sent to Eulenburg in 1897:

> I am completely open, sincere and honest with our dear master. But I don't mean to play schoolmaster towards him. First because it hurts me to see His beautiful sad eyes, but then also because for Him everything depends on His retaining trust and friendship for me. I am entering more and more into His ideas, am trying to turn everything round for the best.

■ Cross-reference

For details of Weltpolitik, refer to pages 77–9.

Bülow was the first chancellor whom the Kaiser trusted absolutely. Bülow visited Wilhelm every morning and used his skills of flattery to remain in the Kaiser's favour. This earned him the nickname of 'the eel'. Bülow abandoned the anti-socialist aspect of Sammlungspolitik and, instead, worked to generate broader political support by focusing on the foreign policy, appealing to the people's patriotism, through Weltpolitik, the development of the fleet and the promotion of Wilhelm II himself as the great emperor. No wonder that, in July 1901, Wilhelm told Eulenburg:

> Since I have him (Bülow), I can sleep peacefully. I leave things to him and know that everything will be alright.

However, Bülow could not escape the controversy that was raging over tariffs when he took control. In 1902, he chose to reverse the tariff reductions arranged by Caprivi, partly to help provide sufficient revenue for the developing navy. A new tariff law restored the 1892 duties on agricultural products and a few key manufactures, which pleased the

Conservative Junkers, although it fell short of what they had demanded. Since industrialists were set to benefit from the huge naval expansion programme that was just developing, this change in economic policy was important in helping to create the alliance of 'steel and rye' that Germany's leaders had been seeking.

However, it was not popular with the socialists, or the electorate, who believed that, by keeping out cheap Russian grain, it would increase the price of foodstuffs. Perhaps not surprisingly, in the 1903 elections, the SPD's vote jumped from 2 to 3 million, and the party gained an impressive 81 seats.

Nevertheless, Posadowsky-Wehner had abandoned his earlier attempts to crush the socialists with repression. Instead, he diverted his energies to developing social security, and introduced a series of social reforms, rather as Bismarck had done.

- In 1900, the period for which workers could claim accident insurance was lengthened.
- In 1901, industrial arbitration courts were made compulsory for towns with a population of more than 20,000.
- In 1903, health insurance was extended and further controls imposed on child labour.

Other reforms included the introduction of a polling booth law, which improved the secret ballot in 1904 and the establishment of payment for Reichstag deputies in 1906.

However, despite such change, Bülow was fundamentally a Conservative and a nationalist, who was intolerant of the national minorities and enthusiastically reversed Caprivi's policies. Following Bismarck's example, Bülow returned to enforced Germanisation in the east. He made German the only teaching language in Prussian schools and in 1908 an expropriation law was passed in Prussia which made possible the confiscation of Polish property, which was then given to German farmers. It was during these years also that an increasing interest was shown in quasi-scientific studies, which purported to show the superiority of the German race. Houston Stewart Chamberlain's *Foundations of the Nineteenth Century* was published in 1899, and its anti-Semitic message certainly found favour with some Conservatives, although its overall influence was limited.

Bülow's difficulties

By 1905–6, relations between Bülow and the Kaiser were no longer as harmonious as they had been at the outset of the chancellorship. Bülow had been held responsible for foreign policy failures and he was unable to fulfil the Kaiser's demand for more money for military spending, since it had become clear that he was no better than his predecessor in controlling the Reichstag. The income raised by the new tariff laws proved insufficient, yet when he tried to force increased taxes, Bülow found the Centre Party, on whom he had previously been able to rely, as well as

Fig. 9 *A German cartoon illustrating the formation of the Bülow Bloc in 1907. What is the cartoonist trying to say?*

■ Cross-reference

More detail on right-wing pressure groups such as the Agrarian League is found on page 74.

■ Exploring the detail

The Hottentot election

The election was fought on the issue of support for Bülow's policies in south-west Africa. The Centre Party and SPD had been critical of the government's Imperial policies and it was they who forced this election. However, a huge campaign was mounted against these two parties, branding them as 'unpatriotic' and this swung the vote.

■ Exploring the detail

The Eulenburg affair and Bülow scandal

In 1907–9, the problems of the empire were added to by a series of courts-martial and five trials in which prominent members of Kaiser Wilhelm II's circle were accused of homosexuality. The journalist Maximilian Harden claimed to have discovered evidence of homosexual conduct between Philipp zu Eulenburg and General von Moltke. Another journalist, Brand, claimed that Bülow had been observed kissing and embracing at male gatherings hosted by Eulenburg. Despite rulings which cleared these men, the media interest produced an outcry and caused much speculation. The accusations may have been the product of those jealous of the Kaiser's circle or Bülow's foreign policy but, whatever their origins and truth, the reputations of those implicated were severely damaged.

■ Question

How successful was Bülow in achieving political stability in Germany in the years 1900–9?

the SPD, voting against him. He resorted to a small tax on legacies, in 1906, which both the SPD and Centre voted through, although they complained that it did not go far enough, but the Conservatives and Bundesrat were horrified by such action.

In 1907, Bülow negotiated a new coalition, known as the 'Bülow Bloc', of Conservatives, members of the Agrarian League and Liberals. His aim was to be able to get legislation passed without relying on the Centre Party. Following the 'Hottentot election' of 1907, this Bülow Bloc won an overwhelming victory, leaving the Centre Party with 95 rather than 100 seats and reducing the number of SPD seats from 81 to 43.

Bülow's fall from power

Bülow's reputation had suffered a blow in 1907, when details of a homosexual scandal had been released. However, the specific reason for Bülow's fall was linked to an interview given by the Kaiser to the British newspaper, the *Daily Telegraph*, in October 1908. In this, he suggested that the Germans were anti-British and that he was personally restraining this sentiment. The report of this piece of personal 'meddling' by the Kaiser, which Bülow had been given the opportunity to suppress, but had failed to do so, worsened relations with Britain and led to another furore in the German press. The Reichstag demanded curbs on Wilhelm's activities, forcing Wilhelm to give an undertaking to moderate his conduct in future. Although he would not admit it publicly, the whole affair damaged the Kaiser's confidence in Bülow, so when the latter submitted his resignation after his finance bill had been rejected, Wilhelm readily accepted it.

■ A closer look

The Kaiser and the *Daily Telegraph* Affair

During a visit to Britain in 1907, Wilhelm II stayed with the pro-German Colonel Stuart-Wortley. The latter then produced an article for the *Daily Telegraph* based on his conversations with the Kaiser. He hoped it would improve relations between the two countries. The Kaiser was quoted as saying that during the Boer War, he had remained neutral despite strong anti-British sentiment in Germany and that he had personally prevented the fomation of an anti-British coalition. He claimed that he had also contacted Queen Victoria with advice on how to win the war. The Kaiser suggested that, while he himself was pro-British, German public opinion was not.

Stuart-Wortley had sent the article to the Kaiser to have it checked out before publication, but the Kaiser had passed it to Bülow and the latter had returned it, largely unread. Its publication, on 28 October 1908, brought severe criticism, both in Britain, due to Wilhelm's perceived arrogance, and in Germany, where there were demands for constitutional reform to curb the Kaiser's meddling. Even though the affair was primarily due to Bülow's negligence, once the storm broke, Bülow joined in the attacks on the Kaiser's 'personal government'. Wilhelm was forced to issue a statement saying that he promised to respect the constitution and had complete confidence in his chancellor. However, the damage had been done.

Theobald von Bethmann-Hollweg, 1909–17

Key profile

Theobald von Bethmann-Hollweg

Bethmann-Hollweg (1856–1921) was an aristocrat, educated at the Universities of Strasburg and Leipzig. He entered the Prussian administrative service in 1882 and rose to the position of the President of the Province of Brandenburg in 1899. He served as Prussian Minister of Interior from 1905 to 1907, and as Imperial State Secretary for the Interior from 1907 to 1909. In 1909, Bülow recommended Bethmann-Hollweg to succeed him. Bethmann-Hollweg was intelligent, a careful administrator and a man of honour, but he admitted that he possessed little knowledge of foreign and military affairs and he was far too entrenched in Conservatism to see the need for, still less carry through, fundamental political reforms. He presided over the disastrous July crisis which led Germany into war in 1914 and eventually resigned in 1917 when under pressure from the supreme command led by Hindenburg and Ludendorff. Wilhelm accepted his resignation with reluctance.

Fig. 10 *Theobald von Bethmann-Hollweg, chancellor of Germany 1909–17*

Bülow's fall marked the end of the Kaiser's attempts to conduct a 'personal rule' at least as far as domestic affairs were concerned. He had chosen Bethmann-Hollweg because he was known to be a good administrator and Wilhelm did not mind his lack of experience in military and foreign affairs because this gave him a free rein to take control of such areas himself! Although Wilhelm never had quite the same relationship with Bethmann-Hollweg that he had enjoyed with Bülow, he was still quite enthusiastic about his new appointment, saying:

> He is as true as gold. A man of integrity, also very energetic. He will straighten out the Reichstag for me. Besides, it was with him in Hohenfinow that I shot my first roebuck.

However, despite his personal qualities, Bethmann-Hollweg soon found himself faced not only with a difficult Reichstag, but also with an increasingly uncontrollable and demanding military.

Reform of the Prussian parliament

Although the Imperial Reichstag was elected on a one-man-one-vote system, within the individual states that made up the empire voting systems varied and often favoured the wealthy. In Prussia, for example, the Lower House of parliament was elected on a three-class system by means of an open ballot. This meant that the votes of the lower and middle classes were worth less than those of the Junkers. This ensured that the Junkers were always able to control the Prussian parliament. For example, in the election of 1908, socialist candidates won 23 per cent of the votes, but gained only 7 seats. The Conservatives, on the other hand, who won 16 per cent, gained 212 seats.

Bülow had unsuccessfully suggested reforms in 1908, but Bethmann-Hollweg devised a deliberately more moderate bill in 1910, aiming to strengthen the position of the growing middle class in the electorate. It was a very carefully thought through measure which would have ended

Activity

Thinking point

As you read this section, try to decide whether Bethmann-Hollweg's problems were more:

 the result of Bülow's legacy as chancellor

 the result of his own failings as chancellor.

Cross-reference

Elsewhere in Germany, Bismarck's constitution granted the vote to all men over 25 years – this is discussed on page 15.

Fig. 11 *A German cartoon commentating on the Prussian three-class franchise. Can you interpret its message?*

indirect elections and increased votes to those with educational and other qualifications (although it still retained open voting and three classes). However, his plans met with such hostility that they had to be dropped. They were too radical for the Conservatives and the Centre, while not far-reaching enough for the more forward-thinking parties.

The 1912 elections

The elections of 1912 were a blow to Bethmann-Hollweg's hopes of forging a working majority in the Reichstag. The socialists won 34.8 per cent of the total vote, giving them 110 deputies and making them the largest party in the Lower House. One in three Germans had voted Social Democrat and together with the Progressive Liberals (who received 12.3 per cent of the vote) the left wing formed a majority in the Reichstag. The Conservatives and others supporting Bethmann polled only just over 12 per cent, the Centre 16.4 per cent and National Liberals 13.6 per cent. According to the historian Berghahn:

> After 1912 it was not only the finances of the Reich and the federal states that were coming apart at the seams, but the political system in general.

Increasing indirect taxes, higher tariffs and a rise in the cost of living had all played their part in swinging the vote towards the left, but the result must also have been partly caused by Bethmann-Hollweg's refusal to play on people's patriotism in the way Bülow had done.

The result produced a sense of crisis at the heart of government. The chancellor could not guarantee majorities for his policies and was forced to lobby for support on measures as they arose rather than relying on any fixed groupings of parties.

Military spending

Bethmann-Hollweg faced the impossible task of balancing a budget deficit with demands for increased military expenditure. Between 1909 and 1912, government spending was just about manageable but, with the growth in international tension after 1912, matters grew more acute.

In July 1913, despite fierce opposition from the SPD, the Reichstag was persuaded to agree to a large increase in the size of the army, but there was much argument over the raising of an additional 435m Reichsmarks to finance the measure. Bethmann-Hollweg's solution was a special 'defence tax' on the value of property. This was carried by the votes of the left-wing Liberals and socialists even though the Conservative parties strongly opposed it. Their opposition was such that additional proposals, to increase **inheritance tax**, had, as under Bülow, to be abandoned.

■ **Key term**

Inheritance tax: a tax on the value of land and possessions received after a person's death.

The Army Bill created even more problems for the government:

- The **national debt** had reached 490bn marks and the deficit for 1913 stood at over 400m marks.
- Bethmann-Hollweg had angered the left through his support for army reform, and the right through his support for inheritance tax.

To compound these problems, in December 1917, Bethmann-Hollweg found himself having to defend Wilhelm's behaviour over the Zabern Affair, in which it seemed as though Wilhelm was prepared to allow the military to do as they pleased with no respect for the rule of law. However, although the Reichstag passed a vote of no-confidence against the chancellor by 293 votes to 54, he survived because he still had the Kaiser's support. Nevertheless, the affair highlighted the position which the army had by then acquired and further demonstrated the weakness of the Reichstag.

A closer look

The Zabern Affair

Zabern, a town in Alsace province, was garrisoned by German soldiers with the help of local recruits. It became known that a German officer, 20-year-old Lieutenant von Forstner, who had been teased for his boyish appearance, had, while instructing his men, insulted the French flag and called the Alsatian recruits 'Wackes', a hated nickname meaning 'square-heads'. He had admitted this and had been punished with several days' confinement in a military prison.

A report of the incident appeared in Zabern's two newspapers and there were demonstrations in the town. On 29 November 1913, a crowd assembled in front of the barracks. The soldiers were ordered to disperse the crowd and charged wildly across the square. Fifteen people were arrested, including the president, two judges and the State Attorney of the Zabern Supreme Court, who had just come out from the court building and were caught up in the crowd.

There was outrage in Germany and an outcry against militarism. The army officers were accused of placing the army outside the law. The army claimed that it was answerable to the Kaiser alone – and Wilhelm II condoned the action. The Reichstag was furious but Bethmann-Hollweg refused to side with them and supported the Kaiser and the military. He defended the military authorities saying:

Fig. 12 *The actions of the German soldiers in Alsace during the Zabern Affair, 1913. What type of magazine do you think produced this cartoon?*

The military authorities have always and justly believed that they cannot allow such insults as were directed against them, especially in this affair in which there was not a single incident but a whole chain of similar occurrences. I beg you gentlemen not to forget, in this serious and, in many respects, sad incident, that the Army has the right to protect itself against direct attack. It not only has the right, it has the duty. Otherwise, no army in the world could continue to exist.

4

Activity

Pairs activity

Put together a reply to the Kaiser from the members of the Reichstag who opposed the army's actions.

The massive anti-government feeling in the Reichstag boded ill for the future of Imperial government. Within the Social Democratic party, an active left wing had emerged, that was calling for Marxist revolution. Although the majority socialists remained committed to less radical change, the situation was so tense that it might have led to some sort of revolution, but for the outbreak of war in 1914. The Kaiser's prestige was evaporating, the SPD was growing in support, and after the tax compromises of 1913 Bethmann-Hollweg had given up trying to carry the Reichstag with him and was relying on decrees rather than legislation. The debt crisis was mounting. There were massive strike movements not only for better wages and conditions, but also for the reform of the Prussian voting system. There were problems from minority groups, particularly the Poles who were up in arms against the blatant discrimination they faced, while the working class was critical of the lack of reform and the police were having to resort to repression and censorship to maintain control. In such circumstances, it is easy to see why it might be suggested that the Kaiser was keen to go to war as a way of diverting attention from the growing crisis at home and uniting the nation in a common cause.

Question

How important was the Zabern Affair in the breakdown of constitutional government in Germany before 1914?

Activity

Challenge your thinking

1. Construct a timeline for the period 1890–1914. Plot the key domestic policies, and highlight in red those that you believe were successful. Highlight in green those that you believe were unsuccessful.

2. In groups, decide which chancellor was the most successful in the years 1890–1914 and prepare a speech to justify your choice.

3. When you have heard each other's speeches, produce a report for each chancellor – explaining the grade you have awarded, from A – *highly successful* to C – *in need of much improvement*.

	Grade (A, B, C)	Reason
Caprivi		
Hohenlohe		
Bülow		
Bethmann-Hollweg		

The Kaiser's personal power and influence, 1890–1914

The issue of where power resided in Wilhelmine Germany was at the heart of the many disputes of the period. The Bismarckian constitution, which remained essentially unchanged until the war years, had placed ultimate authority with the Kaiser. Wilhelm II had not only come to power determined to exert that authority, but had maintained a very personal involvement in government, almost to the extent of over-stepping his constitutional position.

His decisions regarding the appointment and dismissal of chancellors, while breaking from the tradition established by Wilhelm I, were nevertheless constitutional. When a chancellor lost Wilhelm's confidence, he was forced from office. Consequently, Caprivi resigned after clashing with Wilhelm over the renewal of the Anti-Socialist Law; Hohenlohe departed after a dispute with Wilhelm over colonial policy;

Bülow was forced out after his lukewarm support over the *Daily Telegraph* Affair; and, although Bethmann-Hollweg limped on into the war years, he was increasingly marginalised and eventually lost his position to the military in 1917, when the Kaiser was forced by new circumstances to dismiss him.

However, there is controversy over whether Wilhelm's other actions between 1897 and 1908, during Bülow's time as chancellor, when the Kaiser reached the high point of 'personal rule', were truly 'constitutional'. During these years he dictated policy, controlled all appointments, all legislation and all diplomatic moves and, whilst it could be argued that he was doing nothing more than the constitution allowed, his behaviour provoked considerable difficulties with another essential part of the constitution – the Reichstag.

Although the Reichstag could not itself introduce, or even amend, legislation, it nevertheless held a very important power within the constitution – the Kaiser and his ministers needed its support for legislation, as a Reichstag majority was necessary to approve or reject a bill. Consequently, government could only work through a system of agreement – or at least compromise – between the Reichstag majority and the Kaiser's ministers. Unless a minister could be sure of a majority in the Reichstag for legislation, he could not get laws agreed to support his policies. The deputies in the Reichstag also saw this logic in reverse. If a majority in the Reichstag wanted a particular policy or law, they felt that ministers should be prepared to respond to their views.

Fig. 13 *Kaiser Wilhelm II addressing the Reichstag in 1890*

Cross-reference

For the workings of the German constitution, refer back to pages 14–15.

Hence, the period of the Kaiser's personal rule provoked endless discussion about power and rights, as outlined in these comments by Friedrich Naumann, a Lutheran pastor and Liberal politician, in 1900:

> In present-day Germany there is no stronger force than the Kaiser. The very complaints of the anti-Kaiser democrats about the growth of personal absolutism are the best proof of this fact, for these complaints are based on the repeated observation that all policy, foreign and internal, stems from the will and word of the Kaiser. No monarch of absolutist times ever had so much real power as the Kaiser has today. He does not achieve everything he wants, but it is still more than anybody would have believed possible in the middle of the last century.

5

The obstruction of the Reichstag and the increasing separation between the 'Kaiser's government' and the demands of the masses – as reflected in the growing socialist vote – made the Bismarckian constitution increasingly difficult to operate. The Reichstag might have been able to exert still more power had the political parties been able to cooperate more effectively together, but while they remained divided, there was always the chance that a chancellor would be able to retain the upper hand.

By 1908, the Kaiser seemed to have given up on trying to make his personal rule work and he subsequently grew less interested in domestic government. He seemed to abdicate responsibility as the political situation grew more difficult, leaving a 'political vacuum' at the head of government, which only made the situation even more chaotic. In the years to 1914, different groups, both within and outside the Reichstag, all jostled for power. His ministers, the Junkers, the industrialists, the civil service, the military, the politicians and people of all classes were all, in different ways, trying to influence the future direction of Germany, and they did so, not only through the obvious constitutional channels, but also through pressure groups, unions, demonstrations and displays of lawless behaviour which made government increasingly difficult.

Ministers dared not demand too much of a Reichstag that they could not control, whilst within the Reichstag, the political parties became polarised between the left and the right, at the expense of the moderate centre. By 1914, Germany had the largest socialist party in Europe, and also the largest army. The support for the SPD was counter-balanced by support for extreme national and anti-Semitic groups. The Kaiser's association with military figures increased the feeling that the government did not represent the wishes of the people and the struggles of the different interest groups made agreement near impossible.

A closer look

Wilhelm II – historiography

John Röhl (*Germany Without Bismarck: The Crisis of Government in the Second Reich 1890–1900*, 1967) leads the school of historians who argue that the Kaiser deliberately set out to create a personal rule and that his personal neuroses had a direct impact on politics. According to this school of thought, the Kaiser was at the heart of power in Germany after 1890. Wilhelm chose 'pliant tools of the imperial will' for key offices and wore down the opposition of his civil servants until, by 1897–8, he had created a centralised government based on himself. This reached its high point in the years 1897–1908. Weltpolitik, anti-Socialism, the navy programme and foreign policy, such historians suggest, were all the outcome of Wilhelm's own personal desires.

Hans-Ulrich Wehler (*The German Empire 1871–1918*, 1997) has adopted a different view, which is sometimes described as 'structuralist' as it sees developments as emerging from the 'structure' of the country at the time. He has argued that the developments of these years all stemmed, not from the Kaiser's personality, but from Germany's rapid economic development. The country failed to adapt to the rapid change and policies were all about elite groups defending their particular interests and trying to cling on to power. The Kaiser, it is argued, was subjected to pressure from the Junkers, the industrialists, the army and the bureaucrats – all of whom wanted to ensure that their interests were upheld in the face of the demands of the growing middle and working classes. They pressed for anti-socialist policies and they encouraged foreign expansion to divert attention away from the circumstances within Germany. According to Wehler's theories, Wilhelm was just a 'shadow emperor' (*Schattenkaiser*) who reigned but did not rule. Wehler has argued that Wilhelm had insufficient ability to lead and direct policy. Although he acknowledged that the Kaiser made a brief bid to establish a personal rule, he has suggested that all he really managed was irrelevant speech making. Germany was, he suggested, a 'leaderless polycracy' – with several competing power centres and a vacuum at the top.

Other supporters of Wehler's ideas include Fritz Fischer (*War of Illusions: German Policies, 1911–1914*, 1975) and V. R. Berghahn (*Imperial Germany 1871–1914: Economy, Society, Culture and Politics*, 1994). Fischer was one of the first to put forward the view that the German Reich was not a stable autocracy (as had formerly been assumed). He blamed the Conservative Junkers for shaping the Reich's domestic struggles and foreign policy, emphasising that the policies of the German Empire were responsible for the outbreak of war in 1914.

Richard Evans (*Society and Politics in Wilhelmine Germany*, 1978) and David Blackbourn and Geoff Eley (*The Peculiarities of German History: Bourgeois Society and Politics in Nineteenth-century Germany*, 1984) have also stressed the complexities of late 19th century German society and have suggested that the real pressure in society came, not from the elites, but from below, from the growing power of the working and lower middle classes. They do not accept that these groups were 'pawns' but that they were assertive and able to influence government policy.

Christopher Clark's biography of Wilhelm II (*Kaiser Wilhelm II (Profiles in Power)*, 2000) has attempted to marry these different viewpoints. However, controversy still rages as to whether the Kaiser and his ministers were forced into policies, for example Weltpolitik and ultimately the First World War, simply to try to maintain control and provide a focus to unite the nation at home, or whether these policies were indeed the product of the Kaiser's own making.

Activity

Research exercise

Try to get hold of some of the books mentioned in *A closer look* above from a library and read for yourself what historians have had to say about this topic. You will then be able to make up your own mind about which you feel is the most convincing interpretation.

■ Activity

Thinking point

Did Kaiser Wilhelm II control decision making in Germany?

Consider the following statements and decide which support the view that Wilhelm had extensive political power, which oppose it and which provide inconclusive evidence. Where possible, think of additional examples that could be used to illustrate the point made and then try to add some further relevant statements of your own.

1 The Kaiser had the right to declare war and conclude peace; control of all important appointments in the administration, especially the chancellor; the right to dissolve the Reichstag; and personal command of the army and navy.

2 The Kaiser had a very limited grasp of politics and was lazy and pleasure seeking. He was never able to settle down to the regular routine of government and much preferred to spend his time playing the ceremonial role of a monarch, travelling or on military manouevres. He was frequently absent from Berlin.

3 Germany contained a number of powerful interest groups: the bureaucracy; the landowners (especially the Prussian Junkers); the army and the judiciary; and the middle-class industrialists – who were strongly opposed to Socialism and full democracy.

4 The Kaiser's chancellors had their own policy agendas. Caprivi carried through the 'new course', and while Bülow flattered the Kaiser to keep his support, he largely devised his own programme.

5 The policies pursued in Wilhelmine Germany were those the Kaiser favoured – naval rearmament, tariff reform and anti-Socialism.

6 Wilhelm had a close relationship with the military. The army swore loyalty exclusively to the Kaiser and he chose the generals and admirals.

7 The Reichstag had a key power over legislation and used it to oppose any measures of which they disapproved.

8 Wilhelm and his government ministers made extensive use of propaganda to help shape public opinion. Press officers were placed in each ministry to provide a favourable slant on any news.

9 Wilhelm intervened in the affairs of government, e.g the *Daily Telegraph* Affair and the Zabern Affair, with little concern for what others thought.

10 The Wilhelmine period was a time of tremendous economic growth in Germany. This brought about an expansion of the lower middle and working classes as well as promoting the growth of Socialism. The SPD increased its support and became the largest single group in the Reichstag from 1912.

■ Cross-reference

The right and left political groups are discussed on pages 71–6.

AQA Examiner's tip

The term 'shadow emperor' is taken from Wehler's thesis (see *A closer look* on pages 64–5) and suggests that Wilhelm lacked power and influence. You will need to use your answers to the Thinking point activity above in order to decide on your answer to this summary question, which is asking you to evaluate Wilhelm's role in government in these years. Ensure you give a balanced answer which includes points that suggest he was a 'shadow emperor' and others that suggest he exercised real personal power. Although you may want to refer to what historians have said, you should not simply recite their views, but should form a personal judgement and argue accordingly.

■ Summary question

How far was Wilhelm II merely a 'shadow emperor'?

4 Economic change and the polarisation of politics

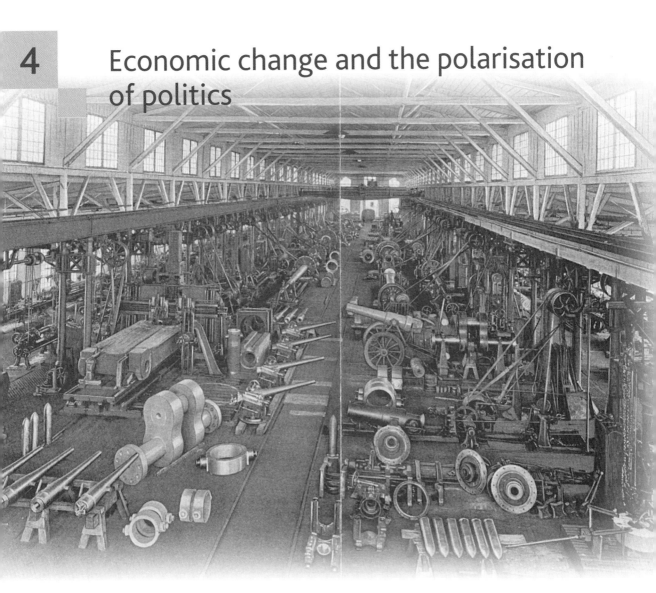

Fig. 1 *The production of cannons in Germany around 1900*

In June 1914, Kaiser Wilhelm II had a full diary of public engagements: the Hanover agricultural fair; an inspection of the Eilweise Wireless station; a day watching army manoeuvres on Lüneberg Heath; and the Elbe regatta. However, the activity he most relished was sailing the royal yacht, the *Hohenzollern*, through the Kiel Canal. This had been recently widened to allow it to take dreadnought class battleships, and the Kaiser was booked to perform the official opening ceremony. This was followed by several days of garden parties, yacht races and dances. However, the festivities ended abruptly when, in the afternoon of Sunday 28 June, Wilhelm was interrupted in the middle of a race aboard the *Hohenzollern* by the arrival of a telegram, bearing the news that Archduke Franz Ferdinand of Austria had been assassinated in Sarajevo. Only two weeks earlier, the Kaiser had visited Franz Ferdinand at his hunting lodge in Bohemia and had spent some time with him there. Now his death, at the hands of Serb terrorists, posed for Wilhelm the crucial question of how Germany should react. The Kaiser knew that news of the assassination would provoke clamours for war from the military in Germany, who would want to support their Austrian ally against Serbia and its Russian protector. Wilhelm's mind was quickly made up and, as he was soon to tell his friend, the industrialist Gustav Krupp, he decided to support action. 'This time,' he declared, 'I shall not give in'.

The Germany of 1914 was a very different Germany from that of 1890. There had been a vast explosion of economic development and this had supported a huge growth in the military. Germany had become the dominant power in Europe and, encouraged by the growth of right-wing pressure groups and uncompromising army officers, Wilhelm was set to lead his country into a war that would bring about his downfall.

■ Economic growth

By 1890, Germany was already well underway towards becoming an industrialised country. The 'first industrial revolution', based on textiles, coal, iron, steel and railways, had already transformed the German economy and the period 1890–1914 saw the second stage of revolution, involving the development of 'new' industries which used more technology, such as electricals, chemicals, machinery and the motor car industry. Between 1890 and 1914, Germany's industrial production tripled and by 1914 Germany was alongside Britain and the USA as one of the world's leading industrial nations.

Underlying the growth was the continuous expansion of the population from nearly 50 million in 1890, to 67 million by 1914. Of all the European countries, only Russia had a larger population. The growth of towns and cities was dramatic and by 1914 more than 60 per cent of Germans lived in towns, compared with 40 per cent in 1890.

The older industries continued their rise as can be seen in Table 1.

■ Cross-reference

To recap on economic development under Bismarck, re-read the section on 'Economic and social change within Germany' on pages 35–42.

Table 1 *A comparison of German and British heavy industrial output 1890–1910*

	Coal production (million tonnes)			Pig iron production (million tonnes)			Steel production (million tonnes)		
	France	Germany	Britain	France	Germany	Britain	France	Germany	Britain
1890	26.1	89	184	2	4.1	8	0.7	2.3	3.6
1900	33.4	149	228	2.7	7.5	9	1.6	6.7	5
1910	38.4	222	268	4	9.5	10	3.4	13.8	5.9

*Adapted from Simpson, W., **The Second Reich – Germany 1871–1918**, 1995*

■ Activity

Statistical analysis

What can you conclude from the statistics shown in Table 1?

The transport system maintained a similar growth. The length of railway network grew from 41,820 km in 1890 to 63,000 km by 1913. While the German merchant marine grew to 3m tonnes by 1913, three times that of the USA, although it was still only a quarter of the size of the British marine.

The growth of the newer industries was, in some respects, even more spectacular. The electrical industry grew most quickly in the Rhine area, where the generators could be powered by the waste gases from the steelworks. The production of electrical energy in this area increased by 150 per cent between 1901 and 1915. Horse-drawn carriages were replaced by electric trolleys and electric lights gradually became more common. By 1913, Germany controlled half the world's trade in electricals. While Germany exported £11m worth of electrical goods, Britain and the USA together only exported £8m.

Germany's expanding chemical industry involved the production of pyrites, common salt and potassium salts, and of 'heavy chemicals' used in manufacturing and as agricultural fertilisers. In 1878, only 1m tonnes of sulphuric acid were being produced in the whole world, yet, by 1907, Germany alone was producing 1,402,000 tonnes. Ammonia production rose from 84,000 tonnes to 287,000 tonnes between 1897 and 1907, and Germany produced more than three-quarters of the world's chemical dyes by 1914, as well as leading the way in pharmaceuticals.

The machinery industry followed the American example. In 1899, Loewe rebuilt his Berlin factory using American ideas of mass production and the Wolf machine works at Magdeburg followed suit. The motor industry was less significant, but advances were being made by Daimler, Diesel, Benz and Mercedes and in the aviation industry by Zeppelin.

As production grew, so did the size of companies and the number of cartels – from 70 in 1887 to 300 by 1900 and 600 by 1911. Nearly every important industry had a cartel. There was one for the chemical trade, and Siemens and AEG both operated cartels in the electrical industry. In coal, the Rhenish-Westphalian Coal Syndicate, formed in 1893, controlled half of Germany's output of coal and coke, while the Steel Union, formed in 1904, comprised 30 large steelworks, including Krupps, by 1911.

Germany's prosperity rested on trade. Food, raw materials and some manufactured goods had to be imported, while chemicals, metal goods, machinery, textiles and coal were sold abroad. German merchants travelled to Africa, Asia, and North and South America. Although there was a 'trade gap' (see Table 2) between imports and exports, the difference was easily made up by the 'invisibles'. These comprised the money earned through foreign investments which were worth over £1,000m and the considerable revenues brought in by shipping and banking.

Activity

Statistical analysis

1. Use the figures in Table 2 to work out Germany's 'balance of trade' (the difference between the cost of imports and exports).

2. Germany also earned money through 'invisible trade' in these years – the profits from services and investments overseas. These figures are given in Table 3. Use them to calculate Germany's overall trade balance. Use these figures to explain what was happening to the German economy in the years 1890–1913.

A closer look

Karl Benz

Karl Friedrich Benz (1844–1929) was born in Karlsruhe, but was brought up in poverty from the age of two when his father, an engine driver, died. His mother was forced to make do and save, in order to provide her son with an education and, in time, an engineering traineeship. Whilst still a student, Benz expressed his exasperation with Germany's muddy roads and dreamt of the day when there would be horseless vehicles to travel in. He established his own machinery company in 1871 supplying metal parts for building trades and by 1879 he had built the first two-stroke engine. In 1883, he created the Benz Company in Mannheim in order to produce industrial engines. He then began work on a 'motor carriage' with a four-stroke engine. By 1885, he had developed an 'automobile' which he was proudly able to drive around Mannheim. It had three wheels and an electric ignition. In January 1866, he took out a patent for his new motor carriage and, by July, he had started selling to the

Table 2 *German imports and exports by value in millions of marks 1890–1910*

	Imports	Exports
1890	2,814	2,923
1900	4,162	3,335
1910	5,769	4,611

Adapted from Farmer, A. and Stiles, A., The Unification of Germany 1815–1919, 2007

Table 3 *Invisible trade by value 1890–1910*

Year	Value (millions of marks)
1890	1,249
1900	1,566
1910	2,211

Adapted from Farmer, A. and Stiles, A., The Unification of Germany 1815–1919, 2007

Activity

Research exercise

Undertake your own research into some of the other great inventors and industrialists of this era. You could give a PowerPoint® presentation to your class.

public. In 1893, the 'Benz Velo' became the world's first, inexpensive, mass-produced car. Benz retired from the company in 1903, although he remained on a supervisory board until his death. Benz and Co. went on to join forces with Daimler in 1926 and Daimler-Benz subsequently became the world's largest automobile manufacturer.

Impact of economic growth

Progress in transportation and the urban infrastructure fuelled an unprecedented growth of towns and cities as the dominance of the industrial economy created a rapidly expanding working class. Whereas in 1890 47 per cent of the population lived in cities, in 1910 it was 60 per cent of the population. While in 1871 only 8 German towns had more than 100,000 inhabitants, in 1910 there were 48. By 1907, the industrial Rhineland and Westphalia had absorbed over 1 million internal immigrants.

This did, of course, still leave large numbers of people whose lives were still predominantly rural. However, no one entirely escaped the relentless thrust of industrial growth which brought, in its wake, new farming techniques, synthetic fertilisers and mechanisation. It is difficult to generalise about the impact of economic growth in the countryside, since conditions varied enormously between one area and another. In some regions large numbers left the rural community to move to the big cities. Elsewhere the rural economy flourished, although changed by the greater dependence on a money-based economy, the spread of communication and education (which brought near-universal literacy) and the influence of central and local state government policies. Overall, the constraints which had made rural life harsh and isolated disappeared and there was greater interaction between town and countryside.

Many workers continued to live in cramped inner-city streets – quite literally on top of one another. Such conditions encouraged protest and, on average, 200,000 trade union workers per year went on strike between 1905 and 1913. However, statistics suggest that standards of living were actually improving for many of these urban dwellers in the post-1890 period. There were new job opportunities, particularly with the spread of white collar positions, and state welfare schemes grew, providing support in times of sickness, accident and old age.

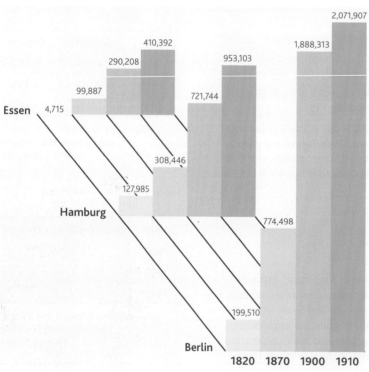

Fig. 2 *Urban population growth, 1820–1910*

Employment rates in the cities were high and average real wages (what could be bought by money wages, taking the cost of living into account) increased by 25 per cent between 1895 and 1913. There were also medical improvements, innoculations and developments in hygiene, which enabled people to live healthier and longer lives. Leisure opportunities improved with the spread of transport and the advent of the cinema and new devices like the telephone, the typewriter and the electric tram network helped speed communications. However, it was the more skilled workers who reaped the greatest benefits and it was probably also the case that the prospect of higher living standards tempted workers to want to improve their lot. If the country was flourishing economically, they wanted a greater share of the wealth that they had helped to create.

Furthermore, despite the improvements, life could be hard and conditions of both living and work compared unfavourably with those in the industrialised Britain and the USA. The average German worked nearly two hours a day longer than the average British worker in the 1890s and, even by 1912, the average working day was longer than the British one in 1877. Despite the wage increases, German workers earned nearly a third less than their British counterparts and there were pockets of acute poverty where families had to share rooms and live with the threat of unemployment just around the corner. It is perhaps unsurprising, therefore, that, although most within the working classes were loyal, diligent and patriotic, many were attracted by the promises of the SPD to improve their lot.

A closer look

The position of women

The spread of Socialism and the questioning of values that characterised German intellectual and artistic movements after 1890 encouraged analyses of what became known as the 'women's question'. There were horror stories of women's sexual exploitation inside and outside the workplace, of the growing numbers of illegitimate or fatherless children in industrial cities and of the believed spread of prostitution. It may be that it was the awareness, rather than the practices, that were becoming more acute at this time but the many restrictions placed on women, for example their loss of property rights on marriage and their limited legal position, were brought into question. The *Bund Deutscher Frauenvereine*, an umbrella organisation which maintained pressure for women's rights, was set up in March 1894. There were campaigns to increase educational opportunities, which led to the founding of female vocational schools and, particularly within the SPD, there were unsuccessful campaigns for a female vote. The socialists Clara Zetkin and August Bebel wrote tracts on female equality which were discussed in bourgeois reading circles, but, as in Great Britain, the female cause advanced little before the First World War, which finally gave women an opportunity to show what they could do.

The growth of political opposition

Despite the limited nature of the constitution and the power which Wilhelm II possessed, he was always concerned about the growth of opposition. He hated to have his will thwarted, yet whilst he could ensure that his chancellors were compliant and deferential, he had a harder job with the Reichstag, which was elected. Wilhelm was always fearful lest his great empire crumble from within and his particular concern was with left-wing opposition, mainly from working-class people. Strangely enough, it was not the left but the right – the army, the Junkers and big business – that was ultimately to destroy his empire by encouraging Wilhelm along the path to war.

Activity

Preparing a presentation

Each group should choose one of the following people and undertake some additional research in order to prepare a short presentation for the rest of the class. Give that person's view of life in Germany between 1890 and 1914. Choose from:

■ a Junker
■ a factory owner
■ a factory worker
■ a farm labourer
■ an unemployed city dweller
■ a middle-class woman.

Fig. 3 *How the left wing viewed the huge Rhenish-Westphalian Coal Syndicate, which seemed to control the lives of thousands of workers in 1904*

Socialism

One significant consequence of economic change was increasing support for Socialism and the SDP. Neither Bismarck's persecution nor the development of 'State Socialism' had prevented the party's growth.

Caprivi's 'new course' (1890–4), during which the Anti-Socialist Laws had lapsed, had merely served to encourage a growth in membership. In the 1890s, the Party organised a series of well-attended conferences, including one in Halle in 1890 and one in Erfurt in 1891.

At the 1891 Erfurt Congress, the party produced a statement of party principles known as the Erfurt Programme:

■ Cross-reference

The emergence of Socialism and Bismark's attempts to repress it are detailed on pages 30–4. Caprivi's change of direction in this area is covered on pages 51–2.

- ■ The Social Democratic Party of Germany fights for the abolition of class rule and of classes themselves and for equal rights and duties for all.

- ■ The Party demands the vote for all men and women over 21.

- ■ The making of new laws and the appointment of high officials to be controlled by the people.

- ■ Decisions for war and peace to be made by the representatives of the people.

- ■ All taxes on goods to be abolished as they are an unfair burden on the poor.

- ■ The costs of government to be paid from income tax, property tax and inheritance tax, to ensure the rich pay most.

- ■ Eight hours to be the maximum working day.

1

■ Activity

Source analysis

Read Source 1.

1 Which of these demands might appear 'revolutionary' and why?

2 Who might be alarmed by this programme?

Despite the apparent radicalism of the Erfurt Programme, the SPD became increasingly moderate in the Wilhelmine era. At the heart of the party were hard-headed practical men – often trade unionists, whose main desire was to help workers in the immediate future, rather than contemplating the overthrow of society. August Bebel, the most prominent party leader, also believed that social reform, better education, housing, and working conditions were most easily achieved through parliamentary action, while other leaders, such as Eduard Bernstein and George Vollmar, spoke of 'gradual Socialism' rather than revolution in order to achieve the socialists' long-term goal of a change in the constitution. Even when the opportunity of a challenge to the established order presented itself, as in the case of the *Daily Telegraph* Affair (1908) or the Zabern Affair (1913), the SPD was reluctant to take advantage of the situation and press for change. When the SPD were presented with their biggest opportunity of all – to hold the Imperial government to ransom when it desperately needed money for the army bills of 1913 – it was passed over.

■ Cross-reference

For the *Daily Telegraph* Affair, see page 58 and for the Zabern Affair, see page 61.

Key profile

August Bebel

August Bebel (1840–1913) was the son of a Rhineland officer who trained as a turner. He met Karl Liebknecht (profiled on page 88) in 1865 and they co-founded the Saxon People's Party, a workers' party. He was elected to the Reichstag of the North German Confederation in 1867 and was the only person to be returned at every election between then and 1912. In 1869, Bebel and Liebknecht formed the Social Democratic Workers' Party (SDAP) which merged with Lassalle's ADAV in 1875 at Gotha. In 1892, Bebel was elected one of the two presidents of the SPD.

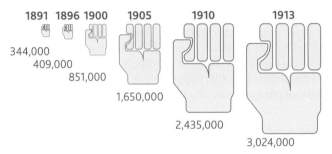

1891	1896	1900	1905	1910	1913

344,000
409,000
851,000
1,650,000
2,435,000
3,024,000

Fig. 5 *Growth of trade unions, 1891–1913*

Fig. 4 *August Bebel, one of the founders of the SPD*

There were, of course, still some traditional Marxists within the ranks who were less easily persuaded that 'gradual Socialism' was the way to go. Socialists such as Karl Liebknecht and Rosa Luxemburg clung on to their belief in more revolutionary methods, and a 'revisionist' amendment to the Erfurt Programme, stating the desire to work through the Reichstag, was defeated in 1900. While, in practice, this made little difference to the course the SPD adopted, the continuance of the party's revolutionary slogans made it harder for other parties, such as the Liberals, to support them and provided an excuse for the Imperial militarist Reich elites to attack them. The government's attempt to combat the socialists' steady rise by portraying them as enemies of the state in 'Sammlungspolitik', however, simply prevented compromise and helped split German society into two opposing extremes.

The SPD's votes steadily increased and, in 1893, it won more votes than any other party. Indeed, it might have won the majority of seats in the Reichstag had the towns and cities, where their support was strongest, been altered to take account of economic changes. The party was popular, not only because it promised to advance the working man's cause in the Reichstag, but also because it helped provide the German working class with a new sense of identity. There were local socialist societies for sport, music and educational purposes. The SPD organised festivals, rallies and holidays, produced newspapers, founded libraries and ran welfare clinics. Their May Day parades were the largest in Europe and a blatant display of working-class solidarity and confidence.

The SPD also helped promote Germany's extensive system of welfare support giving Germany the most comprehensive system of social insurance in Europe by 1913. They pressed successfully for some constitutional changes like the secret ballot (1904) and payment of MPs (1906), which permitted lower middle and working-class men, with no

Did you know?

Trade unions

The trade unions, which grew rapidly in this period, supported the reformist policies of the SPD. The Free Trade Unions – organised in associations for each branch of industry – had 50,000 members in 1890, 680,000 in 1900 and more than 2.5 million in 1913. Under Karl Legien (profiled on page 42) the General Commission, which directed them, became Europe's largest labour organisation. Other associations included the Liberal trade unions and the Christian trade unions and altogether there were c.3.3 million trade unionists by 1914. However, a sizeable body of workers did not belong to a trade union. Known as the *Lumpenproletariat*, some indulged in militant activity, conducting 'lightning' strikes and other violent activity to achieve their ends, while others were the poor and disinterested who remained firmly on the fringes of politics.

Cross-reference

Karl Liebknecht and Rosa Luxemburg are profiled on pages 88 and 93.

■ Cross-reference

Election results between 1890 and 1912 are set out on page 51.

■ Did you know?

A further reason for the hostility of the Kaiser and the elites to Socialism was the type of 'culture' it promoted. Marxism was an international creed, extolling the brotherhood of workers everywhere and the need for pacificism to enable workers to work together against the bourgeoisie. The Kaiser's Germany, however, was a strongly military state. It was dominated by an aristocratic Junker elite and was strongly nationalistic, seeking to extend German domination around the globe. Socialist pacificism was to be challenged in 1914 and many socialists reconciled themselves to warfare since pacificsts were deemed traitors to their country.

■ Question

How successful was the Socialist Party in influencing German politics between 1890 and 1914?

■ Question

Study Table 4. What common themes can you detect in the demands of these right-wing pressure groups?

other income, to put themselves forward as deputies for the Reichstag. In 1911, they supported measures whereby Alsace-Lorraine was given Reichstag representation and universal male suffrage at 21 years was introduced. They also successfully resisted the taxation proposals that would hit the working man harder and promoted progressive taxes, whereby those with the most would be forced to pay more.

From 1912, the SPD were the largest party in the Reichstag, with 110 out of 397 seats. However, they still failed to press for fundamental constitutional change and, in 1914, they accepted a political truce between the parties, known as the *Burgefrieden*, and voted for the funds needed to wage war. The withering of their earlier revolutionary fervour may be partly explained by the rise in living standards which had, by 1900, brought better working and housing conditions and shown that improvements were possible within the constitution of the Reich. However, perhaps even more importantly in these pre-war years was their concern not to appear unpatriotic, at a time when the right were attempting to unite the nation through nationalist campaigns. Fear of being branded as 'anti-German' may well have accounted for the party's apparent timidity to push harder for major changes. However, it is easy to condemn in retrospect and, to understand the limitations of the socialists' leftist opposition, it needs to be balanced against the strength of pressure from the right.

■ The power and influence of the right-wing elites

On the right of politics there were groups which detested the left and were determined to preserve the traditional social hierarchy and the power of the emperor and his armies. The Junkers, military officers and large factory owners shared a common interest in maintaining and extending their own wealth and power. They were fiercely nationalistic and determined to promote the expansion of German influence throughout the world. They saw this as a way of controlling Socialism at home and isolating those minority groups, such as the Poles and the Jews who, they believed, were harming German interests.

The growth of pressure groups

In the course of the 1890s, a number of these right-wing elites formed themselves into pressure groups, with the aim of influencing government policy.

Table 4 *Right-wing pressure groups*

Date	Group	Aim
1876	Central Association of German Industrialists (CVDI)	High tariffs to protect German industry
1882	German Colonial League (DKG)	To promote the development of German colonies
1890	Pan German League (ADV)	Unification of all Germans (to include those living outside the empire)
1893	Agrarian League (BdL)	Tariff protection for agricultural products
1894	German Eastern Marches Society (HKT)	To expand the German Empire
1895	Industrialists' League (BdL)	Tariff reduction – to promote exports
1898	Navy League (DF)	Naval expansion and growth of colonies
1904	Imperial League against Social Democracy	To curb the growth of Socialism
1912	Army League	To promote the expansion of the German army

These patriotic societies and right-wing interest groups came to exert a direct influence on policy making. This was partly because their leadership comprised influential men with wealth and contacts and partly because their concerns were fundamentally in tune with those of the Kaiser and his ministers, though they might wish to push them still further than they were naturally inclined to go. Although there were social differences between the traditional Junker land-owning aristocracy and the newly wealthy industrialists, they shared a common interest in preserving and advancing their own positions. Under their leadership these pressure groups were able to attract other, Conservative elements in society – middle-class bureaucrats, academics, small businessmen, office employees and even members of the working class, particularly in the more rural areas where the peasantry associated their own interests with those of their landlords.

Employers' organisations as well as the Junker-led Agrarian League mounted campaigns for protective tariffs in the wake of Caprivi's relaxing of Bismarck's protectionist laws. Perhaps even more importantly, both Junkers and big business interests came together in the nationalistic and imperialist organisations which sought to expand Germany's wealth and influence overseas and to channel public energies into support for a more aggressive foreign policy. They advocated Weltpolitik and justified and publicised nationalist demands. Among the most radical was the Pan-German League that wanted to unite all ethnic Germans around the world. From *c.*1900, this League became increasingly confrontational and opposed any reformist policies. They called for the suppression of the SPD and stronger leadership, accusing the Kaiser's government of being too moderate.

Its leader, from 1908, was Heinrich Class. He expressed the frustration of the nationalists with what they considered the government's failure to deal with the growing danger of Liberalism, Socialism and Democracy and set out the group's nationalist agenda in his pamphlet 'If I were Kaiser' in 1912.

> The disappointment that all sectors of the population feel about the lack of success and futility of the foreign policy of the German Reich is the most important of the general causes of German discontent. If any state has cause to concern itself with the expansion of power, then it is the German Empire, for its population is rapidly increasing, its industry needs markets and its economy needs soil for the cultivation of raw materials of all kinds.

2

The Pan-German League, like many of the other right-wing pressure groups, expressed overtly anti-Semitic views. They called for a ban on Jewish immigration and restrictions on the rights of Jews, blaming excessive Jewish influence for the growing 'Liberalism' in politics. Such ideas were, in part, influenced by the work of Houston Stewart-Chamberlain, an Englishman resident in Germany, who wrote in 1899:

> True History begins from the moment when the German with mighty hand seizes the inheritance of antiquity. Whoever maintains that Christ was a Jew is either ignorant or dishonest. A deep cleft separates we Europeans from the Jew. We must not be blind to the deep abyss which separates them. The races of mankind are markedly different in the nature and also the extent of their gifts, and the Germanic races belong to the most highly gifted group, usually termed Aryan.

3

Fig. 6 *The* Kaiser Wilhelm der Grösse, *one of Germany's new battleships built under the pressure of the Navy League in 1909*

Right-wing pressure groups lobbied ministers, sought members within the Reichstag, and employed comparatively modern techniques – advertising, the press and even the cinema – to spread their message and win converts. Their campaigning branded opponents as unpatriotic and they were consequently able to attract quite large followings. The Pan-German League could claim membership from 60 right-wing Reichstag members by 1914 and, although it never had more than 25,000 actual members, the status of those members gave it a disproportionately strong influence. The Navy League was deliberately sponsored by the government to promote Germany's claims for a larger navy and win support for the naval laws. By 1900, it had over a million members, which was more than any of the political parties, while the Agrarian League had attracted 250,000. In both cases, they could claim extensive support from the lower classes too.

The overall extent of influence exercised by these groups is still a matter of some controversy. The historian Geoffrey Eley in (1991) *Reshaping the German Right: Radical Nationalism and Political Change after Bismarck*, has suggested that their influence was not as extensive as was once believed, and that they reflected rather than formulated policy decisions. Nevertheless, their very existence adds weight to the view that politics in Germany had become strongly polarised in the early years of the 20th century. Constant pressure from groups determined to promote a strong foreign policy and resist any internal change must have made some contribution to the final breakdown of the Imperial state.

The power and influence of the military

The Prussian officer corps and the military assumed a central role in the Second Reich. This was largely because of the Prussian military tradition and the part that the army had played in the unification of Germany, during which time it had enjoyed glorious victories against the Austrians at Sadowa and the French at Sedan. The new unified Germany perpetuated all the trappings of Prussian military power and most local taverns had a *Stammtisch* or 'regulars' table', where veterans of the wars of unification were accorded due reverence as they met to discuss memories of wartime service. On 'Sedan Day', the anniversary of the 1870 victory, captured French guns were paraded through the streets of Berlin to cheering crowds.

The glorification of war and conquest was also a popular theme in German writing and culture. The socialist leader, August Bebel, claimed:

> The whole nation is still drunk with military glory and there is nothing to be done until some great disaster has sobered us.

The military enjoyed a high prestige and, since money for the army was voted on in the Reichstag only every seven years, the officer corps avoided civilian control. The dominance of this officer corps was, of course, linked to the power of the aristocracy. The higher ranks of the army were dominated by those of Junker class and between 1898

Fig. 7 *A German lance-corporal giving prospective soldiers their first orders, 1910*

and 1918, 56 per cent of all army officers were titled. However, by the time Wilhelm II ascended the throne, it was already evident that the traditional Prussian nobility could no longer supply the number of privileged recruits that a modern army needed. There was an army of half a million men in 1890 and this number was to increase more than eight times by 1914. Consequently, the Kaiser had to ensure that the army retained its prestige by decreeing that the army was infused by a 'nobility of spirit' that demanded respect. This helped perpetuate and ensure popular acceptance of the military's elevated status in society.

It was Wilhelm II himself, with his love of the Prussian tradition, its uniforms, decorative and ritualistic practices and male-dominated culture, that ensured that the power and influence of the military was maintained, and increased. The troops took a personal oath of loyalty to the Kaiser, rather than the state, and this gave him a sense of importance and belonging. In his first public speech as Kaiser, Wilhelm II addressed himself to the German army, rather than the German people, with the words:

> We belong to each other – I and the army – we were born for each other and will always remain loyal to each other, whether it be the will of God to send us calm or storm.

Wilhelm felt more comfortable with military personnel as his companions and he allowed them to become increasingly dominant in policy making whenever questions of importance were discussed. This was particularly the case from the later 1890s as he developed a more personal rule. Civilian decision-makers, Wilhelm believed, could not be relied upon to take tough decisions – only military generals understood how to do that. Count Philipp Eulenburg wrote of Wilhelm II:

> He sucked in like an infant at the breast the tradition that every Prussian officer is not only the height of honour, but of all good breeding, all culture and all intellectual endowment. How a man so clear-sighted as Wilhelm II could have attributed the last two qualities to everyone in guard's uniform has always been a puzzle to me. We will call it a combination of military Hohenzollernism and self-hypnotism.

Cross-reference

The victory at Sedan in 1870 is outlined on pages 4–5.

August Bebel is profiled on page 73.

To recap on the military budget, re-read pages 20 and 52.

Activity

Thinking point

How might you explain Wilhelm II's obsession with, and dependence on, the military?

4

Fig. 8 *The mythical Germania supervises the rise of the German Imperial Navy between 1895 and 1905*

■ Cross-reference

Bülow and Holstein are profiled on pages 56 and 52 respectively.

For more detail on the Navy League, turn to pages 55 and 74–6.

■ Cross-reference

The Schlieffen Plan is introduced on page 52.

The army bills are outlined on pages 52 and 60–1.

Weltpolitik

The Kaiser's ambition for Germany – to win colonies and have German power respected abroad – required military strength, and the expansion of military influence in this period was both the cause and product of Germany's search for world power, or 'Weltpolitik'.

Weltpolitik was encouraged by the right-wing pressure groups, the Pan-German League, the Colonial League and the Navy League, all of which favoured German expansionism and militarism. It was also supported by German industry, which sought raw materials and export markets and, from 1897, Bülow, Tirpitz and Holstein became the protagonists of this 'world policy' with the backing of the military.

Military influence expanded with the passage of the naval laws of 1897, 1900 and 1906. In 1897, Wilhelm had threatened to march the army into the Reichstag and disband it when it had proved reluctant to meet his estimates. However, Admiral von Tirpitz managed to force a change of heart and a year later the Navy League was founded to help win over the public.

The maintenance of the 1892 Schlieffen Plan was another example of the supremacy of the military in decision making. The plan, which had been drawn up as Germany's 'master-plan' in the event of war with Russia and France, involved marching through Belgium in order to defeat France quickly, despite the fact that Belgian neutrality had been guaranteed by Germany, among others, and should therefore never have been considered. It was immoral, since it demanded that Germany break an international agreement. Nevertheless, Bülow raised no objections when it was reconfirmed in 1904 and the Reichstag was not invited to give its views. It thus became the basis for all German military planning and led to army bills being forced through the Reichstag. By 1914, the army had grown to more than 4 million soldiers and expenditure on the army 1913–14 had reached £60m.

Dreadnoughts	1906	1907	1908	1909	1910	1911	1912	1913	1914	Total
Great Britain	1	3	2	2	3	5	3	7	3	29
Germany			4	3	1	3	2	3	1	17

Fig. 9 *The naval race*

Allowing the military to have such dominance that it overrode civilian authority was a very dangerous step. It undermined the democratic institutions which the 1871 constitution had introduced and it placed decision making in the hands of men whose outlook was increasingly at variance from that of the general public.

According to the historian Perry:

> Germany became a state of soldiers and war rather than one of citizens and law. The army not only remained independent of any control, other than that of the monarch himself, but also, through prolonged and universal military service, it was able to influence the thinking of the greater part of the German nation. German society was one in which the upper classes were soaked in the ethos of the barrack square and in which social distinction was measured almost entirely by military rank.

5

Quoted in Wolfson, R., **Years of Change: European History 1890–1945**, *1978*

This military dominance became self-perpetuating. The more Germany became involved in 'world politics' and embroiled in colonial disputes, the more the military were called upon to make crucial decisions about the direction of policy. On 8 December 1912, Wilhelm II convened an infamous war council meeting at his castle in Berlin, during the diplomatic crisis caused by the Balkan Wars. He invited his chief military and naval advisers but excluded civilian decision-makers because he felt the meeting was too important to allow 'mere civilians' to attend. The chancellor, Bethmann-Hollweg, was simply confronted with the decisions made after the event. According to the report of one who was present:

> General von Moltke (chief of the army general staff) said, 'I believe a war is unavoidable. But we ought to do more through the press to encourage the popularity of a war against Russia. The emperor supported this and told the State Secretary Tirpitz to use his press contacts too to work in this direction. In the afternoon I wrote to the Reich chancellor about the influencing of the press.

6

The absence of the civilian leaders and belief of the generals that some form of propaganda was necessary to harness the public's support for war, says much about the power of the military at this time. At the meeting, Helmuth von Moltke, the chief of general staff made it clear that he considered war inevitable and advocated 'the sooner the better', since too much waiting would weaken Germany's chances of a quick victory. However, Admiral Tirpitz, the State Secretary of the Navy actually won the day by asking for an 18-month delay in order to prepare the navy more fully for conflict. Nevertheless, whatever the outcome – and historians disagree about the actual importance of the meeting – the way it was conducted and what it suggests about the mood of Germany's top military decision-makers at the time is clearly important for an understanding of how the Kaiser's reliance on military personnel ultimately led Germany to war.

After the murder of the Austrian Archduke Franz Ferdinand by Bosnian Serbs at Sarajevo in June 1914, it was the German military leaders who urged the politicians to go to war in support of Austria against Serbia's Russian ally. Bethmann-Hollweg, who had always declared his guiding principle to be 'Weltmacht und kein Krieg' – 'World power but no war' – had complained to Wilhelm's son, the Crown Prince, in November 1913, that, 'to rattle the sabre at every diplomatic entanglement is not only blind but criminal'.

Fig. 10 *The arrest of Gavrilo Princip, the assassin responsible for the murder of Archduke Franz Ferdinand at Sarajevo in June 1914*

■ Cross-reference

For the assassination of the Archduke Franz Ferdinand, which triggered the outbreak of the First World War, refer to page 67.

However, he was forced to accept a decision made by generals who argued that Germany's position would only suffer from delay and that war would help counter the threat posed by the growth of the trade unions and the SPD by uniting the country behind the patriotic banner.

On 5 July, after attending a meeting of the Kaiser's military advisers, Bethmann-Hollweg duly told the Austrian ambassador that Austria could 'count safely on Germany's support as an ally and a friend'. This promise was the equivalent of giving Austria a 'blank cheque' or complete freedom to act aggressively by taking a firm line with Serbia and provoking war. It was after Bethmann-Hollweg again met with the military leaders, von Moltke and von Falkenhayn on 30 July, that the decision to declare a state of 'imminent war' in Germany was taken. Whether the generals forced Bethmann-Hollweg's hand or not, we shall never know for sure, but by 4 August, in a spirit of nationalist enthusiasm, Germany found itself at war with Russia, France and Great Britain.

Learning outcomes

Through your study of this section, you should have acquired a good understanding of the influences moulding the development of the Kaiserreich under Wilhelm II. In particular, the position of the Kaiser himself, his chancellors, the various political parties and other influential groups such as the right-wing elites and the army.

You should also understand the key economic developments affecting Germany throughout this period. How the country's relentless drive to modernisation and economic growth sat uneasily alongside a Conservative leadership and a Kaiser and court whose chief interest was in German aggrandisement overseas and whose psychological resentments ran deep.

AQA Examination-style questions

(a)   Explain why new industries developed in Germany in the years after *c*.1890.   *(12 marks)*

 For part (a), try to think of a range of factors which help explain the growth of the new industries. You may want to include some general factors such as the availability of raw materials, but try to be as precise as you can. Think, for example, about the link between technical education and the newer industries, the 'gap' in the market and specific reasons for the demand for these newer goods.

(b)   How far did the economic changes of 1871–1914 transform German society?   *(24 marks)*

 Part (b) is asking you to evaluate the impact of economic change. You will need an introduction which defines any key terms in the question (such as 'economic changes' and 'German society') and suggests the arguments you are going to use. You will need to consider the impact of both industrial and agricultural developments on urban and rural areas, on the class structure, living and working conditions and the emergence of movements such as Socialism and trade unionism. You are being asked to make a judgement, 'how far', so discuss the extent of change and continuity and try to reach a supported conclusion.

5 The abdication of the Kaiser and the difficult birth of a new regime

At 1.30pm on 9 November 1918, in a house adjacent to the German army headquarters in Spa, Belgium, Kaiser Wilhelm II of Germany was brought the news that his abdication had been announced in Berlin. His reign was at an end. He might well cry 'treason', but by 5.00 in the afternoon, he had been forced to accept what had happened. His companions advised him that his only hope of safety was to travel northwards into Holland, which had remained neutral during the war which Germany had been waging on the western front for the last four years against the British and French. Wilhelm, however, was uncertain what to do. His wife, the Empress Dona, was still in Berlin and it was not until just before dawn on 10 November, that a convoy of 10 cars, including the Kaiser's, with its royal insignia removed, set off to the Dutch border at Eysen. Here, the royal party was kept waiting for six hours while the Dutch authorities decided what should happen to such an important visitor, but eventually they were allowed to continue by special train. When Wilhelm met the German ambassador the next day he complained, 'I am a broken man. How can I begin life again? My prospects are hopeless. I have nothing left to believe in.' However, he was informed that Count Betinck was prepared to offer him refuge at his castle at Amerongen and, as Europe celebrated the armistice on 11 November 1918, Wilhelm sat down to 'a good cup of English tea' at his new residence.

The breakdown of government, September 1918

By the end of 1918, Germany was in a sorry state. The war on which the Germans had embarked so confidently in August 1914 had failed to provide the victory that its generals had expected and its people had been led to believe in. As late as March 1918, when the defeated Russians had been forced to sign the punitive Treaty of Brest-Litovsk, the promise of imminent victory could still be used to motivate troops and civilians. With peace in the east, a million men from the German divisions on the Eastern front had been transferred to France, to mount the final 'Ludendorff' or 'Spring Offensive' of March 1918. The German Army Headquarters had been moved to Spa and on 21 March the campaign had been launched with great success. The plan had been to smash through the British and French lines before the fresh young American soldiers, who had already started to arrive in the early months of 1918, swelled the allies' ranks. The plan had, indeed, come near to success, driving the allied armies back to Paris, but by July a million American troops were reinforcing the British and French armies. The final

Fig. 1 *Families were driven to despair by financial and food shortages during the closing stages of the First World War*

offensive, launched on 15 July, collapsed within less than a week and on 8 August, allied tanks had broken through the German lines. The over-stretched, exhausted Germans had been forced into retreat and with the news of the collapse of Germany's allies, the German High Command abandoned hopes of victory.

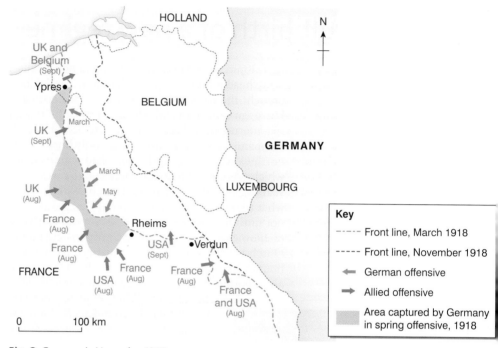

Fig. 2 *Germany in November 1918*

A closer look

The First World War 1914–18

German plans for a quick victory with the Schlieffen Plan in 1914 had failed, and three and a half years of near stalemate on the western front had followed. During this time, Germany had been forced to fight on two fronts, against the British and French in the west and the Russians in the east. However, military success against Russia and the desperate need for peace of the new Bolshevik government (established October/November 1917) allowed Germany to impose vindictive peace terms on Russia in March 1918 and to concentrate its forces in the west. However, in April 1917, the USA had joined the war on the side of the allies, partly in response to the German unrestricted submarine warfare in the Atlantic. America's might, compared with Germany's economic plight, brought about by the British blockade of the German ports, was to tip the scales away from Germany. Furthermore, Germany's allies were in a state of collapse by 1918. Bulgaria was forced to ask for peace on 29 September and Turkey on 30 October. The Austro-Hungarian Empire had broken up under the pressure of war and in September 1918 the break-away Czechoslovak National Council had been recognised by the USA as an independent government. Austria signed an armistice on 3 November and, on 11 November, Germany did the same.

Within Germany, conditions were appalling. The redirection of resources to the war effort, the disruption to agriculture caused by conscription and, above all, the British blockade of German ports which had been in place for the previous two years, had all played their part in creating misery and distress. Ordinary German civilians were reduced to starvation level as food supplies dwindled, leaving most to live on no more than 1,000 calories a day. Compared with 1914, the supply of milk had fallen by 50 per cent and meat and butter by 40 per cent. Bread had been rationed since January 1915 and all necessities were in short supply. In 1916–17, even the supply of potatoes had run out, leaving only turnips to keep the population going through the 'turnip winter', and 1917 and 1918 had both seen poor harvests which had exacerbated problems. Around 750,000 died of starvation or malnutrition through the winter of 1918–19. Electricity supplies were cut to conserve energy, while the public transport system ceased to operate to any reliable schedule. Businesses could not function, the ill and needy could not be attended to and the economy was close to collapse. To make matters worse, an epidemic of Spanish flu, which spread across the whole of Europe, hit the country badly, causing over a million deaths.

News of imminent defeat was kept from the mass of the population by a constant barrage of propaganda and press censorship but, by late September, the German generals knew the game was up and that unless a ceasefire was arranged, Germany itself would be invaded. On 29 September, General Ludendorff and Admiral Paul von Hintze, the foreign secretary, met at Spa to decide the best course of action. They hoped to be able to approach the Americans for an armistice based on Wilson's Fourteen Points, as he had set out in January 1918.

They also agreed that some reform of the German government was necessary before the allies were approached. During the war the government had been allowed to evolve into a military dictatorship, dominated by the army general staff and the 'war lords' Hindenburg and Ludendorff, with the Kaiser as a figurehead. It was known that the Americans, in particular, would never negotiate with such a body. However, this was not the only reason why change was considered necessary. The military leaders also knew that if power were to be handed back to the Reichstag and a more representative government created, this would have to be a primarily socialist (SPD) government. Consequently, a socialist government, rather than the army generals, would have to take responsibility for seeking peace terms. In other words, the military would no longer be held liable for the humiliation of wartime failure nor suffer the anger of the disillusioned German people. As far as Ludendorff was concerned, this seemed to be the only way to save the reputation of the army and the Kaiser, quite apart from persuading the allies to treat Germany more leniently.

A closer look

The impact of the First World War on the Kaiser's government

The outbreak of war had brought *Burgfrieden* – a civil peace in support of the war. Although opposed to an offensive war, the socialists and centre voted for war credits and joined the coalition supporting the government. However, by 1917 this unanimity had broken down. As the war became a war of attrition, the socialists split into three groups. The SPD, which still represented the majority, continued to vote war credits, but the USPD (independent socialists) broke away in April 1917. On the extreme left, the

Exploring the detail

Wilson's Fourteen Points

Woodrow Wilson was an idealist and his Fourteen Points were devised as a means of dealing fairly with the aftermath of war. Some points, such as the return of Alsace-Lorraine to France, were quite specific and punitive towards Germany. However, recommendations such as the establishment of a League of Nations to monitor future disputes and self-determination, whereby different races should rule themselves, together with general disarmament and Wilson's determination to create a peace that would last and prevent another war, gave comfort to the German generals.

■ Cross-reference

To recap on the nature of the government in Germany, refer back to pages 14–16.

Socialism is covered on page 31 and the Spartacists on pages 88, 93 and 95–8.

Spartacists (Communists) broke away in 1916 and opposed war of any kind. They held a demonstration against the war on 1 May 1916 and provoked the first strike of the war.

The Reichstag's 'peace resolution' of 19 July 1917 proposing an end to the war, without annexations, marked the first direct Reichstag intervention into the discussion of war aims. The majority coalition of SPD, centre and progressives was led by Matthias Erzberger of the Centre Party and was critical of the government's conduct of war. The resolution was fiercely opposed by the right and, under the leadership of Tirpitz and Kapp, the Fatherland Party was set up in September 1917, attracting Conservatives, right-wing Liberals, middle classes and the Army High Command. Some belated attempts at constitutional reform failed in the spring of 1917 and Bethmann-Hollweg resigned in July. Control of policy passed into the hands of the military under Hindenburg and Ludendorff. Their unrealistic ambitions and refusal to compromise were to destroy the Second Reich in 1918.

■ **Key profiles**

Erich von Ludendorff

Fig. 3 *Wilhelm II (centre), Hindenburg (left) and Ludendorff (right) imposed a military control over Germany from 1917*

Erich von Ludendorff (1865–1937) acted as second in command on the eastern front in 1914 and was promoted to the position of Quartermaster-General in control of German war policy in 1916. He was a staunch Conservative and, as virtual military dictator (with the older Hindenburg) from 1916, he was responsible for the harsh peace of Brest-Litovsk and the Spring Offensive of 1918. He was dismissed on 26 October 1918, and later became involved in the 1920 Kapp Putsch (see pages 114–15) and 1923 Munich Putsch (see pages 126–7). He sat in the Reichstag as a Nazi deputy 1924–8 and was the Nazi candidate for the presidency in 1925, but he won only one per cent of the vote.

Paul von Hindenburg

Paul von Hindenburg (1847–1934) was recalled from retirement to become Commander in Chief of the German forces in the east in 1914. His success there led to his promotion to the rank of Field Marshal and he took overall command of all German forces from 1916. In August 1918, when he realised the war was lost, he recommended an armistice. He retired again in November 1918, but returned to politics in 1925 when he was elected president. As president he was responsible for appointing Hitler as chancellor in 1933.

Activity

Research exercise

Undertake some personal research into the leadership and activities of Ludendorff and Hindenburg. Try to discover more about their backgrounds, politics and leadership in the war years, particularly in 1918. You might present your findings to the rest of the class and debate the responsibility of these men for Germany's problems by the end of 1918.

The revolution from above

On 2 October, the Reichstag received the totally unexpected news that a new government was to be formed and that Germany was to seek an armistice. The following day, 3 October, the Kaiser appointed Prince Max von Baden as his new chancellor. Max formed a cabinet of ministers with representatives from the majority parties in the Reichstag, including prominent members of the SPD. This was the first stage in the 'revolution from above', sometimes known as the 'October Revolution'. For the first time in its history, Germany had a government led by ministers selected from the Reichstag, rather than chosen by the Kaiser. Max went on to carry through a series of reforms which were designed to remove some of the Kaiser's powers and create a true parliamentary democracy.

- The Prussian three-class franchise was abolished.
- The Reichstag assumed control of the army and navy (instead of the Kaiser).
- The chancellor and government had to account for their actions to the Reichstag (rather than to the Kaiser).

Whether Max introduced these reforms at the generals' prompting, in order to prevent a left-wing revolution and to show the allies that Germany was in the process of democratic reform, or whether he himself was forced into the changes by the Reichstag is uncertain. However, since the Reichstag was actually 'in recess' (not sitting) between 5 and 22 October, this would suggest that the initiative probably came from Max. It is probably no coincidence that these constitutional changes took place in Germany at the same time as the British broke through the last German defence system, the Hindenburg line (6 October), and the need for an armistice became more urgent.

Cross-reference

The various political parties and their beliefs at the end of the First World War are outlined on pages 92–3.

Cross-reference

The Prussian three-class franchise is described on page 59.

Key profile

Prince Max von Baden

Prince Max (1867–1929) was Wilhelm II's cousin. He was a moderate, known for his charitable work with prisoners during the First World War. He had opposed unrestricted submarine warfare and the Kaiser and his generals had hoped that Max's appointment as chancellor might lead to a favourable armistice with the USA. However, Max knew that the government had to be reformed first, and he forced Ludendorff's resignation at the end of October. He also pressed the Kaiser to step down and, receiving no definite answer, announced Wilhelm's abdication – and then his own resignation – on 9 November.

These sudden and unexpected reforms made the German people all too aware that the war was indeed lost. Resentment had been growing for several years, showing itself in the form of food riots and demonstrations.

Now a surge of anger swept through the country. While suffering might have been endured for the sake of victory, once all hopes were dashed, the population wanted to get back to a reasonable state of affairs as soon as possible and sought scapegoats for their troubles. Following a letter from President Wilson on 24 October, which suggested that because the German government was based on an 'autocratic dictatorship' nothing but total surrender would be acceptable to the allies, calls for the abdication of the Kaiser became ever more urgent.

Ludendorff's response to Wilson's letter is given below:

> Wilson's letter is a demand for unconditional surrender. It is thus unacceptable to us soldiers. It proves that our enemies' desire for our destruction, which let loose the war of 1914, still exists undiminished. It proves further that our enemies use the phrase 'a just peace' merely to deceive us and break our resistance. Wilson's letter can thus be nothing for us soldiers, but a challenge to continue our resistance with all our strength.

1

Activity

Source analysis

Read Source 1.

1 Explain why Ludendorff was so angered by Wilson's letter.

2 How accurate are the arguments contained in his response?

3 Imagine you are Prince Max. Write to Ludendorff, expressing your intention to dismiss him and explaining why you believe he has to go.

The revolution from below

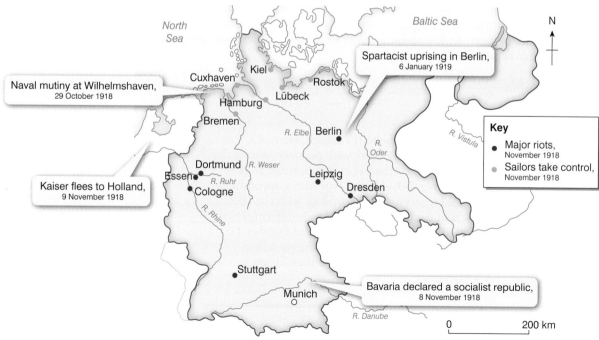

Fig. 4 *Centres of revolt, 1918–19*

Towards the end of October there was an outbreak of strikes and mutinies across Germany. On 28 October, Germany's desperate and fanatical naval commanders ordered the German warships, which had been at anchor in Germany's North Sea ports for most of the war, to be put to sea to fight the British navy. The sailors, already resentful of the harsh discipline of naval life and distrustful of their superior officers, were all too aware of the folly of such a command. It was tantamount to a death sentence. On 29 October, crews on two of the ships moored at Wilhelmshaven mutinied, putting out the fires in the ships' boilers and refusing to sail. They raised the communist red flag and, when the naval commanders ordered their arrest, other sailors demonstrated in support.

Karl Liebknecht, who helped lead the left-wing 'Spartacist' organisation, believed that Germany was on the verge of a communist revolution, similar to that which had occurred in Russia a year earlier. He called on soldiers, workers and other sailors to join in and began plans for a rising in the capital, Berlin. By 31 October, the mutiny had spread to Kiel where sailors took control of the city. On 3 November, eight sailors were shot in demonstrations there and between 6 and 8 November soviet-style councils of workers, sailors and soldiers were set up in several major cities, including Dusseldorf, Cologne, Hanover, Brunswick, Leipzig and the ports of Hamburg, Lubeck and Bremen. On 7–8 November a left-wing socialist republic was proclaimed in Bavaria and by 9 November the revolution had reached Berlin. It certainly seemed to outsiders as though Germany was on the verge of a genuine 'people's revolution' – a 'revolution from below'.

Question

Explain why the 'revolution from above' was followed by a 'revolution from below' in October to November 1918.

Exploring the detail

The Bavarian Socialist Republic

Under the Kaiserreich, Bavaria had retained its own Wittelsbach monarchy. However, on 7 November 1918, the socialist USPD member, Kurt Eisner (1867–1919), led a demonstration through the capital, Munich. His supporters seized public buildings and demanded the end of the monarchy. The Bavarian Democratic and Socialist Republic was proclaimed the next day, with a workers' and soldiers' council in control. Kurt Eisner was elected its Minister-President. However, the USPD were defeated in the elections in Bavaria in January 1919 and, before he could announce his resignation, Eisner was shot by a right-wing aristocrat.

Fig. 5 *Revolutionary activity broke out in cities, where civilians and soldiers joined forces in strikes and mutinies, 1918–19*

Fig. 6 *Karl Liebknecht, the revolutionary SPD/KPD leader*

Karl Liebknecht

Karl Liebknecht (1871–1919) was a revolutionary socialist from Leipzig. He had joined the SPD in 1900 and became an SPD member of the Reichstag in 1912. He was the only Reichstag member to refuse to support the government at the outbreak of war. He joined Rosa Luxemburg (profiled on page 93) in 1916 to lead a left-wing break-away group, named after its journal 'Spartakus'. He was sentenced for treason for leading a peace demonstration in Berlin but released with the general amnesty of October 1918. With Luxemburg, he founded the KPD (German Communist Party) 30 December 1918 to 1 January 1919 and he helped organise the Spartacist rising two weeks later. He was subsequently murdered by the right-wing Freikorps (see page 97).

The Russian Revolution and Communism

The situation in Germany was tense in 1918 because only a year earlier in Russia, which bordered Germany to the east, there had been revolutions which had parallels with what was happening in Germany. In February/March 1917, the hungry workers of St Petersburg had been joined by mutinous soldiers to overthrow the Tsar. Soviets (councils) of workers and soldiers had been set up and these had struggled with the new Provisional government to exert control. Communist and radical ideas, such as the redistribution of land and the destruction of the elites won converts and in October/November the Bolsheviks (Communists) had seized power in the name of the working people. They had confiscated the land and property of the upper classes, nationalised banks and factories and embarked on a civil war in which they terrorised and shot their opponents. It was little wonder that 'Communism' invoked fear and concern in Europe at this time and most particularly among the middle and upper classes of Germany. The government countered Spartacist propaganda with slogans such as 'The tidal wave of Communism threatens our country'. However, the German soviets were generally more moderate than the Russian ones had been. Many were led by members of the USPD who, although more radical than the SPD, still sought democratic governmental change rather than overthrow the established social order and the creation of a workers' dictatorship. The (communist) Spartacist League was not a large or powerful organisation and had barely 1,000 members at the end of 1918.

Prince Max feared events were moving beyond his control and on 8 November he phoned Wilhelm II at Spa to urge his abdication. The Kaiser refused. Consequently, the following day, 9 November, the SPD members of the government announced that they were withdrawing their support. Max knew he could not continue to govern without the SPD so, at 11.30am that day, Max took matters into his own hands.

He released a press statement which read:

The Emperor has abdicated!

His Majesty the Emperor and King has decided to renounce the throne.

The Imperial chancellor will remain in office until all questions relating to the abdication of the emperor; the renunciation of the Crown Prince's claim to the throne of Germany and of Prussia; and the appointment of a regency have been settled.

The chancellor intends to suggest the following measures to the regent: to appoint Deputy Ebert as chancellor; to prepare a bill calling a general election for a constitutional German National assembly, which would be responsible for establishing the future form of the German nation, also encompassing those peoples who wish to be included in the new German state.

2   *Berlin, 9th November 1918. The Imperial chancellor,*
Prince Max von Baden.

Fig. 7 *A German newspaper announces the abdication of the Kaiser, 9 November 1918*

Max simultaneously announced that Ebert, an SPD leader, would take over from him as chancellor. This was an unconstitutional move, since it was the Kaiser's role to appoint the chancellor. However, the times were desperate and as Max willingly chose to hand over his chancellor's position, which had been legally granted, it was accepted as legitimate by the civil servants on whom the government depended.

Question

Explain why the Kaiser was forced to abdicate in November 1918.

 Examiner's tip

As in many 'explain why' questions, the reasons for the Kaiser's abdication can be divided into long and short-term factors. Start by making a plan to identify and distinguish between these. Decide a logical order in which to present the reasons – perhaps starting with the most immediate, or the most important. You should organise your material to provide a logical and convincing answer.

At Spa, Wilhelm had already received a visit from General Groener (the replacement for the disgraced Ludendorff, who had fled in disguise to Sweden on 27 October) who had told him that the army was in no position to support him. When the news of Max's announcement in Berlin came, he was furious but powerless. He left for Holland the following morning and would spend the rest of his life in exile.

Key profiles

Friedrich Ebert

Ebert (1871–1925) had begun his career as a saddler, but he rose to become one of the leaders of the SPD and, in November 1918, chancellor of the new republic. In February 1919, he was elected as its first president and he tried to steer a middle course – keeping the support of the army and Conservatives but trying not to alienate the more radical left wing – but he disappointed many of his former socialist colleagues and never won widespread respect. He died young, of a heart attack in 1925.

Wilhelm Groener

Wilhelm Groener (1876–1939) was a professional soldier who had worked on increasing production during the war. In October 1918, after Ludendorff's resignation, he succeeded him as Quartermaster-General. He advised the Kaiser to abdicate and was prepared to cooperate with the new socialist government. He made the Ebert-Groener pact (see pages 93–4) and took various governmental positions including Minister of Defence 1928–32. He criticised the growing Nazi Party and resigned from government in May 1932.

 Activity

Thinking point

Discuss the terms 'revolution from above' and 'revolution from below'. Is it inevitable that once a 'revolution from above' begins, it will automatically turn into a 'revolution from below'? Can you think of any other historical examples which either fit, or fail to fit, this pattern?

The survival of the republic

The SPD was left in an unenviable position. Although Ebert's political ambition had been to lead a socialist government, the circumstances were hardly a matter for celebration! Neither he nor his co-leader, Philipp Scheidemann, wanted to head a communist revolution and Ebert's personal preference had always been to retain the Kaiser, but with a democratic constitution. However, there was no opportunity for reflection. Whatever Ebert's own views, Scheidemann had taken matters into his own hands and, after the announcement of Ebert's appointment as chancellor, had appeared at a Reichstag window and addressed the crowds, declaring Germany a republic.

Fig. 8 *The proclamation of the Weimar Republic to cheering crowds outside the Reichstag*

Karl Liebknecht, the communist leader, also declared a republic from another balcony just two hours later!

However, the Kaiser's abdication and Ebert's appointment had failed to quell the unrest. Ebert knew that he needed to broaden his support base if he was to curb the activities of the revolutionary soviets, persuade workers to accept his government and stop the revolution from going further. He consequently approached the more left-wing USPD to join him in government and a 'Council of Peoples' Commissars', or People's Representatives (a name deliberately chosen to mimic Soviet Russia and give the illusion that here was a genuinely revolutionary government), with three SPD and three USPD members was established. This body was to take charge until elections could be held for a new assembly.

■ **Cross-reference**

The USPD is described on pages 92–3 and 96–8.

Key term

The left/right: in politics it is quite normal to talk about 'the left' and 'the right' or left and right-wing. This division derives from the time of the French revolution when deputies who supported the monarchy sat on the right, while more radical opponents, who wanted change, sat on the left in the assembly. Thus 'right' has come to mean Conservative – and, at its most extreme, authoritarian and in favour of strong rule – while 'left' means pro-reform, in favour of the workers and, at its most extreme, Communism.

A closer look

Political parties at the end of the First World War

The exceptional conditions of war bred extreme politics. Although the German political parties had come together in support of war in 1914, Ludendorff and Hindenburg's virtual dictatorship from 1916 had brought about a split in the German Socialist Party (SPD). In 1916, some of the more radical SPD members had broken away to form the Spartacist League (which became the KPD or German Communist Party at the end of 1918) while, in April 1917, another group created the USPD (Independent Socialists). Both demanded peace. In September 1917, Admiral Tirpitz and Wolfgang Kapp founded the Fatherland Party to rally support for victory with land annexations. This party disintegrated at the end of the war and the old National Liberal Party also split between the DDP (on **the left**) and DVP and DNVP (on **the right**).

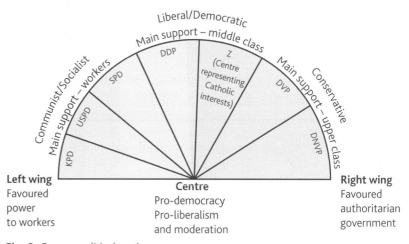

Fig. 9 *German political parties*

Table 1 gives more details on the split in the socialist party.

Table 1 *The German socialists in 1918*

Party	Leader(s) and membership	Aims	Campaigns – November 1918 to January 1919
The Social Democrat Party (SPD)	Friedrich Ebert and Philipp Scheidemann. Membership c.1 million. Formed in 1875 and the largest party in the Reichstag by 1912.	Wanted a moderate socialist republic with democratic elections and a guarantee of basic personal freedoms. Wanted welfare improvements, and the gradual nationalisation of industry. Prepared to work with the army and existing civil service, judiciary and police to maintain continuity and order.	Wanted democratic elections to a Reichstag to draw up a new German constitution.
The Independent Social Democratic Party (USPD)	Hugo Haase and Karl Kautsky. Membership c.300,000. Formed 1917 from SPD members hostile to war.	Wanted a republic with a national Reichstag working in cooperation with workers' and soldiers' councils in every town. Wanted welfare improvements, the nationalisation of industry, the breaking up of large landed estates the reform of the army and the creation of a national militia.	Prepared to cooperate in the election of a Reichstag but also favoured strikes to reinforce need for change.

The Spartacist League. Named after Roman rebel slave Spartacus.	Rosa Luxemburg and Karl Liebknecht. Membership c.5,000. Formed 1916 from radical SPD members opposed to war.	Wanted republican government controlled by workers' and soldiers' councils. Wanted welfare benefits, nationalisation, workers' control of major industries, the disbanding of the army and the creation of local workers' militias.	Refused to cooperate in the proposed elections. Used demonstrations, rallies, strikes, sabotage and assassination.

Key profile

Rosa Luxemburg

Rosa Luxemburg (1870–1919) originally came from Poland. She had fled to Germany in 1898 because of her political views and had married a German socialist simply to be allowed to remain there. (They split immediately after the wedding.) She was an able speaker and became known as 'Red Rosa'. In 1914, she was imprisoned for her opposition to the war. She welcomed Lenin's communist revolution but was against the brutal measures of the Bolsheviks. She helped found the Spartacist League in 1916 and, when she was released from prison in November 1918, returned to Berlin. Although she did not provoke the Spartacist revolt, she gave it her support. She was captured and shot by the Freikorps (see page 97). Her body was dumped in a canal in Berlin.

10 November proved a decisive day for the establishment of Ebert's authority. Firstly, an assembly, elected by the Berlin workers and socialists, approved his new council and, secondly, he received an important phone call from General Groener, the head of the armed forces. Groener recalled:

Fig. 10 *'Red Rosa': Rosa Luxemburg, the socialist who helped found the Spartacist League*

In the evening of 10 November, I telephoned the Reich Chancellery and told Ebert that the army put itself at the disposal of the government and that in return for this, Field Marshall Hindenburg and the officer corps expected the support of the government in the maintenance of order and discipline in the army. The officer corps expected the government to fight against Bolshevism and was ready for the struggle. Ebert accepted my offer of an alliance. From then on, we discussed the measures which were necessary every evening on a secret telephone line between the Reich Chancellery and the High Command. We hoped through our action to gain a share of the power in the new state. If we succeeded, then we should have rescued into the new Germany the best and strongest elements of old Prussia, despite the revolution.

A compromise deal was struck. The army would support the new government if, in return, the government agreed to take steps to crush any revolutionary activity and promised to maintain the authority of existing military officers. This agreement was made with serious reservations on both sides. The army disliked Socialism and probably saw the pact as a temporary measure, while Ebert feared being accused of 'selling out' by his more radical colleagues and followers. In later years, Ebert was accused of 'betraying the revolution' by making this agreement, yet at the time he had very little choice.

Activity

Challenge your thinking

The situation in Germany in November 1918 is sometimes referred to as a 'political vacuum'. What do you think this means? Is it an appropriate description?

■ Activity

Revision exercise

Make a timeline of the main events of the 'German Revolution' between 29 September and 11 November 1918.

Fig. 11 *Friedrich Ebert, the first president of the Weimar Republic*

The armistice, based on terms put forward on 5 November, was signed the following day (11 November). Although it was a ceasefire rather than a peace treaty, the allies were only prepared to agree to it on condition that Germany accepted that it would be required to compensate the allies for all the damage caused to both people and property during the war. Germany had also to promise to withdraw from all occupied territories and overseas colonies, and was required to surrender stock piles of armaments, quantities of railway rolling stock and the entire navy and merchant fleet to the allies. The timing of this armistice meant that the republic, founded just two days earlier, was immediately associated with a humiliating peace which placed the German people entirely at the mercy of the allies. The generals' desire that the socialist politicians be seen as the 'criminals' who signed the armistice had come true.

■ A closer look

The November Criminals and the 'Stab in the Back' myth (*Dolchstosslegende*)

A simple explanation for Germany's defeat soon spread. Germany had been 'stabbed in the back' by the November Criminals who had agreed to the armistice. According to this view, the German army had remained brave and successful to the end. They had not been defeated on the battlefield and no foreign army had ever reached German soil. The army could have won the war but for anti-war agitators who had caused unrest within Germany and sapped morale, and the treacherous politicians who had weakened Germany, created a republic and agreed to a vindictive armistice. Although such an interpretation was blatantly untrue, it was widely believed. In 1919, in his evidence to a government commission, Hindenburg claimed:

> Our repeated requests to the government for strict discipline were never met. Thus our operations were bound to fail. The revolution was only the last straw. An English General rightly said, 'The German army was stabbed in the back'. No blame is to be attached to the German army. Its performances call, like that of the officer corps, for equal admiration. It is perfectly plain on whom the blame rests.

Despite the spreading rumours and accusations, Ebert worked hard to win over the German workers. He met with industrialists, led by Hugo Stinnes, and trade unionists, led by the Social Democrat Karl Legien, to continue negotiations that had already been started in July 1918, to establish good relations between the two. On 15 November all trade unions and employers' associations gave their approval to the Stinnes-Legien Agreement. This said:

■ unions were guaranteed legal recognition

■ workers were granted an eight-hour day

■ workers' committees were to be established in factories, with powers to negotiate with employers over disputes

- a *Zentralarbeitsgemeinschaft* (ZAG) or 'central working association' was set up to arbitrate in industrial disputes
- unions accepted private ownership and a **free market** (rather than communist-style **nationalisation** of industry).

Key profile

Hugo Stinnes

Hugo Stinnes (1870–1924) had developed businesses in coal, iron and electricals during the Kaiserreich. During the republic, he became a DVP (Conservative) member of the Reichstag. He accumulated enormous power by using his personal contacts to borrow from the Reichsbank to buy out struggling competitors. He then paid off his loans in devalued currency. He became known as the 'King of the Ruhr', and owned 1,535 companies and 20 per cent of Germany's industries (including coal, steel, paper, newspapers, chemicals, hotels, land and shipping). His industrial empire collapsed after his death in 1924.

Key term

Free market and nationalisation: a free market is one in which individuals are allowed to compete to make profits and economic enterprise is privately controlled. Whereas nationalisation means the state control of industry, banks, transport and other 'means of production'. In a free enterprise economy, wages are determined by private agreement but under nationalisation they are determined and paid by the state.

Ebert's government also granted freedom of speech, freedom of the press and freedom of assembly. It introduced immediate welfare measures to help ease suffering, provided support for the unemployed, increased housing provision and got food supplies moving again. Although the changes were not as wide ranging as some would have liked, they did help win workers' support and, by 29 November, the 'revolution from above' seemed to have been won. The Council of People's Commissars felt the situation was stable enough to announce that elections would be held for a new National Assembly on 19 January 1919.

The defeat of the left

The changes in government did not quell the left-wing unrest in Germany. In December 1918, the Spartacists tried to push the people's revolution a stage further. Under Liebknecht and Luxemburg, they wanted to use the workers' councils to overthrow the government and create a Bolshevik-style revolution. On 6 December, the league led a demonstration in Berlin in which 16 demonstrators were killed and 12 wounded in clashes with the army.

Cross-reference

Liebknecht, Luxemburg and the Spartacists were introduced on pages 92–3.

Between 16 and 20 December the first national Congress of Workers' and Soldiers' Councils took place, attended by approximately 300 SPD and 100 USPD representatives, as well as some Spartacists and other radicals. It was a tense time, but the congress decided overwhelmingly (344 votes to 98) to support elections to a new Reichstag and to abandon the idea of a government based on councils. This was clearly what Ebert wanted to hear, but he was less delighted by two further resolutions. The congress called on Ebert to nationalise industries and replace the army with a 'people's militia' in which soldiers elected their own officers. Such radical demands would have involved the breaking of both the Ebert–Groener and Stinnes–Legien pacts, to which Ebert could not agree.

The split in the working-class movement was further illustrated by an incident involving Ebert's SPD colleague, Otto Wels, who found himself in dispute with a group of radical sailors, aided by the USPD.

As a result of the incident, on 29 December, the three USPD members of the Council of People's Commissars resigned. They were under pressure

Exploring the detail

Otto Wels and the USPD

In November 1918, Ebert had appointed Otto Wels as city commandant in Berlin. He controlled the Republican Soldiers' Army which was responsible for putting down radical left-wing demonstrations. Wels had ordered a group of radical sailors from Kiel, who had set up their headquarters in the stables of the former Royal Palace in Berlin, to move out. When they refused, the government soldiers took action; two sailors were killed and Wels was taken prisoner by the naval division. On Ebert's instructions, Groener sent in regular troops to bombard the naval division's headquarters. They would have succeeded had not Eichhorn, the USPD police president in Berlin, sent reinforcements to help the sailors. The army had to withdraw and the SPD was forced to come to a settlement with the sailors. Wels was released but had to resign as city commandant.

Fig. 12 *Armed soldiers in Charlottenstrasse during the Spartacist uprising in Berlin*

from their own left-wing supporters to end their cooperation with Ebert, but their action did little to help the democratic cause. Indeed, by leaving the government at this time they removed any chance the government had of bridging the gulf between themselves and the extreme left Spartacist movement. It split Socialism between the majority SPD and the small, but ardent Spartacist group who felt the 'revolution' had failed them. At the end of December, these Spartacists chose to link with other radicals to form the KPD – the German Communist Party. They also decided to boycott the elections scheduled for 19 January.

The SPD responded to the USPD's defection by dismissing all prominent USPD officials, including Emil Eichhorn, the Berlin Chief of Police. This sparked off a left-wing demonstration on 5 January which, although not originally started by the Spartacists, was to become known as the 'Spartacist Rebellion'. Karl Liebknecht and Rosa Luxemburg gave speeches to encourage the workers' rebellion and inspire them to overthrow the SPD government before the new elections could take place. The SPD's newspaper offices were occupied and a revolutionary committee formed.

Ebert turned to General Noske, recently appointed as defence minister, to deal with the incident. Noske issued the following declaration:

> Worker! Soldier! Citizen! Today at one o'clock, 3,000 men with heavy artillery and machine guns marched through Berlin and Charlottenburg. Through them, the Government showed that it has the power to carry out your will which demands an end to the Spartacist gangs. The Reich government has entrusted me with the leadership of the Republican soldiers. I promise that no unnecessary blood will be spilled. With the new Republican Army, I want to bring you freedom and peace. The working class must stand united against the Spartacists if democracy and socialism are not to be lost.

5

Key profile

Gustav Noske

Gustav Noske (1868–1946) came from a working-class background and had entered the Reichstag as an SPD member in 1906. After the war he helped crush the Kiel mutiny. He joined the Council of People's Commissars in December 1918, after the departure of the USPD members, and from 1919 to 1920 was Reich defence minister. His brutal repression of the radical left won him the admiration of the right, but lost him support among the SPD movement. After the 1920 Kapp Putsch (see pages 114–15) was defeated by the workers, they demanded his resignation. He became Governor of Hanover and was later implicated in the 1944 July bomb plot against Hitler.

Despite his promises, Noske acted with great severity. He used not only the republican army but also bands of Freikorps, tough ex-soldiers who hated Communists. Between 10 and 12 January there was savage street fighting in which the Spartacists were treated with great brutality. More than 100 workers were killed. Liebknecht and Luxemburg were captured on 12 January and, despite government orders to the contrary, met mysterious deaths on their way to prison. The uprising was crushed but it left a bitter legacy. The left wing no longer saw the SPD as their saviour, but as their enemy and they felt horribly betrayed.

A closer look

The deaths of Rosa Luxemburg and Karl Liebknecht

With the collapse of the Spartacist revolt, Luxemburg and Liebknecht were arrested and taken for interrogation in the Eden Hotel, which was acting as the Berlin Headquarters of the Freikorps. As they left the building, supposedly to be taken to prison, Private Runge hit them on the head with a rifle and they were dragged off into two separate cars. Liebknecht was thrown from his car as it drove through the Berlin Tiergarten (a public park) and was then shot for 'trying to escape'. His corpse was taken to a local mortuary without identification. Luxemburg was shot by Lieutenant Vogel and her body thrown in a canal, where it was not discovered until May. Ebert was said to be horrified by the deaths and ordered an investigation into the murders. Lieutenant Vogel was found guilty of failing to report a death and illegally disposing of a body, but he was easily able to flee justice. He escaped to Holland and, after lying low for a few months, quietly returned to Germany. Private Runge served a light sentence of a few months for 'attempted manslaughter'.

Exploring the detail

Freikorps

The 'Free corps' comprised around 200 groups of volunteers – c. 4,000 soldiers in total. They were mostly recruited from demobilised soldiers and officers and were tough men of right-wing, nationalist sympathies. They were largely paid for by supporters of the old empire and, although they proved useful to the government in suppressing left-wing revolts, they showed their political bias by refusing to act against the right wing. Many members later joined Hitler's *Sturmabteilung* (stormtroopers).

Activity

Research exercise

Research further into the lives of the two Spartacist leaders and write an obituary for either Rosa Luxemburg or Karl Liebknecht. You will want to refer to their hopes in 1918–19 and the circumstances of their deaths. Try to comment on their legacy and what they had/hadn't achieved.

In the aftermath of all this tension, the long-promised election took place on 19 January. Thirty million Germans cast their votes and the number of seats gained are shown in Table 2.

Table 2 *Election results, January 1919*

Party	Number of seats gained
USPD	22
SPD *	163
DDP *	75
Centre Party *	91
DVP	44
Others	7

Note: parties marked * are the pro-republican parties. They gained 76 per cent of the vote.

The result was a strong victory for the pro-republican parties and in particular the SPD. The Centre Party and DDP won roughly equal numbers of seats to the SPD, so creating a moderate central group. This pattern was actually quite similar to the election of 1912. The KPD, which had boycotted the elections, encouraged workers to strike in defence of the workers' councils and in March the USPD agreed to support the councils in preference to parliamentary democracy. The government had again to call on the Freikorps to curb the street fighting and in Berlin over a thousand people were killed. However, Bavaria was the only area to experience a successful left-wing rebellion. Kurt Eisner was assassinated in February and, after some confusion, a republic of workers' councils was declared in Munich. Nevertheless, even here, success only lasted until May, when the new regime was also defeated by the army and Freikorps.

The Weimar Republic had certainly experienced a difficult birth and, in trying to establish a stable government for Germany, many of the high hopes of November 1918 for a changed society had evaporated. By the time of the elections, the radical phase of the revolution had passed and many had already become embittered anti-republicans. In the words of the historian Immanuel Geiss, 'once the dust had settled, it soon emerged that precious little had changed'.

Activity

Thinking point

In groups, consider what the consequences for the Weimar Republic might have been if:

- Ebert had not made a pact with General Groener
- the USPD members had not resigned from the Council of Peoples' Commissars.

Activity

Class debate

Divide the class into groups representing the various factions in Germany in November 1918.

- A sailor from Kiel.
- An army general.
- A member of the Spartacist League.
- A member of the SPD.
- A member of the Freikorps.
- A member of the USPD.

Within your group, prepare a speech to persuade others that you know the best way forward. Hold a balloon debate to see which group is the most convincing.

Summary questions

1 How far do the events of 1918–19 in Germany warrant the title 'revolution'?

2 Why did the Weimar Republic survive through the years 1919–20?

A new constitution and a hated peace treaty

Der Rat der Volksbeauftragten

Fig. 1 *Members of the Provisional government. Left to right: Dittmann (USPD); Landsberg (SPD); Haase (USPD); Edbert (SPD); Barth (USPD); Scheidemann (SPD)*

In this chapter you will learn about:

■ the strengths and weaknesses of the new constitution of the Weimar Republic

■ the circumstances in which Germany accepted the terms of the Treaty of Versailles

■ the impact of the Versailles Peace Treaty on Germany.

Cross-reference

The location of Weimar is shown on the map on page 107.

If the empire was born out of the brilliance of victory, the German Republic was born out of its terrible defeat. This difference in origin cast a dark shadow on the new political regime, although, at first, most still felt that the new order was necessary for the rebirth of Germany. The criminal madness of the imposed Versailles settlement was a shameless blow in the face of such hopes.

> **1**   *Hugo Preuss, author of the Weimar constitution, speaking in 1923*

■ The republican constitution

The new German Reichstag met on 6 February 1919. Because of the fighting between the Spartacists and Freikorps in Berlin, it assembled in Weimar, south of Berlin in central Germany. The town had a long-standing intellectual tradition. It was the home of the writer Goethe and it was thought to be a suitable setting for the new republic, as it helped to associate it with the German cultural, rather than military, tradition. The result, of course, was that the name 'Weimar Republic' was given to the new regime.

The main task of this new Reichstag was to draw up a constitution for Germany to replace that which had allowed the Kaiser and his chosen ministers to exercise enormous power. Hugo Preuss, a Liberal law professor, had already been instructed to begin consideration of a new democratic constitution, even before the Reichstag met.

Key profile

Hugo Preuss

Preuss (1860–1925) was a left-wing Liberal and Professor of law who had been appointed Secretary of State by Ebert in November 1918. He had hoped to create a constitution that would have broken up the federal nature of Germany and created a single central government (a unitary state). However, the Reichstag, which contained representatives from fiercely independent states like Bavaria, did not favour this idea and it was defeated.

Consequently, the first draft was made available to consider straight away, although the finalised version was not produced until August, when it was accepted by 262 to 75 votes. Its provisions were as follows:

■ Germany was to remain a federal state, with a central Reich government and separate 'state' (*Land*, plural *Länder*) governments in the states which comprised the nation. However, the Länder lost some of their former powers and Prussia and Bavaria were no longer to have monarchies. Control of taxation, rail and postal services and the military was transferred from the Länder to the central government, but the local states retained control of their own police services, education and judges. The Reich government was to control the army (in contrast to the Bismarckian constitution).

■ **Cross-reference**

To compare the previous constitution, established by Bismarck in 1871, re-read pages 14–15.

Fig. 2 *The Länder under the Weimar constitution, 1919*

Exploring the detail

Proportional representation

Germany had 35 equal electoral districts with almost a million voters in each area. Voters voted for parties, not candidates, and for every 60,000 votes for a party in each district, that party gained a seat. The parties drew up lists of candidates and seats were duly distributed.

If a party failed to gain 60,000 votes in any district, but gained 30,000 or more in different districts, the votes were added together and deputies allocated. The number of deputies in the Reichstag was not fixed and varied according to the number of votes cast.

Germany was to have a president with a range of powers (see Figure 3), including the right to use armed force against any of the Länder which refused to obey the laws of the Reich. Partly because of the instability in Bavaria, Preuss included 'Article 48' which stated, 'If public safety and order in the Federation are materially disturbed or endangered, the president may take the necessary measures to restore public safety and order.' This allowed the president to make decrees which had the force of law, without consulting the Reichstag. The president also had power to dissolve the Reichstag and call new elections.

Elections for both the Länder and the Reich were to take place using a system of proportional representation. All men and women over 20 were to have the right to vote. The head of government would be the chancellor, who, along with his ministers, was to be chosen from among the elected Reichstag deputies by the president. However, the president could only appoint a chancellor who had a majority of over 50 per cent in the Reichstag, and both chancellor and ministers were to be answerable to the Reichstag for their actions. The chancellor and government were to draft laws for the Reichstag to debate and vote on.

There was to be a second chamber, the *Reichsrat*, to provide advice and act as a check on the Reichstag, but its powers were limited. It was to consist of representatives of the governments of the various Länder with each Land (state), except Prussia, receiving votes in proportion to its population. Prussia was to be allowed a maximum of two-fifths of the total. Members of the state delegations were to be able to vote individually (and not as a single unit, as in the old Bundesrat) and legislation rejected by the Reichsrat could still be made law by a two-thirds majority in the Reichstag (so again, unlike the Bundesrat, there was to be no absolute veto).

Referendums could be called for by the president, the Reichsrat or by 'people's request' if a tenth of the electorate applied for one.

The 'Fundamental Rights and Duties of German citizens' were guaranteed in the second part of the constitution. Statements included: 'all Germans are equal before the law'; 'personal liberty is inviolable'; 'censorship is forbidden'; 'the right of property is guaranteed'; and 'all inhabitants enjoy full religious freedom'. It gave illegitimate children the same rights as legitimate ones and promised 'economic freedom for the individual'. It also contained provision for the nationalisation

Activity

Revision exercise

Review the terms of, and comments on, the new constitution and copy and complete the table below to make your own assessment of its strengths and weaknesses. Leave plenty of space so that, when you read the next section, you can add any further ideas.

Aspects of the constitution	Strengths	Weaknesses
The federal state		
The powers of the president		
The voters and the system of elections		
Other aspects		

President – Head of State

- Elected by voters every seven years.
- Appointed/dismissed the chancellor.
- Could dissolve Reichstag and call new elections.
- Commanded the army.
- In an emergency could issue laws by decree, without the Reichstag's consent.

Appoints

Chancellor

- Had to have the support of at least half the Reichstag.
- Proposes new laws to the Reichstag.

Provides advice

Needs 50% majority before appointed

Drafts laws for the Reichstag to debate

The Reichsrat

- An assembly of 67 representatives of the 17 states of Germany (whose governments were individually elected by all over 20 years every four years).
- Could provide advice on, and veto, laws but could be overridden by the Reichstag.

Representatives from the Länder

The Reichstag

- Elected by all Germans over 20 years.
- One deputy per 60,000 votes (average 528 deputies) on a basis of proportional representation.
- Elections every four years.
- Votes on the budget and new laws.
- Members can be government ministers.

- All men and women over 20 could vote for the Reichstag every four years using proportional representation.

Voters

- Vote for their local state assembly every four years.
- Vote for the president every seven years.
- Vote in plebiscites – occasional votes on important issues.

- There was also to be a supreme court independent of the Reichstag and president and a federal system whereby there were separate governments in the 17 'Länder' or local states of Germany.

Fig. 3 *The Weimar constitution*

of industry and some modern social rights such as: 'all Germans have the right to form unions and societies'; 'Labour is under the special protection of the federation'; 'the Reich shall organise a comprehensive system of social insurance'; 'every German shall be given the opportunity to earn his living through productive work and, if no suitable opportunity can be found, the means necessary for his livelihood will be provided'; 'workers and employees are called upon to cooperate, on an equal footing, with employers in the regulation of wages and of the conditions of labour'.

Strengths and weaknesses of the constitution

Some historians have provided powerful criticisms of this new constitution. Consider the words of the historian K. D. Bracher:

> The structure of the Weimar constitution aimed at perfection but proved unable to unite the disrupted nation and secure the transition to a democratic society. A tendency to Presidential governments was encouraged by the vast powers which the Constitution granted to the office of President. Designed as a counter-balance to the parliamentary system, the Presidency actually served as a kind of substitute for the lost absolute monarchy. The forming and functioning of government coalitions proved increasingly difficult. The public became used to feeble cabinets. The constitutional structure of Weimar preserved powerful elements of the absolutist state including the continuation of anti-democratic forces, especially the civil servants who were opposed to the idea of democracy and anti-party.

2   *Adapted from Bracher, K. D., **The Nazi Take-over: History of the Twentieth Century No. 48***

Bracher's criticism of the power of the president is often cited as the constitution's main weakness and Article 48, in particular, is considered out of place in an otherwise democratic constitution. However, in 1919 (and until 1928), no one took much notice of this article. The presidential powers were considered vital for stability and the new presidency was generally regarded as 'weak' (although this is not what Preuss had wanted) in comparison with the 'strong' presidency in America. Ebert was chosen as the first president with Scheidemann as his first chancellor and, in Ebert's hands, the constitution did indeed work well. Ebert used his powers wisely throughout his time in office to 1925.

Bracher's second criticism is of proportional representation. This system made it almost impossible for a single party to gain a majority in the Reichstag, so government had to be by groups of parties working together in 'coalition'. However, coalition governments are prone to collapse and do not always produce an obvious chancellor, so enhancing the power of the president. A proportional representation system will also allow extremist parties to gain election to the Reichstag. Nevertheless, proportional representation has worked, and still works, in many other countries and its establishment in Germany marked a laudable attempt to get away from the 'sham constitutionalism' established by Bismarck. The instability in the early years of the Weimar Republic was actually less to do with proportional representation than the product of wider conflicts within society, whereby a substantial number were opposed to the republic altogether. Certainly,

Cross-reference

To recap on Bismarck's 'sham constitutionalism', re-read pages 14–17 and 43–4.

the 1919 election, held under proportional representation, produced results that were little different from 1912, held under a different system, and by allowing minorities to exert some influence, no one could accuse the constitution of being undemocratic.

Finally, Bracher suggests that the Weimar constitution did not go far enough. It allowed the old Länder to remain, but with fewer powers, and it satisfied neither those who had preferred the old system, nor those who wanted a new 'unitarian' (single state) government. It made no attempt to reform the civil service or judiciary and it allowed opponents of constitutional government to retain power. However, whilst it is easy to criticise what was done in retrospect, it is hard to see how any different arrangements might have been considered better at the time. The civil servants and judges were needed for government to continue and wholesale dismissals would surely have brought still more chaos. It must be remembered that the new Weimar constitution was the most democratic constitution in Europe at the time. Few countries permitted such widespread rights and freedoms and few, including Britain, gave women a vote on equal terms with men.

The impact of the Treaty of Versailles on Germany

The armistice of 11 November 1918 had brought about a ceasefire but it was not until June 1919 that the peace treaty concluding the First World War was finally signed in the Hall of Mirrors at Versailles. Negotiations between the victorious allies had been in progress since 18 January but Germany had not been invited to attend. Although a few details were leaked before the German representatives were summoned to sign the document, the terms were not officially seen by the German government until 7 May. The Germans were given 15 days (which was actually extended to 21) to consider the treaty and make written comments. The shocked government responded with some suggested amendments but these led only to a few minor changes. On 16 June, Germany received the final terms requiring acceptance within seven days.

Fig. 4 *The Versailles Peace Conference in the Hall of Mirrors at Versailles, 1919*

Activity

Challenge your thinking

Although K. D. Bracher puts forward some powerful arguments to suggest that the Weimar constitution was flawed and that, as under the Second Reich, the Germans failed to achieve effective democracy, it is important not to accept particular interpretations such as this unthinkingly. Bracher belongs to a school of historians who believe that the ease with which Germany came to accept Nazi domination from 1933 was the result of its particular historical development and its lack of democratic tradition. However, this 'determinist' view of history is certainly open to challenge. Do you agree that the way people behave and the actions they take are always conditioned by their history?

Activity

Revision exercise

Write a critical appraisal of the Weimar constitution for a newspaper editorial in 1919. Remember that, although you may point to potential weaknesses, you will have no idea what the future may bring. You may choose to be optimistic or pessimistic depending on the stance you choose to adopt!

A closer look

The allies at Versailles

The Paris Peace Conference opened on 12 January 1919 and meetings were held at various locations in and around Paris until 20 January 1920. Leaders of 32 states, representing about 75 per cent of the world's population, attended but the defeated powers were excluded and all the major decisions were taken by the four most influential leaders: President Woodrow Wilson of the USA; David Lloyd George, Prime Minister of Great Britain; Georges Clemenceau, Prime Minister of France and conference chairman; and Vittorio Orlando, Prime Minister of Italy. All of these leaders were subject to varying aims and pressures from their own people. Lloyd George had recently won the 1918 election with promises of 'squeezing Germany until the pips squeak', while Clemenceau had seen the north of his country ravaged by war with 300,000 buildings and 21,000 km² of French farmland destroyed. Long-standing disputes over the Rhineland and revenge for Germany's seizure of Alsace-Lorraine in 1871 made Clemenceau the most vengeful of the delegates. Wilson had more idealistic concerns including disarmament and the setting up of a League of Nations to ensure a means of settling disputes peacefully in the future, but he was determined to prevent the possibility of Germany starting another war and wanted an arrangement that ensured the massive loans which the USA had given to the allies could be repaid. All were influenced by the harsh treaty which Germany had imposed on Russia at Brest-Litovsk in March 1918. Had Germany won, they argued, the Germans would have had no compunction in treating the allies harshly.

■ **Cross-reference**

The Treaty of Brest-Litovsk is introduced on page 81.

Fig. 5 *The new constitution provoked a major election campaign, as the SPD fought to retain control in 1919*

The terms were regarded with horror. The armistice of November 1918 had not been an unconditional surrender and, although the Germans knew they would have to face some harsh demands, there had been a promise of peace 'between equals'. It is of little surprise, therefore, that, when faced with a treaty that put the total blame for the war on Germany and proceeded to demand retribution as a result, the German government felt that the allies were acting with undue vengeance and were unfairly trying to cripple a Germany which had already thrown off its Imperial past and was trying to follow the path

The terms of the Treaty of Versailles

The treaty removed over 70,000 km² (13 per cent) of German territory and all Germany's overseas colonies. This meant the loss of 75 per cent of Germany's iron ore; 68 per cent of its zinc ore; 26 per cent of its coal and 15 per cent of its arable land. Also lost were the entire Alsatian potash and textile industries and the communications system built around Alsace-Lorraine and Upper Silesia. 6.5 million (10 per cent) were lost from Germany's population, around half, ethnic Germans. 1.5 million Germans were left in the new Poland, whose lands split Germany in two. The Poles were given access to the sea at Danzig and although Danzig was German speaking, it was made a free port under the control of the League of Nations. Germans in the Sudetenland found themselves in the new country of Czechoslovakia and despite the Germans living there, North Schleswig went to Denmark, Upper Silesia to Poland and Memel to Lithuania. At the same time, Anschluss (union) with the ethnic Germans of Austria was expressly forbidden, despite the vote in the Austrian Provincial assembly in November 1918 favouring union with Germany. In theory the colonies were ruled under a 'mandate' from the League of Nations for the benefit of the colonial peoples but in practice they went to Germany's colonial rivals who received the mandates.

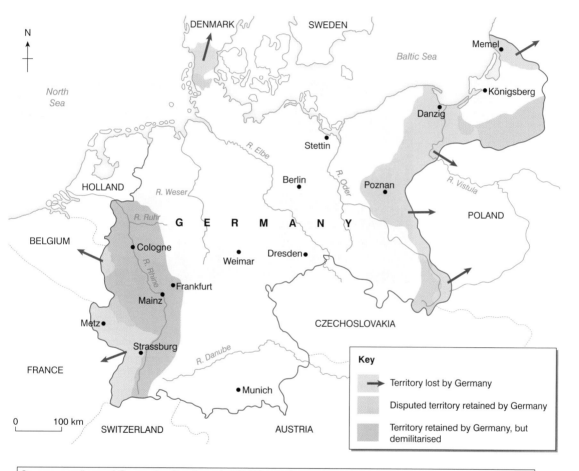

Key

→ Territory lost by Germany

Disputed territory retained by Germany

Territory retained by Germany, but demilitarised

Germany was disarmed. Germany's military forces (c.300,000 men in 1919) were to be cut by 31 March 1920 to 100,000 men in the army of which no more than 4,000 could be officers. Germany was to be allowed no tanks or military aircraft; 6 battleships, 6 cruisers, 12 destroyers, 12 torpedo boats; no submarines; no airforce and have no conscription. Allied armies, under an allied commission of control, were to occupy the west bank of the Rhine for 15 years to ensure the treaty was obeyed and the whole of the Rhineland area was to be permanently demilitarised. This meant that no fortifications or German forces could be placed within 50 km of the east side of the river. Germany was also not allowed to join the League of Nations.

Germany was blamed for starting the war in the infamous 'clause 231', the 'war guilt clause'. This was used to justify the demand for reparations (compensation) to enable the allies to repair their own war damage. An immediate 20,000m marks worth of reparations – payable mostly in industrial goods – were demanded and Germany lost many economic assets. The coal mines of the Saar were to be run by the French (under the auspices of the League of Nations) for 15 years, so that Germany would supply France, Belgium and Italy with free coal. After this a plebiscite was to decide their ultimate fate. All ships over 1,600 tonnes (90 per cent of the fleet) in the German merchant navy were to be surrendered to the allies as well as shipping facilities, railway rolling stock, patents and overseas investments and property. A five-year ban on protective tariffs was also imposed. The final amount of reparations was to be left to a commission to decide and was not finalised until 1921, but it was ultimately fixed at £6.6bn (132,000m gold marks) over 30 years.

Fig. 6 *Terms of the Treaty of Versailles, 1919*

of democracy. Hindenburg argued that the Germans should take to the battlefield again, and that a heroic defeat would be preferable to such a humiliation. However, this was not a realistic choice. To refuse the terms would have meant an allied attack, and most probably the disintegration of Germany as some states were seized and others declared independence.

The cabinet met throughout the night of 18–19 June and emerged split with seven members in favour of signing and seven against. On 20 June, Chancellor Scheidemann resigned rather than agree to the terms, but Ebert remained and appointed Gustav Bauer (SPD) to replace him. Bauer created a new coalition government without the Conservative DDP which would not accept the treaty. Erzberger, the leader of the Centre Party, won a vote to try to persuade the allies to drop the clause placing the sole responsibility for the war on Germany and demanding the handover of the Kaiser and other leaders for trial, in return for agreement on the other clauses, but this was refused. The allies proved even more resolute after the action of the naval commanders at Scapa Flow who scuttled the German

■ Cross-reference

Matthias Erzberger is profiled on page 116.

■ Activity

Thinking point

Before reading further, discuss the terms of the Treaty of Versailles with a partner and try to identify the main reasons why the Germans regarded the treaty as unfair. (Remember it was not unusual at this time for the loser of a war to have to accept some responsibility and pay some costs; it was simply the scale of this war which was new.)

Fig. 7 *The French were determined to see their long-standing enemy crushed. They had taken great pleasure in presenting medals to French soldiers in front of the statue of Wilhelm I in Bonn in 1918*

Fig. 8 *Alsace-Lorraine had been taken back under French control at the end of the war*

fleet to prevent having to surrender it as agreed under the armistice terms. News of the burning of some captured battle honours due to be returned to France by Freikorps members in Berlin added to their feelings of mistrust.

On the day the ultimatum expired, 22 June, the Reichstag voted to accept the terms by 237 to 138 votes. Even then, the non-coalition parties were asked to sign a document accepting that the government was acting against its will. On 28 June Hermann Müller (SPD), the foreign minister, and Johannes Bell (Centre Party), the justice minister, went to Versailles to sign.

The German reaction to the treaty

Since few Germans understood the military situation at the end of the war, news of their government's acceptance of this harsh treaty brought demonstrations and a funereal atmosphere as places of recreation and amusement closed. The German people had been led to believe that they had been fighting a 'just' war against the aggression of Britain, France and Russia and they particularly resented the establishment of the 'Polish corridor', cutting Germany in two, the war guilt clause and the issue of reparations.

Furthermore, the territorial settlement seemed to ignore the main provisions of Wilson's Fourteen Points whilst Germany, as the only nation to be disarmed and kept out of the League, was not given equality of status internationally. The Germans felt as though their country was being controlled and exploited by the allied commission. They referred to the treaty as a 'diktat', meaning a treaty which had been dictated to Germany without consultation.

The feelings of hostility were not only directed against the allies, however; they were also aimed at the politicians who had unwillingly agreed terms. The Weimar government was accused of betraying the German nation yet again.

However, whilst it is easy to sympathise with the German reaction, in some ways it was more extreme than it should have been. Wilson's Fourteen Points and the armistice agreement had made it clear that Alsace-Lorraine would have to be returned to France, that a new state of Poland with access to the sea would be created, that Germany would be expected to hand over some of her assets and that considerable German disarmament was to be expected. Indeed, the allied blockade of German ports had been maintained for the very purpose of ensuring such terms would be met, so the Germans had not been kept in total ignorance.

Furthermore, the treaty was not as severe as it might have been. Had Clemenceau had his way, he would have extended the French border to the Rhine, or annexed the Saar coalfields and created an independent Rhineland. The Germans must have been naive to think that the French would allow a union with Austria, which would have created a Germany that was larger than it had been before the war, when Germany already had a population that was half as large again as that of France. Territory was removed from Germany, but nowhere did it contain a majority German population. Germany was not broken up; the allies were too wary of the spread of Communism for that. In fact, Germany's relative position in Europe was potentially stronger than it had been pre-1914, with the collapse of the old Austro-Hungarian and Russian Empires. Germany still had sufficient resources to re-emerge as a major European power and, despite

■ **Exploring the detail**

War guilt

War guilt became a strongly emotive issue. The German foreign office even subsidised a special group – the *Kriegsschuldreferat* – to help prove German innocence, and academics at home and overseas were canvassed for opinions that weakened the case for Germany's guilt. The evidence of Karl Kautsky, a USPD member, commissioned by Ebert to investigate the question in 1919, which showed, through a series of documents, that the Imperial government had been behind the ultimatum to Serbia which had provoked the war, was never published. The endless discussion and publicity helped undermine the moral basis of the settlement and reinforced the idea of the 'unjust peace'.

■ Cross-reference

Wilson's Fourteen Points are explained on page 83.

To recap on the myth that politicians had 'stabbed Germany in the back', re-read pages 94–5.

■ Cross-reference

The economic situation in 1923 is discussed on pages 119–21.

The Treaty of Brest-Litovsk is introduced on page 81.

a setback in 1923, German industry was able to recover fairly quickly. It has even been suggested that the problem with the treaty was not that it punished Germany too harshly, but that it was not harsh enough!

The Treaty of Versailles was not as punishing as that of Brest-Litovsk, nor did it take from Germany what Bethmann-Hollweg had planned to take from his defeated enemies in 1914. Had Germany succeeded, his plans would have imposed reparations on the allies that were four times greater than those actually imposed on Germany. The German politicans who agreed to the treaty did so in the expectation that their cooperation would help persuade the allies of Germany's good intentions and lead to a revision at some point in the future. They may have hated the terms, but knowing of the disagreements between the allies, they believed there would soon be possibilities for re-negotiation.

Significance of the treaty

The Treaty of Versailles was, in some respects, less important for what it did, than for what it represented. It gave the anti-republican right wing yet another stick with which to beat the new government. It was to provoke further right-wing challenges to the republic government and to worsen the country's economic situation. Even more importantly, however, it turned some of those who, up to that point had supported the Weimar Republic, against it. Its real damage was in alienating moderates who had been happy to accept the new constitution and its promises of a 'better' Germany, but who could not stomach politicians who appeared to have betrayed an unbeaten country. The treaty caused political demoralisation at the very centre of government, associating the republic once again with weakness and failure. The politicians who agreed it were forced to become defensive and, to the public at large, the gains of the revolution seemed unimpressive. The historian A. J. Ryder called it 'the death warrant of German democracy'.

Consider this comment by the modern historian, A. J. Nicholls:

> The political gains of the revolution had actually been considerable, but in the public mind, they remained unimpressive. The Germans had a new constitution; to many of them the old one had seemed good enough. They had more freedom politically, but most of them had thought of themselves as free before. They had a responsible government; this responsibility seemed to mean confusion and even bloodshed in home affairs. The one thing that the new order had brought them – peace – had been transformed by a settlement which their newspapers and political leaders all agreed was a form of prolonged slavery for Germany. It was not an encouraging start.

3 *Adapted from Nicholls, A. J.,* **Weimar and the Rise of Hitler***, 2000*

Cross-reference

Right-wing challenges included the Kapp Putsch, detailed on pages 114–15 and the Munich Putsch, detailed on pages 126–7.

Activity

Thinking point

1 Read Source 3. Why did many Germans feel that the revolution had brought them little gain?

2 Which is the more important in history – what actually happened or what people at the time felt and believed?

Learning outcomes

In this section you have learnt how the Kaiserreich collapsed in 1918 and how a new style of democratic government was established in Germany out of the 'incomplete' revolution of November 1918. You have considered some of the problems surrounding the new government and how it was beset by opposition from both the left and the right. You should be aware of how the Spartacists (Communists) on the left challenged the republic at its very inception and of how the nationalists on the right found it hard to come to terms with democratic government.

You have looked at the strengths and weaknesses of the constitution and seen how, by preserving the power of the right wing, the Weimar Republic laid down troubles for itself in the future.

Finally, you have looked at the impact of the Treaty of Versailles on Germany and the 'stab in the back' myth. Whether the republic was doomed from the start or not is an issue of some historical debate, and you may like to bear this in mind as you look at the final section.

 Examination-style questions

(a) Explain why proportional representation was introduced in the new republican constitution of 1919.

(12 marks)

For part (a), you will need to identify why proportional representation was considered as a suitable means of representation in 1919. The reasons for its introduction would also require reference to what had gone before and to what the new constitution makers were trying to achieve. Take care not to recite how the system worked – nor to spend time on its shortcomings. What you need to show here is an understanding of why the decision was made in 1919. You might refer to the desire to break with the past, practical considerations, and socialist democratic ideas. Try to show how your reasons interlink and provide a supported conclusion.

(b) How important was the Treaty of Versailles in creating opposition to the Weimar Republic by 1920?

(24 marks)

For part (b), you will need to focus on the ways in which the Treaty of Versailles provoked opposition to the Weimar Republic, but you should also consider other factors which caused opposition. Left-wing opposition, for example, was not directly attributable to the treaty and there was plenty of right-wing opposition even before June 1919! Weigh up the evidence to produce a balanced answer which leads to a convincing conclusion.

7 Instability, extremism and financial collapse, 1919–23

In this chapter you will learn about:

■ the challenges posed to the Weimar government from both the right and left between 1919 and 1923

■ the development of Weimar government 1919–23

■ the reasons for the economic collapse of 1923

■ the economic and political impact of the collapse of 1923.

Fig. 1 *Look at this election poster for 1919. What message is the SPD trying to convey?*

■ ## The instability of the republic

The challenge from the left

The defeat of the Spartacists did not end the left-wing rebellion. The workers, who had celebrated the overthrow of the Kaiser in November 1918, had been disillusioned by the 'revolution' that followed and frustrated that the 'new' government of the Weimar Republic seemed too ready to compromise with the right. Economic conditions also bred disorder while demobilised soldiers often found it hard to adjust back to civilian life. Marxists considered Germany ripe for revolution and the Comintern encouraged the communist activity. Consequently, worker activism remained a constant concern for the government.

In March 1919, there was another Spartacist rising in Berlin, while in troubled Bavaria a communist government based on workers' councils and protected by a guard of armed workers was established.

In April 1919, there was a wave of strikes in Halle and the Ruhr valley, the industrial heartland of Germany which supplied *c*.80 per cent of the country's coal. As well as asking for shorter hours, the strikers demanded more control over their own industries and a government based on workers' councils.

However, while the KPD provided encouragement, it lacked the leadership and organisation to coordinate the protests. The Weimar government was able to call on the Freikorps and army to use force to suppress these activities and 1,200 workers were killed in Berlin in March, and a further 700 in Bavaria in May when the new communist government was in turn overthrown in favour of a right-wing regime.

The troubles continued into 1920, and after the workers had shown their power in defeating the right-wing Kapp Putsch with a general strike in Berlin in March, Communists formed a 'Red Army' of 50,000 workers and seized control of the Ruhr. A virtual civil war followed as the regular army and Freikorps struggled to crush the rising. Troubles also broke out in Halle and Dresden and over 1,000 workers and 250 soldiers and police were killed. More disturbances in Saxony and Thuringia, where the workers organised self-defence units, were also put down in April.

After December 1920 when the USPD voted to join forces with the Communist Party, the KPD grew more confident. Consequently, in March 1921, it tried to force a revolution, beginning with a rising in Merseburg in Saxony. The strike disruption spread to Hamburg and the Ruhr but, once again, hesitancy allowed the risings to be crushed by the police and 145 were killed in the Ruhr.

There was a further bout of strike activity in 1923, at the time of Germany's economic collapse. This was again centred in Saxony and Hamburg, but it too was suppressed. The government survived, and was never severely threatened, although there were many occasions when events might have turned out differently had the KPD been less cautious. Nevertheless, the continued spate of working-class rebellion did its political damage. The fear of a 'red revolution', at a time when civil war was raging in Russia and the consequences of Communism appeared grim, served to frighten the law-abiding middle classes. Once again, it was the 'moderates' who were most affected and most inclined to feel that their government was not fully in control.

Exploring the detail

Comintern

The Comintern was the Communist International set up in 1919 to oversee the actions of Marxist parties throughout the world. Socialist groups from other countries were invited to join and receive support but leadership was in the hands of the Russians.

Cross-reference

The Kapp Putsch is described on pages 114–15.

Cross-references

The economic crisis of 1923 is covered later in this chapter, on pages 119–21.

Fig. 2 *Anti-communist propaganda tried to show the dangers of the 'Bolshevik serpent' which brings war, ruin, hunger and death*

■ Exploring the detail

The values of the Weimar Republic

The Weimar Republic was the product of the Social Democrats' belief in democracy and the freedom of the individual. Consequently, the republican government became associated with challenges to traditional values, tolerance of diversity, experimentation and Liberal moral standards. To those on the right, this represented an unpatriotic undermining of German traditions and culture.

■ Cross-reference

General Ludendorff is profiled on page 84.

Fig. 3 *The right-wing nationalist Wolfgang Kapp, who led a putsch in Berlin in 1920*

The challenge from the right

The powerful Conservative right wing posed at least as big a, if not a bigger, threat to the Weimar government than the left. Many of those on the right had been hostile to the republic from the outset. They did not share its values, and their disgust at the way the war had been brought to an end was compounded by their hatred of the Versailles Treaty and the 'weaknessness' of the government in failing to crush Communists once and for all. Yet the republic depended upon such people. Right-wing ideas were strong amongst members of the Freikorps and in the army, whilst the large landowners, industrialists, civil servants, police and judges on the whom the republic relied were also traditional Conservative anti-republicans. Because of their wealth and influence, these forces of the right wielded a disproportionate amount of power and some chose, quite literally, to take the law into their own hands – by rebellion or, for example, by showing their partiality in the administration of justice. In such cases, there was very little the republic could do.

The government was obliged to put into effect the terms of the Treaty of Versailles in January 1920, and, consequently, started to reduce the size of the army and to disband some of the Freikorps units, which were no longer deemed necessary.

In February 1920, the defence minister, Noske, ordered two Freikorps units, comprising 12,000 men, to disband. These units had recently returned from the Baltic and were stationed 12 miles from Berlin. When General Walther von Lüttwitz, the commanding general, refused to disband one of them, the government ordered his arrest. Lüttwitz and the Freikorps leader, Captain Hermann Erhardt, decided to march their troops to Berlin in protest and other officers sympathetic to Lüttwitz offered their support. Lüttwitz was also supported by the right-wing civil servant and politician Wolfgang Kapp, who was intent on the overthrow of the government. Crucially, however, Hans von Seeckt and Ludendorff remained non-committal. They sympathised but were aware of the dangers of voicing open support.

Key profiles

Hans von Seeckt

Hans von Seeckt (1886–1936) was a career soldier who had been placed in charge of the German forces in East Prussia at the end of the war. He was a member of the German delegation to Versailles and was appointed head of the *Truppenamt*, which replaced the forbidden army general staff. He replaced General Reinhardt as Commander of the *Reichswehr* (army) from 1920. He was instrumental in disbanding the Freikorps units and trying to keep the army out of politics as much as possible. Nevertheless, under his command, 1920–6, the army became a privileged elite beyond accountability.

Wolfgang Kapp

Wolfgang Kapp (1868–1922) had trained in law and worked as a civil servant. He was attracted to right-wing politics and co-founded the Fatherland Party in 1917 (see page 84). He was a monarchist and in 1919 was elected to the Reichstag for the nationalist DNVP. He attempted a putsch in 1920 and tried to set himself up as chancellor but, after its failure, he fled to Sweden. He returned to Germany in 1922 but died in Leipzig whilst awaiting trial.

On March 12, the 12,000 Freikorps troops marched into Berlin unopposed, and the next day Wolfgang Kapp issued a proclamation:

> The Reich and nation are in grave danger. With terrible speed we are approaching the complete collapse of the state and of law and order. Prices are rising unchecked. Hardship is growing. The government, lacking in authority and in league with corruption, is incapable of overcoming the danger. From the East we are threatened by war-like Bolshevism. Is this government capable of resisting it? How are we to escape internal and external collapse?
>
> Only by re-erecting a strong state. There is no other way but a government of action. In the best German tradition, the state must stand above the conflict of classes and parties. We recognise only German citizens. Everyone must do his duty!

1   *The Reich Chancellor, Wolfgang Kapp, 13 March 1920*

Ebert's government was forced to withdraw to Dresden and when Ebert and his chancellor, Bauer, called on the regular army to crush the rising, Seeckt famously told Ebert:

> Troops do not fire on troops; when Reichswehr fires on Reichswehr, all comradeship within the officer corps has vanished.

The situation appeared dangerous, but there was actually considerable tension between the military and civilian elements of the putsch and it failed to gain widespread support, even from the Conservative right wing. Civil servants and bankers remained at best lukewarm and often hostile, whilst ordinary workers, encouraged both by some of the socialist members of Ebert's government and by the trade unions, called a general strike which spread across the whole of Germany. Berlin was brought to a standstill and within four days, the putsch collapsed and Kapp and Lüttwitz were forced to flee. Ebert's government returned, but not quite with the air of triumph that might have been expected.

The putsch had taught a number of lessons. The army was not to be trusted, civil servants could be disloyal, the workers as a group could show their power (a realisation which gave renewed vigour to the communist movement) and, without the army's support, the Weimar government was weak. The leniency shown by right-wing judges towards those brought to trial in the aftermath of the putsch contrasted strongly to the harsh treatment suffered by the left wing, and their behaviour too sent the message that the government was not really in control.

Political assassinations

The violence continued as right-wing nationalists organised themselves into leagues, committed to the elimination of prominent politicians and others associated with the 'betrayal' of Germany. These *Vaterländische Verbände*, or Patriotic Leagues, were often formed out of the old Freikorps units and acted as fiercely anti-republican paramilitaries. They were potentially very powerful and some were actively supported by members of the regular German army. One early victim of the assassins' bullets was Hugo Haase, a USPD member who had been a member of the Council of People's Commissars and was shot in front of the Reichstag in October 1919. He died of his wounds a month later.

Exploring the detail

The Kapp Putsch trials

Of the 705 involved in the putsch that were brought to trial, 412 were granted amnesty, 285 had their 'proceedings discontinued', 7 had their 'proceedings reviewed' and just 1 was punished. Lüttwitz was retired from service and provided with a general's pension, while Kapp died awaiting trial. The Chancellor Bauer, Defence Minister Noske and General Reinhardt, Commander of the Reichswehr who had favoured military action together with some civil servants, were forced to resign. However, Seeckt was promoted to replace Reinhardt! He, and other army leaders, went unpunished because the government knew it might need their support in the future.

In August 1921, the former finance minister, Matthias Erzberger, was assassinated in the Black Forest by two members of the terrorist league 'Organisation Consul'. He had already been shot at in January and left wounded, but the assassins were determined to complete the job. Erzberger had both led the German delegation for the signing of the armistice and had signed the Treaty of Versailles. He was also Germany's representative on the reparations committee. Even after he was buried, his widow continued to receive abusive letters – including threats to defile his grave.

■ Key profile

Matthias Erzberger

Matthias Erzberger (1875–1921) had entered the Reichstag as a deputy for the Centre Party in 1903. He had supported the Peace Resolution of 1917 and became a member of Prince Max's government in 1918. He led the German delegation to sign the armistice and had signed the Versailles Treaty on behalf of the German government in 1919. He was Reich finance minister from June 1919 to March 1920 and had carried out a major reform of the German taxation system. He had been subject to frequent attacks in the Conservative press and was a prime target for assassination.

On 24 June 1922, it was the turn of the foreign minister, Walther Rathenau. Rathenau was in an open-top car, driving to work from his home in Grünewald, when four assassins from Organisation Consul shot at him and hurled a hand grenade for good measure. The reasons are not difficult to fathom. Rathenau's crimes were to be a Jew and a leading minister in the republican government. He had participated in the signing of the armistice, had negotiated with the allies to try to improve the Treaty of Versailles and had negotiated the 1922 Treaty of Rapallo with communist Russia. Nevertheless, Rathenau had been a popular figure and the following day over 700,000 protestors lined the streets of Berlin. The assassination had an impact abroad too and the value of the mark fell, as other countries feared the repercussions.

■ Key profile

Walther Rathenau

Walther Rathenau (1867–1922) was a physicist and chemist by training and head of AEG electricals. He had entered politics as a Liberal. In 1919, he had joined the DDP and became Minister of Reconstruction in 1921 and foreign minister in 1922. He recommended the fulfilment of the Treaty of Versailles.

■ Exploring the detail

The Treaty of Rapallo

In 1922, Germany and the Soviet Union were both outsiders in Europe. Rathenau negotiated this treaty to provide mutual benefits. The treaty brought the claims from both sides for compensation for the First World War damage to an end, and set up trade links between the two states. Secret military links were also established which allowed Germany to circumvent the terms of the Versailles Treaty by allowing for the training of German forces in Russia.

Altogether, between 1919 and 1923 there were 376 political assassinations, 22 carried out by the left wing, 354 by the right. In an attempt to call a halt to this rising tide of lawlessness, in July 1922, the Reichstag passed a law which was to last five years, 'For the Protection of the Republic'. This placed severe penalties on those involved in conspiracy to murder and prohibited extremist organisations.

Organisation Consul was forced to disband, but the law was not as effective as it might have been because the judges who were required to put it into practice were often right-wing sympathisers. In Bavaria, the staunchly Conservative government even refused to implement it and so unwittingly allowed the Nazi movement to establish itself). Rathenau's killers and their accomplices received an average of only four years each in prison and whilst 326 of the right-wing murderers went unpunished, and only one was convicted and sentenced to severe punishment until 1923, 10 left-wing murderers were sentenced to death.

Ernst von Salomon, a German nationalist writer who received five years' imprisonment for his part in the murder, had this to say of the right-wing nationalist activities:

> There was one political common denominator that held the whole of the 'national movement' together – to make an end to the policy of accepting the Versailles Treaty and cooperating with the West. We had no wish to become a political party but we did desire basic change. The only course open was to eliminate every politician who believed in 'fulfilment' [the policy of cooperating with the West]. We had a list – a single dirty sheet of paper with names scribbled all over it in pencil, some crossed out, some written in again. Many of the names meant absolutely nothing to me and I had to take quite a lot of trouble to find out who the people were. I remember thinking that there were a lot of Jewish names. One name, Wassermann, I crossed out myself because I thought it meant Jacob Wassermann, the writer. In fact it was Oskar Wassermann, the banker, a man of whom I knew nothing. The whole thing was drawn up in a fantastically casual way.

2

Although the right-wing activity failed to destroy the republic, the developments of the 1919–22 period had bolstered the confidence and arrogance of those right wingers who believed they could (quite literally) get away with murder. Since the Weimar politicians seemed constantly to exaggerate the threat from the left and to underestimate that from the right, this meant that the right wing was able to establish itself very firmly in the new German state.

> I grew up in the midst of this atmosphere. In our high school in Stuttgart, as indeed in most of the secondary schools in Germany after 1918, a noticeable rightist trend prevailed, which most of the teachers followed. We believed that it was the stab in the back alone that had prevented a German victory. We were convinced that one could be patriotic only on the rightist side. We were taught to hate the French and the British and to despise the Americans. We did not see that the socialist workers had also sacrificed their blood for Germany – for a country that had never really given them a chance. We were brought up for a world that no longer existed and we took up nationalistic slogans, while the Republic of which we were trying to make fun was trying to pull the wagon out of the mud.

3   *Fritz Ernst, a German historian, recalling his own experience of the early years of the Weimar Republic*

Activity

Challenge your thinking

Salomon was an educated man and, after his release from prison, he became a celebrated German author. Discuss with a partner why men like Salomon became involved in terrorist activities. Try to jot down a list of reasons as to why there was such a marked decline in civilised political behaviour in Germany in the 1919–22 period.

Questions

1 Explain the views of Fritz Ernst and, in particular, the phrases 'stab in the back', 'rightist' and 'trying to pull the wagon out of the mud'.

2 Why do you think middle-class boys were encouraged to think in this way?

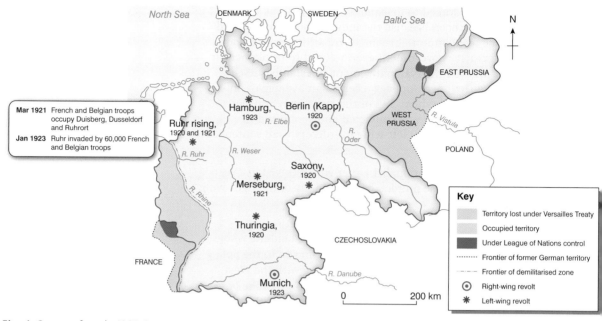

Fig. 4 *Centres of revolt, 1920–3*

Statistical analysis

Study Table 1.

1. What do these results show?

2. Identify the three parties which supported the republic and comment on the results for these.

3. Overall, what has happened to the 'political balance'?

Fig. 5 *The People's Party in Bavaria invokes the dangers of Communism in this election poster*

The 1920 elections

Once the new constitution had been approved, elections had to take place for a new Reichstag. These were held in June 1920 and the results showed a different picture from those of January 1919, as can be seen in Table 1. Study these results carefully and answer the questions alongside before reading on.

Table 1 *National assembly elections, January 1919 and June 1920*

Party	Seats (January 1919)	Seats (June 1920)
USPD	22	83
SPD	163	103
DDP	75	39
Zentrum (Centre Party)	91	64
DVP	19	65
DNVP	44	71
KPD	0	4

You should have spotted that the SPD, DDP and Zentrum (pro-republican parties) all lost seats.

The SPD vote fell from 37.9 per cent in 1919 to 21.7 per cent in 1920; the DDP vote from 18.5 per cent to 8.3 per cent; and the Zentrum vote from 19.7 per cent to 13.6 per cent. Meanwhile, the vote of the USPD soared and the KPD established itself, while the votes for the parties on the right also grew (DVP, DNVP).

These results show a loss of support for the moderate centre – which had formed the first coalition government – and a growth in support for the more extreme views of the left and right. Clearly, the impact of the Treaty of Versailles, together with the developments of 1919–20, had played its part in disillusioning the voters. The pro-republicans (linked in the public mind with shame and weakness) could no longer dominate the government and create a workable coalition; the DVP had to be called upon. Their decision to participate in a coalition government for the first time was in some ways a promising sign, since it suggested that they were prepared to accept the republic, but it also meant that there was such a cross-section of opinion in the government itself that decisions were difficult to come to and stable government extremely difficult to achieve.

Table 2 shows the many government changes that occurred between 1919 and 1923.

Table 2 *Government instability*

Appointment	Chancellor	Party	Members of governing coalition	Fall
February 1919	Philipp Scheidemann	SPD	SPD, Z, DDP (modern socialist-centre)	Treaty of Versailles
June 1919	Gustav Bauer	SPD	SPD, Z, DDP (from Oct) (modern socialist-centre)	Kapp Putsch
March 1920	Hermann Müller	SPD	SPD, Z, DDP (modern socialist-centre)	Election result
June 1920	Konstantin Fehrenbach	Z	DDP, Z, DVP (centre-right)	Reparations ultimatum
May 1921	Josef Wirth	Z	SPD, Z, DDP (modern socialist-centre)	Cabinet resigned over partition of Upper Silesia
October 1921	Josef Wirth	Z	SPD, Z, DDP (modern socialist-centre)	
November 1922	Wilhelm Cuno	No party	DDP, Z, DVP, BVP (centre-right)	Economic crisis
August 1923	Gustav Stresemann	DVP	SPD, Z, DDP, DVP (centre-right with socialists – the 'Great Coalition')	
October 1923	Gustav Stresemann	DVP	SPD, Z, DDP, DVP ('Great Coalition')	SDP left coalition
November 1923	Wilhelm Marx	Z	DDP, Z, DVP (centre-right)	

The economy, hyperinflation and the currency collapse of 1923

To finance the war, the government of the Kaiserreich had decided against imposing new taxes or raising money by increasing taxation on the more wealthy. Instead, it put more money into circulation. This had meant abandoning the link between paper money and gold reserves that had existed before the war. The German government borrowed heavily from anyone prepared to provide 'war loans', as many patriotic Germans were, and they were promised repayment, with interest, after the war.

The amount of paper money in circulation increased from 2,000m marks in 1913 to 45,000m in 1919. At the same time, the amount of money owed by the government (the national debt), had grown from 5,000m to 144,000m marks in the same period. When there is more money in circulation, without an increase in productivity, the value of the currency will fall. This is what happened to the German mark. In 1919, it was worth less than 20 per cent of its pre-war value. Shortages of goods also helped push prices up and the price of basic foodstuffs and consumer

Questions

1 Explain why the right wing posed a threat to the stability of the Weimar Republic in the years 1919–22.

2 How successful were the Weimar governments in dealing with the threats posed by the left and right wing in the years 1919–22?

Fig. 6 *A 100,000 Reichsmark note from February 1923. The continued use of Reichsmarks and the use of the Imperial symbol, the double-headed eagle, are evidence of the continued support for the empire and lack of support for the Weimar democracy from key institutions like the banks*

■ Cross-reference

The new welfare benefits introduced in this period are discussed on pages 134–5.

■ Cross-reference

One powerful industrialist who grew rich by borrowing from the Reichsbank and repaying his loans in devalued currency was Hugo Stinnes, who is profiled on page 95.

goods increased by three or four times. In other words, Germany was suffering from inflation. This might not have been a problem had the war ended with the victory the Germans had hoped for. Annexations and reparations would have provided sufficient income for the loans to be paid back. However, in practice this, of course, was not to be.

Not only did Germany lose the war (and with it the territory and money it had already begun to take from the Russians), the Germans themselves suffered the loss of valuable lands and were themselves faced with a reparations bill. Nevertheless, government borrowing continued. Fearing the political consequences, the new government dared not devalue the currency. This would have made the paper money in circulation worthless and reduced the value of savings. In any case, Germany needed capital to rebuild industry and re-start trade as well as meeting the post-war pensions bill and paying compensation to those who had lost land under the Treaty of Versailles. There were also the new welfare benefits to meet, while payments to civil servants had to be maintained, not least to retain their political support.

Given the acute difficulties which Germany faced in the immediate aftermath of war, it is hardly surprising that the fledgling Weimar Republic did not try to address economic issues with radical new measures, and some have gone so far as to suggest that allowing some inflation to continue was economically wise. Unemployment had virtually disappeared by 1921 and there was a rapid recovery in economic activity. However, it may be less clear to see why the new government of 1920 did not respond to the mounting inflation. After all, prices, which had doubled between 1918 and 1919, had quadrupled again between 1919 and 1920, reaching a point 14 times higher than in 1913. The answer is partly political. The 1920 coalition was dominated by the Centre Party which was supported by many of the powerful German industrialists. They were benefiting from the inflation by taking short-term loans from Germany's central bank to expand their businesses. They could then repay these with inflated currency. Furthermore, inflation had the effect of lessening the government's burden of debt (although the reparations themselves were not affected because these were paid in gold marks or goods) and it is often suggested that the German politicians had a vested interest in allowing it to continue unchecked.

In some ways inflation was beneficial. It stimulated economic activity and, compared with Britain, unemployment rates were quite low. By 1921, there was only 1.8 per cent unemployment in Germany compared with nearly 17 per cent in Great Britain. This in turn encouraged investment, especially from the USA. However, left unchecked, inflation will eventually become uncontrollable. This happened in Germany in 1923 and high inflation became hyperinflation.

The reason why inflation – caused by long-term structural problems – turned into hyperinflation was related to the issue of reparations.

Reparations

The Treaty of Versailles had made it clear that Germany would have to pay reparations – payments in cash and goods – but had not stipulated the total amount. A reparations commission had been set up to determine the scale of damage caused by Germany and an initial payment of 20bn gold marks was demanded. By the time the commission reached its decision in May 1921, the allies estimated that they had received 2.6bn gold marks worth of goods (made up of almost the entire German merchant fleet, 5,000 railway locomotives and over 100,000 each of railway wagons, horses, cattle and agricultural machines). France also had the value of the Saarland coalfields – worth a further 2.5bn marks. However, the Germans claimed to have already made payments of *c*.37bn marks!

Cross-reference

The Treaty of Rapallo is covered on page 116.

Table 3 *The course of the reparation decisions and their consequences*

March 1921	April/May 1921	1922	1923
London conference held to consider reparations proposals. The Germans asked that the Rhineland be evacuated and Upper Silesia restored as the price of their compliance. The allies refused and occupied three Ruhr towns, claiming that Germany was already in breach of an interim payment of £1,000m.	The Reparations Commission presented its final report. The amount was set at 132bn gold marks or £6.6bn. The first 50bn gold marks were to be paid in annual instalments of 2bn gold marks (£100m) plus 26% of the value of German exports. The ultimatum was presented on 5 May. The Germans were given six days in which to accept. Chancellor Fehrenbach resigned and Josef Wirth took office. He signed the ultimatum 20 hours before it expired. Germany paid its first reparations installment (£50m) at the end of May.	By January 1922 Germany was in such economic difficulties that the Reparations Commission granted a moratorium (postponement) on the January and February installments. In July, the German government asked for a further suspension of the payments due that year. In November 1922, it asked to be released from obligations for three to four years in order to stabilise its currency and also asked for a loan of 500m gold marks. The French were deeply suspicious that this was simply an excuse. Their suspicions were made worse because of the Treaty of Rapallo which contained provision for economic cooperation between Germany and Russia.	The Paris Conference of January 1923 tried to resolve the problems. On 9 January the commission declared that Germany had deliberately defaulted over coal deliveries. On 11 January French and Belgian troops were sent to the Ruhr. The occupation devastated the economy and sparked hyperinflation.

The British economist Maynard Keynes feared the repercussions of reparations:

> The policy of reducing Germany to servitude for a generation, of degrading the lives of millions of human beings, and of depriving a whole nation of happiness should be abhorrent and detestable. Some preach it in the name of justice. In the great events of man's history, justice is not so simple.

4 *Quoted in Howarth, T.,* **Twentieth Century History: the world since 1900***, 1987*

The modern historian Peukert (1991) has argued that the eventual reparations demand that was placed on Germany was actually quite

Questions

1 Explain why Britain, France and the USA might consider reparations 'just'. (You may need to refer back to Chapter 1 to provide a full answer here.)

2 Keynes disagreed, but not solely out of sympathy. Can you think of any other reasons why an economist might regard reparations as 'detestable'?

Cross-reference

For pensions and social welfare payment, look ahead to pages 134–5.

Walther Rathenau is profiled on page 116. Stresemann is introduced on pages 128–9.

Exploring the detail

Fulfilment

Fulfilment, or cooperation with the Versailles Treaty, characterised Weimar foreign policy and is particularly associated with Stresemann. Right-wing nationalists regarded it as a mark of weakness. It also received a setback in October 1921 when the League of Nations decided to partition Upper Silesia, giving the more industrial area in the east to Poland and the larger, but less valuable, section in the west to Germany. This was despite over 60 per cent of the inhabitants voting in a referendum to remain part of Germany. The Treaty of Rapallo (see page 116) in April 1922 broke from the policy of fulfilment.

manageable. It only amounted to two per cent of Germany's national output, so he feels the consequences have been exaggerated. However, there were other important economic problems:

- In order to acquire currency with which to pay the 'cash' demands of the reparations, Germany needed to export goods. However, Germany's traditional western European trading partners were anxious to rebuild their own economies and did not want to buy German goods.

- The western European nations were in debt to the USA. The receipt of reparations did not help stimulate the European economies (and consequently European trade with Germany) but tended to go straight to the USA.

- Reparations came at a time when Germany was already facing large payments for the interest on loans raised during the war, for pensions and for social welfare payments.

While Walther Rathenau was the Minister of Reconstruction in 1921, he tried to cooperate with the allies hoping that a willingness to meet demands would win sympathy. He fully expected that, once it became clear that reparation demands were beyond Germany's capabilities, the allies would revise them. This policy became known as 'fulfilment' and it naturally encouraged politicians to leave the economy alone. Had Germany shown that it could manage the payments, the whole purpose of the 'fulfilment' policy would disappear!

Germany paid its first reparations installment at the end of May 1921 (£50m) but in January 1922 (see Figure 7) it tried to negotiate for more time and a further loan, and by December 1922 Germany was behind with its deliveries of timber to France.

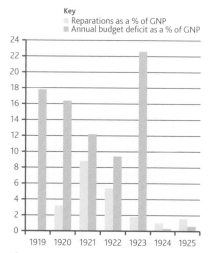

Fig. 7 *Reparations and annual budget deficits as a percentage of Gross National Product, 1919–25*

Fig. 8 *The French army marching through the German Ruhr in 1923*

Consequently the French and Belgians, with the support of the Italians, sent a team of engineers – 'protected' by five French and one Belgian division of 60,000 men – to the Ruhr on 11 January 1923. Their aim was to seize the area's coal, steel and manufactured goods as reparations. These troops occupied the whole Ruhr area and, in the course of 1923, the numbers in the occupying forces grew to 100,000. They took control of all the mines, factories, steelworks and railways, demanded food from the shops and set up machine-gun posts in the streets.

Chancellor Cuno knew the Germans could not fight back. The Versailles Treaty had reduced the size of the German army and the Rhineland was, in any case, demilitarised. Instead, he responded by stopping all reparations payments and ordering a policy of 'passive resistance' whereby no one living in the area, from businessmen and postal workers to railwaymen and miners, would cooperate with the French authorities.

The developments are described here by a German industrialist, Fritz Thyssen:

> The government had forbidden the coal deliveries. The officials had been instructed to refuse to obey the order of the occupation authorities. The railway employees went on strike. Navigation on the Rhine was stopped. The French army occupied the mouths of many of the mines. When this happened the miners stopped work. In other collieries the work continued but the coal accummulated in great heaps on the surface. No train, no boat transported any of it to Belgium or to France. In order to break the resistance the occupation authorities established a customs barrier between the occupied territories and the rest of Germany. No merchandise was allowed to leave.

5
*Quoted in Howarth, T., **Twentieth Century History: the world since 1900**, 1987*

Workers were promised that their wages would continue if they obeyed the call to passive resistance while paramilitary troops working with the Reichswehr secretly organised acts of sabotage against the French. They crossed the customs barrier secretly at night and blew up railways, sank barges and destroyed bridges in order to disrupt the French effort. The scale of the French operation grew in response.

The French set up military courts and punished mine owners, miners and civil servants who would not comply with their authority. Around 150,000 Germans were expelled from the area. Worse still, some miners were shot after clashes with police. Altogether, 132 Germans were shot in the eight months of the occupation, including a seven-year-old boy, whom the French claimed to have been shot in error by a French officer cleaning his rifle, although the German newspapers claimed he was killed in cold blood. The French also brought in their own workers to man the railways and get coal out of the Ruhr, but this did not prove particularly effective. In May 1923, deliveries were only a third of the average monthly deliveries in 1922 and output in the Ruhr had fallen to around a fifth of its pre-occupation output.

The Ruhr occupation worsened the country's economic situation in a number of different ways:

- Paying the wages or providing goods for striking workers was a further drain on government money.
- Tax revenue was lost from those whose businesses ceased and workers who became unemployed.
- Germany had to import coal and pay for it from the limited foreign currency reserves within Germany.
- Shortage of goods pushed prices up further.
- International confidence in the value of the mark collapsed.

The scale of the damage may be seen in Figure 9.

Essentially, by November 1923, the currency was worthless. 300 paper mills and 2,000 printers were working day and night to provide sufficient paper money, and notes of ever higher denominations had to

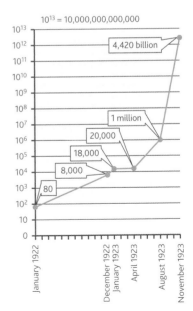

Fig. 9 *Annual German inflation rate, 1919–23, marks to the dollar (logarithmic scale)*

be printed. Workers were having to be paid daily or even twice daily as prices rose by the hour. Once received, the paper notes were spent as fast as possible, before the currency devalued further, but, it was not always easy to find goods to buy. There were serious food shortages, since farmers were not prepared to sell their produce for worthless money. Barter became common. Sometimes workers bought the first goods they could lay their hands on, then used these to barter with until they could obtain what they needed. Other town dwellers set off to visit the surrounding fields to try to 'glean' food, whilst some better organised employers paid their workers in goods (in kind) rather than in money.

Konrad Heiden, then a German student, described the situation:

> The printing presses of the government could no longer keep pace. You could see mail carriers on the streets with sacks on their backs or pushing prams before them, loaded with paper money that would be devalued the next day. Life was madness, nightmare, desperation, chaos. Communities printed their own money, based on goods, on a certain amount of potatoes, of rye, for instance. Shoe factories paid their workers in bonds which they could exchange at the bakery for bread or at the meat market for meat.

Fig. 10 *Cartoon illustrating the impact of hyperinflation*

The results of hyperinflation

Hyperinflation was not a disaster for everyone – there were both winners and losers.

Winners

Those who had debts, mortgages and loans did well since they could pay off the money they owed in worthless currency. Hyperinflation also helped enterprising business people who took out new loans and repaid them once the currency had devalued further. Those who had property on long-term fixed rents gained, because the real value of their rents decreased. Owners of foreign exchange and foreigners living in Germany could also benefit. Sometimes the benefits trickled down to those lower in the social hierarchy too. In the countryside, farmers coped well since food was in demand and money was less important in rural communities anyway. Shopkeepers and craftspeople could also do good business.

Losers

Those relying on savings, investments, fixed income or welfare support lost out. Among these were the students, the retired and the sick. Pensioners were particularly badly hit and this included war widows living on a state pension too. Those who had patriotically lent money to the government in wartime by purchasing fixed interest rate 'war bonds' also lost because the interest payments decreased in value. Landlords reliant on fixed rents were similarly hit. Of the workers as a whole, the unskilled fared the worst. Although workers were given wage increases, these did not keep up with the rising prices so standards of living declined, but did not completely collapse.

There were many variables and the effects of hyperinflation depended on the different parts of the country and the different means of earning a living that Germans had. Nevertheless it was an 'unreal' time which left many people uncertain about where they stood or what the future might hold. Of course, there were those who blamed the government, perhaps with some justification, for what happened. Once the French invaded and inflation started to spiral out of control, the government seemed to make little effort to stop the crisis and it has been suggested that they were happy to see a situation which would prove to the allies the futility of demanding reparations. However, it is extremely unlikely that the German government really wanted its people to suffer to prove this point and the responsibility for the final collapse of the German economy must lie, to some extent, with the allies and particularly the French.

Uprisings

The inflationary crises inflicted yet another blow to the political and social stability of the republic. Unemployment rose and there was an increase in crime. Unrest reached a new peak and President Ebert had to rely on his powers of emergency legislation under Article 48 to maintain control. In September, he transferred power from local governments to regional military commanders. Democracy itself seemed in danger as the government's desperate need for the support of the army to control the nation fuelled fears (and, for some, hopes) of another military dictatorship.

The Reichswehr had to be sent into Saxony and Thuringia in October and November, to crush communist risings. In Saxony, a new Reich Commissioner was appointed under Article 48 in defiance of the elected (SPD) prime minister who had refused to dismiss the KPD members of his government. On the right, there was an attempted putsch by General Buchrucker in northern Germany in October 1923 which was crushed by the army, but a month later came another in Munich in Bavaria – by Hitler and the Nazis.

After the left wing had been ousted in May 1919, Bavaria had been led by a strongly right-wing government, which had allowed secret paramilitary organisations to flourish despite the legislation passed in the wake of Rathenau's assassination. When, in August 1923, Gustav Stresemann was appointed chancellor and chose to call off passive resistance, nationalist feelings were outraged. There were conspiracies at the very heart of the Land government. Otto von Lossow, the head of the Bavarian Reichswehr, and General von Kahr, the State Governor, considered marching on Berlin to replace the central government, but they held back when they saw the Weimar government's success in driving the Communists from Saxony and Thuringia.

Fig. 11 *Hitler and his stormtroopers carry the Swastika flag as they prepare for the Munich Beer Hall Putsch of 9 November 1923*

Activity

Group activity

Divide into two groups. One group should prepare a speech blaming the allies and the French for the troubles of the German economy in 1923. The other group should prepare a case accusing the German government of creating the problems. Hold a debate and see which side is able to put forward the more convincing argument.

Activity

Talking point

Should other nations have intervened or done more to help Germany control its economy in 1919–23? Explain your ideas.

Exploring the detail

The use of Article 48

Article 48 is often criticised as a weakness of the Weimar constitution. Nevertheless, under President Ebert it proved a valuable way of dealing with the crises which the republic faced between 1919 and 1923. Ebert invoked it to deal with the Kapp and Munich Putsches on the right and the Spartacist, Ruhr and Saxon threats on the left. The transfer of military power to regional military commanders under order from the Ministry of Defence in Berlin in 1923 enabled the republic to survive the unrest of that year.

Cross-reference

Reference to the situation in Bavaria in 1919 is found on page 113.

For the assassination of Rathenau, refer back to page 116.

Gustav Stresemann is profiled on page 128.

■ Key profiles

General Otto von Lossow

Lieutenant-General Otto von Lossow (1868–1938) was the commander of the Reichswehr in Bavaria. He was a staunch Conservative and favoured a strong national state. He refused to obey orders from the Reichswehr Ministry in Berlin and only obeyed instructions from von Kahr, with whom he was plotting to establish a new regime in Berlin. However, he was ready to be patient – unlike Hitler – and how convinced he really was by Hitler's attempted putsch is not known.

General von Kahr

Gustave Ritter von Kahr (1862–1934) was a right-wing Conservative politician who had been Minister-President (1920–1) of the right-wing government that had been established in Bavaria. He had stepped down after disagreements with the Reich government but, in 1923, he had been appointed State-Commissioner General and was given wide powers by the Munich government. He favoured a strong Bavarian state with its own monarchy once more and he had hoped to use the Nazi Party to this end. However, although sympathetic to Hitler, he was an unwilling participant in the Beer Hall Putsch of November 1923. He spent the rest of his career as president of the Bavarian administrative court, but was murdered in 1934 during Hitler's 'Night of the Long Knives'.

In November 1923, it was the turn of the little known, right-wing rebel, Hitler, to try to seize power. Hitler knew that a putsch could only succeed if he had the weight of powerful figures behind it so, having secured the support of Ludendorff, he set out to win over Kahr and von Lossow in direct fashion. On 8 November, he burst into a Munich Beer Hall, where the two were addressing a meeting of 2,000, surrounding it with his stormtroopers and announcing that the revolution had begun. At gunpoint, in a side room, Kahr and von Lossow were persuaded to agree to his plan to march on Berlin and to install Ludendorff as the new Commander in Chief. However, their support evaporated overnight and so too did some of Hitler's success in persuading others to support him. Crucially, the stormtroopers were unable to gain control of the Munich army barracks and by the next day, 9 November, it was clear that Hitler's original plan had failed. Nevertheless, he went ahead with a march through Munich.

The ensuing gun battle with the police later became part of the folklore of the 'courageous' Nazis who marched fearlessly through the streets into the arms of a police cordon. Hitler fell and dislocated his shoulder, possibly in response to the shooting of his companion with whom he had linked arms. He fled, only to be captured the next day, whilst Ludendorff walked straight up to the police and allowed himself to be arrested.

The incident again showed the importance of the army to the political survival of the regime. Seeckt sent in Weimar troops to deal with the aftermath of the abortive putsch, and central control over the wayward republic was soon re-imposed. The Nazis were banned and Hitler imprisoned (although only for five years, of which he served nine months).

Once again, the republic survived.

A closer look

Adolf Hitler and the Nazi Party

Adolf Hitler (1889–1945) had stayed in the army after seeing service delivering messages between trenches on the western front. He obtained a job in the army political department in Munich, spying on the new political groups and parties that were emerging in Bavaria at this time. In 1919, when sent to observe the DAP, a new right-wing workers' party, he decided to join it. In 1920, the party was renamed the National Socialist German Workers' Party (NSDAP – Nazi Party) and Hitler became its chairman in July 1921. By 1923, the party had 55,000 members and a paramilitary wing – the stormtroopers, or SA. Its demands were laid down in a 25-point programme of 1920, of which some of the terms are given below:

- We demand the union of all Germans to form a greater Germany.
- We demand the abolition of the peace treaties of Versailles and **St Germain**.
- We demand land and territory for the nourishment of our people.
- None but those of German blood may be members of the German nation. No Jew, therefore, may be a member of the German nation.
- We demand the abolition of incomes unearned by work.
- We demand profit-sharing in the big industries.
- We demand the creation of a strong central government in Germany.

7   *From the Nazi Party 25-point programme of 1920*

Key term

The Treaty of St Germain (1919): this was the post-war peace treaty with Austria which, like that of Versailles, had forced Austria to pay reparations and give up land.

Questions

1 The Nazi Party claimed to be a 'National Socialist' party. Identify which terms are nationalist and which socialist.

2 Who might have been attracted by the party programme and why?

Summary question

Explain why democratic government was able to survive the political crises of 1923 in Germany.

AQA Examiner's tip

Obviously, democratic government survived in large measure because of its use of the army, but you also need to ask yourself whether there was ever any real alternative to the survival of democratic government. With French troops in the Ruhr and the collapse of the mark, neither the confrontational approach of the right wing nor the revolutionary stance of the left was likely to win widespread support. Try to comment on the weakness of the opposition as well as the strength of the democratic government to show your understanding of the issues.

Fig. 12 *The leaders of the Munich Beer Hall Putsch pose before their trial. Left to right: Dr Freidrich Weber; Wilhelm Frick; Hermann Kriebel; General Erich Ludendorff; Adolf Hitler; Wilhelm Brueckner; Ernst Röhm. Notice that only Hitler and Frick are dressed as civilians: what does this imply?*

8 Financial recovery and the Weimar Republic in 1925

In August 1923, Germany acquired a new chancellor – Gustav Stresemann. Stresemann is often regarded as 'the man who saved the republic' and the 'good German'. Here is the verdict of the historian William Carr:

> Stresemann's 'hundred days' as Chancellor marked a real turning-point in the Republic's history. He took office when the Republic was at its lowest ebb politically and economically but by the time the 'great coalition' collapsed in November 1923, the Republic was well on the road to recovery. Stresemann was one of the few really outstanding political figures in the Weimar period. A statesmanlike figure of immense ability and industry, he was a gifted orator and a dynamic and vigorous personality with some of the mental qualities and attitudes of Winston Churchill, whom he resembled both in temperament and physique.

1

Adapted from Carr, W., **A History of Germany**, *1991*

Key profile

Gustav Stresemann

Gustav Stresemann (1878–1929) studied economics at Berlin University and set up a manufacturers' association to promote the interests of small businesses in Saxony. He was elected to the Reichstag as a National Liberal in 1907 and, at 28 years, was its youngest member. He was a good speaker and a nationalist, a member of the Navy League and a supporter of the colonial empire. During the war, he supported those who wanted German victory with annexations and unrestricted submarine warfare. In 1917, he became leader of the National Liberals until its break up in November 1918. At the end of the war most National Liberals became the (moderate) DDP but Stresemann was excluded because of his Conservative stance. He therefore set up his own party – the DVP – which was at first hostile to the revolution and republic and wanted the return of the monarchy, although with its powers curbed. He seems to have been favourably inclined towards Kapp but changed his attitude after Rathenau's assassination, because he realised the dangers of chaos. His party represented many of the leading industrialists and Stresemann was both an able speaker and effective politician. Consequently, he became chancellor on 13 August 1923. His 100 days in office ran until 23 November 1923, when the SPD left the coalition on which he relied for his government. Nevertheless he continued as foreign secretary. He won the Nobel Peace Prize in 1926 and remained in office until his death in October 1929.

Fig. 1 *Gustav Stresemann, the 'good German'?*

Activity

Thinking point

As you read this chapter, you should consider whether Stresemann's positive reputation was fully deserved.

Financial recovery: the work of Schacht and Stresemann

Gustav Stresemann, leader of the DVP Party, and a man with right-wing sympathies, was appointed chancellor in August 1923, in the midst of the economic crisis. He was determined to see a revision of the Treaty of Versailles and reduction, or abolition, of reparations payments but he was prepared to lead a coalition including the Centre and SPD, since these formed the majority parties in the Reichstag and he knew that without their support he would be unable to restore Germany's fortunes. The crippling inflation had to be brought to an end, and since this could only be achieved by coming to terms with the French, and settling the outstanding international problems which Germany faced, he adopted a policy of 'fulfilment' as previously espoused by Rathenau.

- In September, Stresemann called off passive resistance unconditionally. This was a brave move since it had been a popular action and ending it appeared to be a 'surrender'. Its ending stirred up yet more nationalist hostility, as seen, for example, in the Munich Putsch in November 1923, but ultimately it was the only way to normalise the German position.
- Stresemann cut government expenditure – dismissing many civil servants in an attempt to show that Germany was being reasonable and trying to put its own house in order.

Schacht and the stabilisation of the currency

Stresemann appointed the expert Hjalmar Schacht as Reich Currency Commissioner. In November 1923, Schacht introduced the *Rentenmark*, valued at one Rentenmark to one trillion old marks. This new currency was backed by land and industrial resources (rather than by gold) and was exchangeable for bonds in land and industrial plant. Its supply was also strictly limited so it was regarded as safe, as being of worth and consequently it held its value.

Key profile

Hjalmar Schacht

Hjalmar Schacht (1877–1970) had been director of the National Bank from 1916 and was a co-founder of the DDP, which emerged from the old National Liberal Party in November 1918. In 1923, he became Reich Currency Commissioner and head of the Reichsbank and introduced the Rentenmark. He helped negotiate the Dawes and Young Plans. He later became economics minister under the Nazis (1934–7) but lost favour and was removed from the Reichsbank in 1939. He was implicated in the 1944 July Bomb Plot against Hitler, and was tried at Nuremberg, but was subsequently acquitted and returned to banking.

Schacht also took over the leadership of the Reichsbank which was an important role, particularly in the early months when the stability of the new currency could not be taken for granted. A range of fiscal measures were adopted to keep inflation and the exchange rate at reasonable levels and to balance expenditure against income. The government stopped offering credit to industry. This had been an encouragement to speculation and inflation and, by reducing borrowing, the circulation of

Key chronology

The Stresemann era

1923

August	Stresemann becomes chancellor.
September	Passive resistance is called off.
October	The left-wing governments in Saxony and Thuringia are overthrown.
November	Hitler's Munich (Beer Hall) Putsch fails.
	The Rentenmark is introduced and inflation curbed; Stresemann's government falls but he remains as foreign minister.

1924

April	Dawes Plan reorganises reparations in Germany's favour.
May	Election: extremist parties improve position.
December	Election: moderate parties improve position – extremists do less well.

1925

February	President Ebert dies.
April	Field Marshal Hindenburg is elected president.
October	Locarno Conference; Germany accepts the western borders.

Cross-reference

'Fulfilment' is described on page 122.

You can read about the Dawes Plan on pages 130–1.

The Munich Putsch is outlined on pages 126–7.

money returned to 'normal' levels. The government also altered its policy with regard to the printing of money, which, previously, had increased as inflation had risen. Schacht's task was to keep the amount of money in circulation limited to the real worth of the economy.

Lending rates were controlled. In one month they rose from 30 to 45 per cent, while overdraft charges rose from 40 to 80 per cent. All this was combined with a range of new taxes which increased the taxation paid by both individuals and companies, so reducing spending power. This enabled the government to reinvest a larger proportion of the nation's wealth. Schacht worked so hard to restrict the money supply that the German government-operated post office and railways formed their own banks in which they built up the capital they needed for investment.

These changes made a considerable difference to the way that the German economy operated. Well-managed companies, that were run prudently and were careful not to build up excessive debt continued to prosper, but those that relied on credit crumbled. The number of companies that went bankrupt in Germany rose from 233 in 1923 to over 6,000 in 1924. This made the economy more efficient and faith in the Reichsbank returned.

Schacht later wrote in his autobiography:

> The speculators had learnt that the Reichsbank was now able, if it decided to do so, to put an end to all speculation on the foreign exchange market. The success of the campaign meant an immeasurable increase in the confidence of the public in the stabilisation of the mark.

| 2 | *Adapted from Schacht, H.,* **Stabilizing the Mark**, *1927* |

The old inflated marks were gradually cashed in and in August 1924 the Rentenmark became the Reichsmark, and was backed by the German gold reserve, which had to be maintained at 30 per cent of the value of the Reichsmarks in circulation. Inflation ceased to be a problem and the value of the new currency was established at home and abroad.

Stresemann's policy of 'fulfilment' and the Dawes Plan

The stabilisation of Germany's position was as much dependent on settling Germany's relations with the allies as it was on the domestic decisions. Ending inflation demanded a solution to the problems caused by the reparations issue. In November 1923, Stresemann asked the Allies' Reparations Committee to set up a committee of financial experts to address Germany's repayment concerns. Since America had a vested interest in getting Germany back into a position where reparations could be made to France, as much was then passed on to the USA to repay loans, the American banker Charles Dawes acted as the chairman.

By the time the committee reported with the Dawes Plan of April 1924, Stresemann's government had fallen, but he remained as foreign secretary and took credit for much of what was achieved. Although the Dawes Plan confirmed the original figure of a total reparations payment of £6.6bn (132,000m gold marks), it made the payments more manageable. It recommended that:

■ the amount paid each year by Germany should be reduced until 1929, when the situation would be reappraised. It proposed that Germany

Activity

Thinking point

Schacht is often praised for his contribution to the restoration of the German economy. What difficulties do you suppose he might have faced in winning public support for his policies?

should re-start reparations by paying 1,000m marks (a fraction of what had been expected before), and that this sum should be raised by annual increments over five years to 2,500m marks per year. After this, the sum paid should be related to German industrial performance.

Germany should receive a large loan of 800m marks from the USA to help get the plan started and to allow for heavy investment in the German infrastructure.

Linked to this was the reorganisation of the Reichsbank (under allied supervision) and the replacement of the old German mark with the Rentenmark. The Dawes Plan also agreed that any sanctions for non-payment of reparations would need to be taken after consultation between all the allies (not just France acting alone).

There was a heated debate in the Reichstag over the plan. The 'national opposition' (mainly the DNVP, but also smaller right-wing groups like the Nazi movement) bitterly attacked this policy of compromise since they believed Germany should defy the Versailles Treaty and abandon reparations altogether. However, it was eventually agreed and accepted by both Germany and the allies in July 1924. It brought several benefits to Germany:

The allies accepted that Germany's problems with the payment of reparations were real.

Loans were granted, with which new machinery, factories, houses and jobs could be provided and the German economy rebuilt.

The evacuation of the Ruhr, and better relations with France were established. The French gradually left the Ruhr during 1924–5, once it became clear that Germany was going to restart paying reparations and the occupation could no longer be regarded as legitimate. Such measures contributed to German optimism that their country was once again its own master.

The Locarno treaties

Stresemann's other major step came in October 1925, when the western European powers met, at Germany's suggestion, at a conference in the Italian city of Locarno. Stresemann was anxious to restore Germany's position internationally and avoid any hostile alliance between Britain and France, particularly as the latter began to feel threatened by Germany's industrial recovery. France was suspicious of the move, but eventually agreed to attend, along with the USA and Germany's former enemies, save for Russia. The discussions led to the Rhineland Pact and Arbitration Treaties, usually known as the Locarno Pact, although they were finally signed in London on 1 December 1925.

Fig. 2 *A view into the conference room during the final sitting of the Locarno meeting, with Stresemann at the head*

Under the Rhineland Pact:

- Germany, France and Belgium promised to respect the western frontier – as drawn up at Versailles in 1919. These frontiers were to be regarded as fixed and internationally guaranteed.
- Germany agreed to keep its troops out of the Rhineland, as demanded at Versailles.
- Britain and Italy promised to aid Germany, France or Belgium if attacked by its neighbours.

Under the Arbitration Treaties:

- Germany agreed with France, Belgium, Poland and Czechoslovakia that any dispute between them should be settled by a conciliation committee.
- France signed treaties of 'mutual guarantee' with Poland and Czechoslovakia. These said that France would make sure Germany did not break the agreement above.

It was also agreed that any conflicts regarding the western borders should be referred to the League of Nations and that France would not be permitted to cross into Germany should there be any dispute between Poland or Czechoslovakia.

The Locarno Pact was hailed as a major triumph in many quarters. It was the first time that Germany had recognised the western border imposed at Versailles and accepted the loss of Alsace-Lorraine and Eupen-Malmédy to Belgium. For the French, there was a guarantee of support from the British, should there ever be another German attack, while for the Germans, it meant the 1923 invasion could never be repeated. The French agreed to withdraw the forces occupying the Rhineland and, although this was initially postponed in January 1925 because of Germany's refusal to comply with the disarmament obligations imposed at Versailles, it was achieved over the next five years and without Stresemann giving any assurances that Germany would disarm. The city of Cologne, for example, was evacuated by the French in 1926.

However, although the Arbitration Treaties with Poland and Czechoslovakia offered some guarantees, the eastern borders were not recognised in the same way. For Stresemann, this might be a triumph of diplomacy, but for the 'new' states in the east, the pact seemed far less satisfactory and almost a recognition of the disinterestedness of powers like Britain and the USA as to their future. The real reason behind the omission was that Britain and Italy were not sure they could enforce decisions there, particularly since the USSR was not part of the negotiations.

Stresemann regarded Locarno as his greatest achievement – and he was rewarded by Germany's acceptance into the League of Nations as a permanent member of the council and the Nobel Peace Prize in 1926.

In his address to the League of Nations in September 1926, Stresemann said:

> In many respects the League is the heir and executor of the treaties of 1919. Out of these treaties there have arisen in the past, I may say frankly, many differences between the League and Germany. I hope that our cooperation within the League will make it easier in future to discuss these questions. In this respect mutual confidence will, from a political point of view, be found a greater creative force than anything else. Germany desires to cooperate on the basis of mutual confidence with all nations represented in the League.

3

Of course, not all Germans agreed with Stresemann's analysis of what was needed or how to go about it. Stresemann's apparent willingness to conciliate offended the nationalists and particularly those army officers, such as Seeckt, the Commander in Chief of the German army who believed that Germany should work with Russia to overthrow the independent Poland created in 1919 and set out to avoid all disarmament through collaboration with the Red Army. Until his dismissal in 1926, Seeckt was a bitter opponent of Stresemann.

However, Stresemann could take pride in the fact that he had established Germany's position as an equal partner in diplomatic negotiations with the three major western powers – France, Britain and the USA and, strategically, he had achieved a good deal with very little loss to Germany. He might expect a revision of the eastern frontier to follow in due course and, in the meantime, Germany could quietly work through the Treaty of Rapallo with the Soviet Union, to undermine some of the military provisions of Versailles. Indeed, in 1926, the two countries signed the Treaty of Berlin which confirmed the earlier Rapallo agreement.

Cross-reference

For the Treaty of Rapallo, refer to page 116.

Assessment of Stresemann

Clearly, Stresemann was both an able politican and a skilful and influential diplomat, but whether he was fully deserving of the praise given by Carr in Source 1 remains in dispute. While he liked to appear the champion of European cooperation, his long-term aim was a revision of the Versailles Treaty. He had, after all, been an outspoken nationalist during the First World War and he desperately wanted to make Germany a great, and perhaps, dominant, power once more. It could be argued that his commitment to 'fulfilment' was no more than a devious policy to cover up his nationalist agenda and it must be remembered that Stresemann's policies provided Germany with far more than the country gave up – American money and protection from a French invasion together with hopes of revisions to the eastern borders. What is more, he maintained the secret military arrangements with the USSR and so laid the basis for Hitler's later foreign policy. However, this judgement may be too harsh. Stresemann certainly chose to follow the route of negotiation and compromise and was fully aware that Germany's recovery depended on moderation and on maintaining good relations with the West. He never regarded the Russian alliance as any substitute for that and in his actions he showed courage in the face of opposition, intelligence in the way he set about his tasks and determination in the way he saw them through.

Activity

Talking point

Write a speech to support or oppose the view that: 'Gustav Stresemann did not deserve the Nobel Peace Prize'. Give your speeches to the rest of the class and try to come to a class decision as to whether or not this statement is true.

Question

How successful was Stresemann as chancellor and foreign minister in serving Germany between August 1923 and the end of 1925?

The economic and political strength of the Weimar Republic by 1925

Economic recovery

By 1925, Germany appeared more stable and more prosperous. The combination of the new currency, the Dawes Plan, Schacht's work at the Reichsbank where interest rates were kept high to attract foreign investment, and the Locarno agreements helped improve Germany's situation enormously. American loans helped kickstart the economy. Industrial output had, in any case, reached its pre-war levels again by 1923 and it grew rapidly from 1924 (and was to double by 1929).

Fig. 3 *Mass production in Germany in the 1920s*

■ Cross-reference

The growth of cartels in the pre-war years is outlined on pages 37 and 69.

■ **Did you know?**

Cartels

Cartels are formed from industries engaged in similar or allied productive processes. They reduce competition, protect prices and allow more of the profits to be reinvested, for example, in research. 'IG Farbenindustrie', set up in 1925, monopolised the country's chemical and drugs industry and was the largest industrial business in Europe. Its firms produced goods ranging from synthetic dyes and artificial textiles (e.g. rayon) to nitrogen production and dynamite. *Vereinigte Stahlwerke'* linked firms engaged in the production of coal, iron and steel and controlled more than 40 per cent of Germany's iron and steel production and 36 per cent of its coal.

German industry underwent extensive 'rationalisation' as new management and production techniques were introduced, and antiquated equipment replaced with new modern machinery. The fact that Germany had to hand over many of its materials as reparations at the end of the war opened the way for this new start and, with American finance, the big industrialists began to buy out or forge cooperative agreements with smaller firms to form cartels. By 1925, there were around 3,000 such cartel arrangements in operation including 90 per cent of Germany's coal and steel production.

Advances were made in the chemical industry, often the result of wartime research, as, for example, in the large-scale production of artificial fertilisers at the Leuna works near Merseburg. The car and aeroplane industries also developed, although they were still too expensive for the average German.

The inflation rate was close to zero and living standards rose as wages began to increase from 1924 and loans helped to finance roads, schools, municipal buildings, public works and the provision of housing. Massive population growth had created an acute housing shortage in Germany by the early 20th century and the overcrowding and insanitary conditions of working-class city accommodation had been linked to political instability. Consequently, state initiatives to provide affordable homes were of great importance for future stability. 178,930 dwellings were built in 1925 – over 70,000 more than in the previous year – and in 1926 there were to be 205,793 more new homes. Money was spent on welfare payments and health improvements and in 1924 new schemes of relief were launched. A new system of binding arbitration introduced in October 1923, whereby an outside arbitrator had the final say in industrial disputes (in accordance with the provisions of the constitution), also reduced the number of strikes. Women also found they had an increasingly central role to play as economic improvements opened up more opportunities, both for unskilled and professional women.

Key

...... Industrial production

--- Coal production

— Steel production

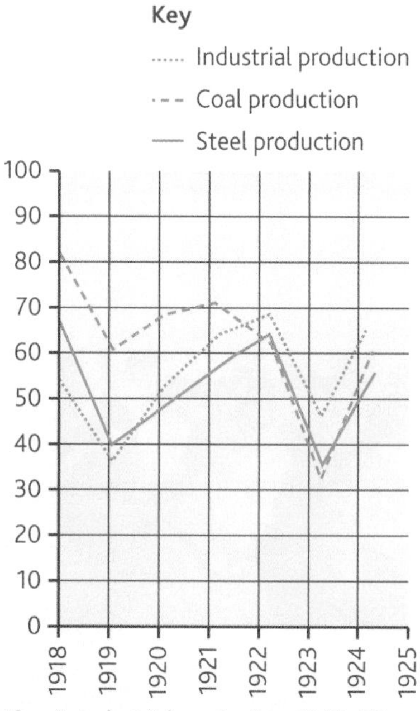

Fig. 4 *Industrial production, 1918–25*

■ **A closer look**

Welfare reforms of the Weimar Republic

The Weimar Republic saw a huge expansion of social welfare programmes, in accordance with the terms of the second section of the Weimar constitution. In 1920, war victims' benefits were added to the social welfare system already established under the Second Reich. In 1922, a Youth Welfare Act was passed, and in 1923, in the wake of the economic troubles of that year, unemployment relief was consolidated into a regular programme of assistance, financed by employees and employers. 1923 also saw the 1913 agreement between doctors and insurance providers over the treatment of state-supported patients integrated into a new National Insurance Code, and a single agency for the administration of social insurance programmes for miners was set up, replacing the 110 separate associations which had controlled miners' insurance schemes before this. In 1924, a modern public assistance programme was introduced to replace older poor relief legislation and, in 1925, the accident insurance programme was reformed, allowing diseases linked to certain types of work to become insurable risks. In 1927, a national unemployment insurance programme was also established. Such welfare programmes were a heavy burden on the state, which had to increase taxes to help pay for them. In 1923, when many became unemployed during the period of passive resistance and yet claimed unemployment benefit, the system nearly collapsed.

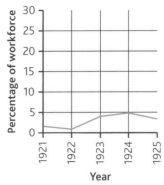

Fig. 5 *Unemployment, 1921–5*

A closer look

The Rhineland

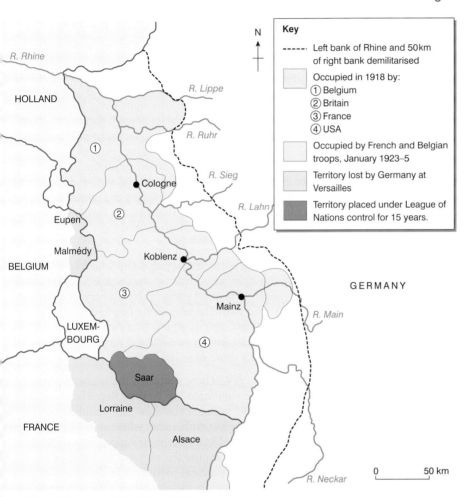

Fig. 6 *The Rhineland and the Ruhr by 1925*

The Rhineland was of an area of major economic and strategic importance to Germany. Between the rivers Rhine and Main lay the Ruhr valley coalfields, the 'Powerhouse of Germany' and the heart of German industry. This was also the area which bordered Belgium, Luxembourg and France and which the French had insisted was demilitarised by the Treaty of Versailles. Furthermore, Germany had lost Eupen-Malmédy, Alsace and Lorraine by that treaty while it had been agreed that the Saar would be run by the League of Nations for the benefit of the French for 15 years. The whole area was also occupied by allied troops to ensure German compliance.

Cross-reference

For more detail on industrial disputes and the political extremism of 1919–22, see pages 112–17.

■ Activity

Research exercise

The 1920s are often referred to as the 'golden age' of Weimar culture. The removal of censorship allowed for a flowering of cultural activity in painting, film, art and architecture and music. Select one of these areas to research and prepare a PowerPoint® presentation for the rest of your group. Pay particular attention to what your art form can teach about political attitudes at the time.

The Ruhr became the centre of troubles in 1923 when French and Belgian troops occupied the area to force the payment of reparations, but gradually over the years 1924–5 the situation improved for Germany. Stresemann's attempts at 'fulfilment' led to the French withdrawal from the Ruhr and, by agreeing to the western borders and permanent demilitarisation in the Locarno Pact of 1925, the allies also began to withdraw their occupying troops. However, the area still contained some occupying forces as late as 1930 and the Saarland did not return to Germany until 1935.

Political developments

In the improved economic climate from 1924, extremism on both the left and right declined. There was a fall in the number of right-wing paramilitary organisations and the threat of political assassination receded. Public opinion had been much swayed by the murder of Walther Rathenau in 1922 and, although the Munich Putsch of 1923 had been a reminder of the continuing grievances of the right wing, by 1924 the glamour and appeal of the militaristic right had faded. By encouraging terror and murder, the right-wing paramilitaries had sent public opinion firmly on to the side of the republic and the brighter outlook engendered by economic stability, international understanding and intellectual freedom encouraged greater hope and confidence. As well as having less popular support, there were fewer opportunities for the opposition to criticise the democratic government, and many of the earlier extremist leaders were, in any case, either dead or imprisoned.

The establishment of the *Reichsbanner*, a republican defence force, in 1924, provided a new rallying point, attracting some who had previously been more disposed to the right-wing military organisations and helped spread pro-republican sentiment in all parts of the country. It attracted over a million members who swore to honour its flag and constitution. In the Reichstag too, the political picture grew more stable after May 1924, as cabinets held office for longer periods and the parties of the governing coalition kept their share of seats.

There were two elections in 1924. These indicated the greater support returning to the parties which supported the Weimar Republic – the SPD, DDP, DVP and Centre. Over 61 per cent voted for pro-republican parties in May 1924, and 67 per cent in December and, whereas in May the Nazis polled 6.5 per cent of the vote, by December their support was down to 3 per cent. The Communist Party on the left also saw its fortunes fall after May 1924, whilst the nationalist political parties of the right, who began to accept the republic and work within, rather than against it, found their electoral position weakening from December. The Conservative right-wing DNVP joined a Reich coalition government in January 1925.

The greater stability of the governments of these years can be seen in Table 2 on page 137.

■ Activity

Statistical analysis

Study Table 1. Work with a partner to explain these election results. Different pairs may like to explain different elections. You will need to consider the historical context of each election and should also comment on the implications of the result for the republic.

Table 1 *Political parties in Germany*

Number of MPs elected	Left wing				Centre		Right wing	
	Communist (KPD)	Independent Social Democratic Party (USPD)	Social Democrat Party (SPD)	Democratic Party (DDP)	Centre (Catholic) Zentrum	Conservative (DVP)	Nationalist (DNVP)	Nazi (NSDAP)
1919	0	22	165	75	91	19	44	0
1920	4	84	102	39	85	65	71	0
May 1924	62	-	100	28	81	45	95	32
December 1924	45	-	131	32	88	51	103	14
1928	54	-	153	25	78	45	73	12

*Taken from Murphy, D., Morris, T. and Fulbrook, M., **Germany 1848–1991**, 2008*

Table 2 *Chancellors and ruling coalitions, 1923–5*

Appointment	Chancellor	Party	Members of governing coalition
November 1923	Wilhelm Marx	Z	DDP, Z, DVP (centre-right)
June 1924	Wilhelm Marx	Z	DDP, Z, DVP (centre-right)
January 1925	Hans Luther	No party	DDP, Z, BVP, DVP, DNVP (centre-right)

*Adapted from Hite, J. and Hinton, C. **Weimar and Nazi Germany**, 2000*

Key profiles

Wilhelm Marx

Wilhelm Marx (1863–1946) was from a middle-class background and had served as a lawyer and judge. He became a member of the Centre Party and was first elected to the Reichstag in 1910. He was appointed chancellor of Germany in November 1923 after Stresemann annoyed the Social Democrats by refusing to deal firmly with the perpetrators of the Munich Putsch. They left the coalition and caused its collapse. Stresemann remained as foreign secretary and Hans Luther as finance minister. However, in the general election of December 1924, decline in support for the Catholic Centre Party forced Marx from office. After a spell as prime minister of Prussia, he once again became chancellor of Germany in May 1926.

Hans Luther

Hans Luther (1885–1962) came from a wealthy business background. He had studied law before joining Berlin's civil service. He served as a town councillor and mayor. He was a moderate and not affiliated to a particular political party but was recognised as a good administrator. Consequently, in December 1922, he was appointed Minister of Food and Agriculture. He went on to become finance minister under Stresemann and Marx and, in 1924, was involved in the negotiation of the Dawes Plan. Luther replaced Marx as chancellor in December 1924 and joined with Stresemann in negotiating the Locarno Pact in 1925. The signing of this treaty resulted in the DNVP withdrawing its support for the government and Luther was forced to resign.

■ Cross-reference

Field Marshal von Hindenburg is profiled on page 84.

Fig. 7 *Field Marshal Paul von Hindenburg as president of Germany*

■ Activity

Revision exercise

Write a newspaper article commenting on the recent election of Paul von Hindenburg as president of Germany. As well as presenting the 'news', you could include some biographical details and editorial comment. Decide what type of paper you are writing for before you begin. Different members of the group could write for a communist, a socialist, a Conservative and a Nazi newspaper and the articles could be compared.

In 1925, following Ebert's death, Germany got its first popularly elected Reich president. The choice of 77-year-old Field Marshal Paul von Hindenburg, a military figure of strongly Conservative views, might not appear to have been the most promising step forward, yet he acted constitutionally and his position helped reconcile many on the right to acceptance of the regime, giving it an air of respectability.

The presidential election of 1925

Ebert, the first president of the Weimar Republic, died on 28 February 1925. He had been indirectly elected by the National Assembly, but his successor would need to be elected according to the terms of the Weimar constitution, which meant that a full German election would have to be held. Under the terms of the constitution, unless a candidate received more than 50 per cent of the vote in the first round of voting, there had to be a second ballot and it was possible to nominate alternative candidates in this second ballot. Hindenburg did not stand in the first round of voting on 29 March, when there were seven candidates including Wilhelm Marx for the Centre, Thälmann for the Communists and Ludendorff, who stood as a Nazi Party candidate. No clear winner emerged and in the second round the candidate on the political right, Karl Jarres, withdrew in favour of Hindenburg. Hindenburg allegedly consulted the exiled ex-Kaiser before he, reluctantly, agreed to stand. The number of nominees was reduced to just three – Hindenburg, Marx and Thälmann and, because the SPD had agreed to support Marx, it was thought that Marx had a good chance of winning. However, because of Thälmann, the left vote was split and in the election on 26 April, Hindenburg won with 48.3 per cent to Marx's 45.3 per cent (Thälmann trailed with 6.4 per cent). Some of his supporters hoped he would destroy Weimar democracy but they were to be disappointed.

The extent of stability in 1925

Despite all the promising signs, the Weimar Republic was not economically stable in 1925 and, although much had improved, the German economy suffered from a number of underlying weaknesses. Firstly, it relied extensively on foreign credit. After America had agreed to supply large sums under the Dawes Plan, other foreign investors were quick to see the potential of lending to Germany. They offered highly precarious short-term loans at a time when the internal credit squeeze made domestic investment more difficult. Overseas investors hoped to get rich quick, from a country with huge economic potential, but the extent of Germany's dependence made it extremely vulnerable to any recession in the world markets.

Secondly, Germany was living beyond its means. The welfare state developments overstrained resources and the pensions burden made huge demands on state finance. Furthermore, the government tried to provide some compensation to those who had lost out from hyperinflation, but it was unable to meet expectations and was even forced to set up a lottery to decide the order in which it might try to meet its commitments! Trade unions and state arbitration forced wage increases, regardless of productivity, whilst cartels stifled competition and kept prices high for the domestic consumer. Although industrial disputes were kept in check by government intervention, not all workers were better off and unemployment after 1925 was considerably higher than before it – reaching 10 per cent in 1926.

Nor were economic improvements universal. Agriculture remained in recession because of foreign competition and, with worldwide over-production after the war and a combination of high farm indebtedness, low prices for agricultural produce and high taxes drove some farmers into bankruptcy and political radicalism.

Finally, Germany's economic performance compared to that of the rest of the world was not particularly impressive (as shown in Table 3).

Table 3 *Comparative economic performance from a baseline of 1913 = 100*

	1920	1925
World	93	121
USA	122	148
Germany	59	95
UK	93	86
France	70	114
USSR	13	70
Italy	95	157
Japan	176	222
Sweden	97	113

Political stability was equally, if not more, elusive. The aftermath of hyperinflation had left a bitter aftertaste affecting large numbers, particularly among the middle classes who had previously been republican supporters, and the bitterness over who got compensation and at what levels kept some resentments alive. Furthermore, extremism survived. Although Hitler was in prison in 1924, he was busy writing *Mein Kampf,* while his supporters were developing clearer policies and organisation, and being galvanised to fight elections. Their success in May 1924 proved a positive encouragement and, as the election results show, extremism on both left and right remained as a very real presence. The Communists still had a relatively strong following in certain working-class areas and it was common for extremists to disturb the meetings of opposing groups.

The 'Grand Coalition' which brought Stresemann to prominence as chancellor was not to last and, although actual cabinets may have been more continuous, the pattern of short-lived coalitions continued as parties struggled to make satisfactory working agreements. Such coalition governments were often 'minority' governments and there were frequent changes of allegiance. More worryingly, politics saw an increasing dominance of the right. The Centre Party and DDP (which split after its poor showing in 1924) moved further to the right, while the DVP suffered disunity. The DNVP participated in the 1925 coalition, yet still retained an anti-republican outlook. Consequently, although the SPD remained the biggest single party, it did not serve in any government from November 1923. It was poorly led and tended to move leftwards (in reaction to the other parties), leaving the way open for this right-wing dominance.

Failure to take steps to reform the judiciary, civil service and universities also left a powerful right-inclined elite, which remained strongly anti-republican. Judges continued to interpret legislation in their own fashion, undermining the credibility of republican legislation and justice. The traditional elites still managed the economy and dominated industry, and right-wing dominance was also reinforced in the way the army continued to evade the Treaty of Versailles. A general staff organisation was secretly maintained and German officers trained with the Red Army in Russia, using tanks and aircraft forbidden at home.

The election of President Paul von Hindenburg was another manifestation of this growth of nationalist and Conservative feeling. He was hardly a promising choice for future political stability. A monarchist in outlook, he was fundamentally opposed to republican government. Furthermore, he was old and had little understanding of economics.

> Even during the years of relative stabilisation all was not well with the Weimar Republic. The profound social, economic, political and psychological destabilisation which had set in with the First World War had not really been overcome; underlying economic problems remained, and the relative political stability of Weimar's 'golden years' rested on shaky foundations.

4   *Adapted from Fulbrook, M. (ed.),* **German History Since 1800**, *1997*

Fig. 8 *The golden years of 1920s production*

Activity

Thinking point

1 Using the information you have read, copy and complete the table below to show the strengths and weaknesses of the Weimar Republic in 1925.

2 Given the position in 1925, is it possible that the Weimar Republic could have survived?

	Strengths	Weaknesses
Economic		
Political		
Social		
Other		

Activity

Revision exercise

At the end of the previous section, you were invited to consider whether the Weimar Republic was 'doomed from the start'. In order to answer this question, copy and complete the table below as fully as you can, with reference to the development of the republic 1918–25.

Criticism	How true?	How important?
The November 1918 revolution was too 'incomplete'		
The constitution contained many flaws		
The Treaty of Versailles destroyed the republic		
Economic problems were too great for the republic to cope with		
The republic had too many political enemies		
The leaders and parties of the republic had insufficient commitment to make it work		

Learning outcomes

In this section you have learnt how the Weimar Republic dealt with the challenges it faced from both the left and right wing after 1919, and how, after the experience of hyperinflation and currency collapse, it recovered and was strengthened by the work of Schacht and Stresemann. You have considered the strengths and weaknesses of the republic by 1925 and should now be in a position to advance your own views as to the reasons for its survival and its prospects for the future.

 Examination-style questions

(a)   Explain why the German currency collapsed in 1923.   *(12 marks)*

 For part (a), you will need to explain both the long and short-term causes of the currency collapse. Refer briefly to the problems created by wartime financing and post-war borrowing. The main part of your answer, however, should address 1923 and should consider the impact of the French invasion of the Ruhr and why this damaged the currency further. Don't forget to supply a supported conclusion.

(b)   How far did the work of Schacht and Stresemann bring financial recovery to the Weimar Republic by 1925?   *(24 marks)*

 For part (b), you will need to assess the measures taken by Schacht and Stresemann to restore the German economy and look at both their strengths and weaknesses. You should decide what your answer will be before you start writing and should try to make some judgement about their success.

Between 1871 and 1925, Germany struggled to find political stability. The proclamation of the German Empire in 1871 had been greeted by the Liberals, who had sought unification for so long, as the dawn of a new modern era by which Germany would travel down the path to full democracy. However, the Conservative Prussian elites viewed it differently. For them, this was the final stage in Prussia's aggrandisement and a confirmation of Prussian values and military prowess. This unsteady combination of traditional Conservatism and progressive Liberalism provided the uncertain foundations upon which the new Germany was founded and, even in 1925, these same two forces of right and left were threatening to tear the country apart should the soothing blanket provided by the economic recovery of 1924–5 be taken away.

The German Empire of 1871–1918 never lived up to the Liberals' political aims of a democratic constitutional state based on the sovereignty of the people. Instead, it developed as an outmoded authoritarian regime, based on the power and influence of the Prussian monarchy and propped up by the military and the traditional elites. Circumstances were rendered all the more difficult by the enormous industrial growth that Germany experienced in this period, which changed the basis of the economy and transformed society. However, rather than accepting and adapting to such change, the kaisers, chancellors and ministers saw it as their duty to uphold the traditional Prussian social order, and the dominance of the Junker military officers and bureaucrats.

Germany's social and political structure prevented newer progressive forces from playing an effective part in national life. Instead, the forward-thinking political groupings – the left-wing (progressive) Liberals, the

Social Democrats and the Catholic Centre party – were branded by Bismarck as 'enemies of the Reich' and the cooperation of the mass of workers and middle ranking business interests through responsible political parties was rejected. Whereas in other industrialising nations such as Britain or the USA a prosperous middle class formed the backbone of Liberal constitutional government, in Germany such developments were prevented.

From 1878, Bismarck's Anti-Socialist Law prevented the working man from playing his part in the politics of the state and, although Bismarck's social welfare reforms were designed to reconcile the workers to the state, divisions along class lines and resentments remained strong. To control the empire, from 1878–9 Bismarck tried to strengthen Conservatism and increasingly worked to muzzle the Reichstag that he had helped to create. His attempt to forge an alliance of 'steel and rye' between the industrialists and landowning elites simply reinforced the Prussian tradition and, from this time onwards, the Second Reich was marked by a deep discrepancy between its social make-up and its political system. The historian Michael Bracher has suggested that:

> A great modern state was being governed according to the ideas and forms of a pre-industrial and pre-democratic autocracy.

The historian J. M. Roberts has written along similar lines:

> In Berlin, trade unionists and businessmen bowed and scraped to a haphazard collection of courtiers and soldiers who clanked about in the trappings of the Middle Ages and strove to keep alive an ideology and an ethos that had vanished with the Stuarts in Great Britain and with the Revolution of 1789 in France.

Bismarck's dismissal in 1890 precipitated further crisis. The empire of 1871 had been based on a very special relationship between Bismarck and Kaiser Wilhelm I. Once that had gone, the German political system was fully exposed to the defects of the Imperial structure. Wilhelm II was far less adept than Bismarck at juggling the conflicting forces around him and his attempts to set up a personal rule, whereby his ministers would simply be his servants, proved a disastrous failure. The chaos at the centre of government affected German foreign policy too, and a kaiser who could not resolve tensions at home turned instead to Weltpolitik and the creation of a large navy. He pursued a policy of gesture, bluff and intimidation on the European stage and called on national forces at home to 'rally round' his leadership.

The ploy again failed, creating enemies abroad and doing little to relieve internal problems. Ultimately, it plunged Germany into the disaster of the First World War and, although this brought momentary relief in the *Burgfrieden* or truce between the differing political interests in 1914, its effects did not last for long. The prolonged war intensified the divisions over domestic policy which had never gone away and, what is more, they became entwined with war aims and made the divisions between left and right more marked than ever before.

In the autumn of 1918, after four exhausting years of warfare, the Nationalism that had appeared to unite the country in 1914 had evaporated and Germany was returned once more to its divided state, as spontaneous revolutionary risings brought the Second Reich to its humiliating end on 9 November 1918. The military collapse appeared to have opened the way for a new beginning and, with the Social Democrats as the main leading political force, a return to the Liberal ideals of 1871 seemed possible. However, similar mistakes were repeated. In their desire to avoid extreme left-wing radicalism and a slide into Communism as had been witnessed in Russia in 1917, the socialists were prepared to strike bargains with the old elites, who were never destroyed as a political force. They cooperated with the army, permitted and used the Freikorps, allowed judges and civil servants to retain their positions and kept their demands for reform moderate, so as not to offend the old Imperial establishment.

Whilst a new constitution brought the long-awaited parliamentary democracy and gave the German people direct influence over their own politicians, the political future was clouded by the decisions taken at Versailles and the spread of the 'stab in the back' legend by those right-wingers who could not reconcile themselves to a new-style government. Putsches, assassinations and strong feelings on both the left and right were intensified by economic crises and a French invasion of the Ruhr, which led to the catastrophic hyperinflation of 1923. By the time the revaluation of the mark had helped bring stabilisation, the Weimar Republic had already lost many of its original middle-class supporters, who had witnessed the depreciation of their savings.

By 1925, Germany had undergone a degree of economic and political recovery, fuelled by foreign loans and international agreements. There was a new spirit of optimism as minds were filled by the illusory image of the 'golden twenties'. However, the dispute between the state and its component territories, the attitude of the judiciary and conflict with the armed forces were all reminders that authoritarianism had not been destroyed. Furthermore, it was the figurehead of these Conservative forces, Field Marshal Paul von Hindenburg, who had remained loyal to the emperor after Wilhelm II's abdication in 1918, and was openly anti-republican, who was elected by a majority of the German people to become the second president of the republic in 1925.

The old struggles were far from dead. Throughout this 1871–1925 period, Germany had been more reactionary than revolutionary. Although the Weimar Republic had given the illusion of being progressive, in fact, limited real change had occurred and the old political and social struggles remained. The leaders of the Weimar Republic had left the fundamentals of German political life as they had found them, and had consequently allowed the balance of internal political power to continue undisturbed.

It is hoped that, through your reading of this book, you are now able to answer the question which has underpinned this history of the development of Germany from 1871 to 1925: why was Germany never able to develop as a stable Liberal parliamentary democracy? You will appreciate that the answer to this question is multi-faceted and far from straightforward, and yet it is fundamental, not only to an understanding of subsequent German history, but also to an appreciation of the problems which beset emergent states in the present-day world. By exploring the many aspects of Germany's development over this period of 55 years, you should be able to appreciate the complexity of interests and ideas which affected Germany and understand the forces which restricted the decision-makers' freedom of manoeuvre. You should, in short, be in a position to form judgements of your own about the issues, events and developments which this book explores and, in so doing, appreciate the lessons that are there to be learnt from this study of continuity and change within Germany.

Glossary

absolutism: this refers to complete and undisputed authority in the hands of a monarch. This was the normal style of government in 18th century Europe, although some rulers, such as Friedrich II of Prussia (1740–86), turned their monarchies towards 'enlightened absolutism', by granting some freedoms.

ADAV: German Workers' Association. This group was led by Ferdinand Lassalle, and was committed to a socialist programme which included the redistribution of wealth and the abolition of private property. It had 15,000 members by the middle of the 1870s.

Agrarian League: this was a pressure group founded in 1893 to represent the interests of the large landowners of Germany. It was politically Conservative and sought protectionist tariffs.

B

Bundesrat: this is the name given to the Federal Council of the North German Confederation established by Bismarck in 1867 and, from 1871, of the empire. It had 43 members during the time of the Confederation and 58 under the empire. In both cases, Prussia had 17 of the seats and the rest were divided between the other Länder. It is sometimes referred to as the Reichsrat.

C

Centre Party: this refers to the party founded in 1870 to represent the German Catholics and the minorities opposed to Bismarck. It is known in German as the *Zentrum* or Z. The party was strong in the southern German states, particularly Bavaria and also in the Rhineland. It was determined to preserve the position of the Catholic Church, especially in education. It was Conservative regarding the constitution and favoured greater decentralisation, but it was quite Liberal in its attitude to social reform. The party moved further to the left during the First World War and was an important force during the Weimar Republic. It survived until its voluntary dissolution under Hitler in 1933.

chancellor: the chancellor was the head of the government. In the German Empire he was deemed the 'highest official of the Reich'. He was appointed by the Kaiser and led a government directed by 'state secretaries'. He presided over the Bundesrat (or Reichsrat). Most chancellors were also Minister–President of Prussia, although Bismarck gave up that post briefly in 1872–3 and Caprivi 1892–4. In the Weimar Republic, the Reich chancellor and, on his advice, Reich ministers, were appointed and dismissed directly by the Reich president. The chancellor was responsible to the Reichstag and had to resign if faced with a parliamentary vote of no confidence. He presided over a cabinet and determined policy.

Communism: Communism is derived from Marxism and refers to an economic and social system in which everyone works together for the common good. In a perfect communist society, all would be equal and there would be no need for any money. Government and states would wither away and society would be classless. Communists saw this 'perfect' state as the ultimate stage in human history.

F

Free Conservatives or (from 1871) *Reichspartei* **(FKP):** the *Freikonservative Partei* was founded in 1866. It represented landowners, industrialists and businessmen. Its members were strong supporters of Bismarck and it attracted a number of former Liberals. It changed its name in 1871 but had no real party organisation or programme until 1906. It had an influence greater than its numbers and favoured an assertive foreign policy. It opposed radical reform at home, although it was prepared to accept cautious modernisation.

Freikorps: literally the Free Corps, this was the term given to the right–wing paramilitary units which served in the early years of the Weimar Republic. They mainly comprised ex–officers and they were involved in campaigns of political terror. They were also used by local governments as auxiliary forces to put down left–wing rebellion.

G

German Communist Party (*Kommunistische Partei Deutschlands* **or KPD):** this was founded in December 1918/January 1919 by a merger of the radical left and the Spartacist League. It was primarily the party of the unskilled working class and the unemployed and it became involved in political rebellions in the 1920s.

German Conservative Party (*Deutsche Konservative Partei* **or DKP):** this party adopted the name in 1876. It mainly represented the Protestant and aristocratic Prussian Junker landowners. It was the most right wing of the political groups of the Imperial period and detested the Reichstag because it was elected by universal suffrage. It was dominant in the Prussian Landtag (state government).

German Democratic Party (*Deutsche Demokratische Partei* **or DDP):** this was a Liberal party of the Weimar Republic.

It was founded by a group of intellectuals and businessmen in November 1918 and merged the Progressive Liberal Party of the Imperial period with the left wing of the National Liberal Party. Its members helped draft the Weimar constitution.

German Nationalist People's Party (*Deutschnationale Volkspartei* or DNVP): this nationalist party of the Weimar Republic was founded in November 1918 and brought together the Conservative and extreme right–wing elements of the Imperial period. It also attracted supporters from the right wing of the former National Liberal Party. Its leaders represented the landed interest and sections of heavy industry. It was a monarchist party, hostile to the Weimar Republic and opposed to Versailles.

German People's Party (*Deutsche Volkspartei* or DVP): this was a middle–class Conservative party during the Weimar Republic. Founded in December 1918 and led by Gustav Stresemann, it attracted those national Liberals who felt excluded by the DDP. It was anti–republican and committed to a revision of the Treaty of Versailles, but it joined Weimar coalition governments and defended the interests of businessmen and the upper middle classes.

Junker: this was a term used to describe Prussian aristocrats. The Junker class was specifically the class of large Prussian landowners who lived east of the river Elbe and dominated the institutions of Prussia, and more indirectly, of the Reich. They were involved in running the army and manning the bureaucracy and were Conservative in outlook.

Kaiser: this is the German word for emperor (deriving from the Latin 'Caesar', which also gives rise to the word Czar).

Kulturkampf: this means literally

a struggle for culture and was, in practice, Bismarck's attack on the Catholic Church and its political influence in Germany.

L

Liberal/Liberalism: Liberalism was a political concept spread by the French revolution that encouraged personal and economic freedom. Personal freedoms included the right to property and the freedom of speech, of religion and of participation in politics. Economic freedoms included free trade and non–interference in working relationships. The term 'liberal' came to imply those in favour of representative, elected government. In Germany, the Liberals came to form the National Liberal Party (see below).

N

National Liberal Party (*Nationalliberale Partei* or NL): this party was founded in November 1866 by members of the Progressive Party in the Prussian *diet* who left to support Bismarck. This was the party of the Protestant middle classes. It was supported by wealthy, well–educated men such as bankers, merchants and civil servants. It favoured free trade, a strong Germany and a constitutional Liberal state. After 1875 it grew more Conservative as its members felt threatened by the growing strength of the Social Democratic Party.

Nationalism: this implies loyalty to a nation, rather than to a ruler or ideology and it became a major force in 19th century Europe, following the defeat of Napoleon and the economic changes of that century. Nationalism manifested itself in the unification of both Germany and Italy, in the drive to enlarge the empire through colonisation and in the determination to acquire and maintain 'great power' status.

Navy League: the *Deutscher Flottenverein* was founded in 1898 following the campaign for the first navy law and was one of a number of right–wing pressure groups at that time. It was mainly

controlled by businessmen and Conservative politicians with a lower middle–class nationalist following. By 1914 it had over a million members.

P

Progress Party (*Deutsche Fortschrittspartei* or DFP, also known as the Progressives): this was founded in June 1861 by a radical group that broke away from the Liberals in the Prussian Landtag. It was led by landowners and educated middle classes and precipitated the crisis over the Army Bill, which brought Bismarck to power, by refusing to approve Wilhelm I's budget. The party believed in a Liberal, constitutional state but disliked centralism and militarism and so was not very supportive of Bismarck. Its members wanted to extend the powers of the Reichstag and, in 1884, the left wing broke away in more open opposition. This was the only middle–class grouping to oppose Bismarck.

putsch: this is the German word for a sudden, violent political uprising such as the Kapp Putsch (1920) or Munich Putsch (1923).

R

Reich: this is the German word for an empire or state. It was used to describe the Holy Roman Empire (the First Reich), the German Empire of 1871–1918 (the Second Reich) and the Nazi regime of 1933–45 (the Third Reich). It was also sometimes used of the Weimar Republic, referring to the state.

Reichsbank: also known as the *Deutsche Reichsbank*, this was Germany's central bank from 1875–1945. It became independent of the state in 1924, in accordance with the terms of the Dawes Plan, although the Nazis reassumed state control in 1937.

Reichsfeinde: this was a term used in the Bismarckian era to describe 'enemies of the Reich'. In practice these were the more progressive forces in the state, such as the Progressive Liberals, the socialists and the Centre Party.

By labelling such as *Reichsfeinde*, Bismarck inhibited the growth of responsible political parties representing all areas of life.

Reichsrat: the Reichsrat was the Upper House of the German parliament during the Weimar Republic (although it is occasionally used of the Bundesrat under the empire). It represented and was indirectly elected by the federal states, which each had at least one vote on legislation within it. Although it participated in law–making, the Lower House (the Reichstag) could override its decisions by a two–thirds majority.

Reichstag: this term was used of the parliament of the North German Confederation from 1867 and then the parliament of Germany from 1871–1945. From 1871, the Reichstag was the principal parliamentary body. It was directly elected on the basis of a franchise for all males over 25 years. However, it was not fully representative as there was no redistribution of seats to take account of demographic change. It also had only limited power over the chancellor's government (until the last weeks of the First World War). During the Weimar Republic, electoral procedures were reformed, women were given the vote on an equal basis with men from the age of 20 and proportional representation was introduced.

right wing/left wing: in politics it is quite normal to talk about 'the left' and the 'right' or left– and right–wing. This division derives from the time of the French Revolution when deputies who supported the monarchy sat on the right, while more radical opponents, who wanted change, sat on the left in the assembly. Thus 'right' has come to mean Conservative – and, at its most extreme, authoritarian and in favour of strong rule – while left means pro–reform, in favour of the workers and, at its most extreme, Communism.

S

Social Democratic Party (*Sozialdemokratische Partei Deutschlands* or SPD (also SAPD)): formed in 1875 in Gotha by the merger of the General Workers' Association (ADAV) and the Social Democratic Workers' Party (SDAP), the new party was at first known as the SAPD. This party represented the working classes and worked with the trade unions. It supported a reduction in the power of the elites and the extension of welfare reforms. Its most extreme members wanted a total overthrow of the constitution, but the majority were prepared to work within it in order to bring about better conditions for the masses. It developed its own subculture of clubs, cooperatives and educational and leisure associations. The SPD played a decisive role in the creation of the Weimar Republic.

Socialism: Socialism seeks to achieve greater equality by reducing private profit, extending opportunities and spreading welfare reforms. In its most extreme form, Socialism is generally referred to as Marxism or Communism. However, more moderate forms of Socialism are less violent.

soviet: a soviet was a council, usually of workers, soldiers, sailors and perhaps peasants, who tried to take control of the local area. They were left–wing bodies modelled on those set up in Russia at the time of the revolutions of 1917, but their leadership was not always communist.

U

USPD: this refers to the Independent Social Democratic Party (*Unabhängige Sozialdemokratische Partei Deutschlands*) which was formed in April 1917 by a radical group of Social Democrats who broke away from the majority party, in frustration at the SPD's continuing support for the Imperial government. It became a significant political party by the end of the war and, in November 1918, joined with the SPD in the Council of People's Representatives, although it left after a few weeks. It broke up in October 1920 when the majority of its members joined the KPD

Bibliography

Students

Abrams, L. (1995) *Bismarck and the German Empire*, Routledge.

Farmer, A. and Stiles, A. (2007) *The Unification of Germany 1815–1919*, Hodder Murray.

Hite, J. and Hinton, C. (2000) *Weimar and Nazi Germany*, Hodder Murray.

Layton, G. (2005) *Weimar and the Rise of Nazi Germany 1918–1933*, Hodder Murray.

Layton, G. (1995) *From Bismarck to Hitler, Germany 1890–1933*, Hodder Murray.

Lee, S. J. (1999) *Imperial Germany 1871–1918*, Routledge.

Lee, S. J. (1998) *The Weimar Republic*, Routledge.

Teachers and extension
General reference and broad coverage

Berghahn, V. R. (1987) *Modern Germany: Society, economy and politics in the twentieth century*, 2nd edition, Cambridge University Press.

Blackbourn, D. (1997) *The Fontana History of Germany 1780–1918: The Long Nineteenth Century*, Fontana–Harper–Collins.

Carr, W. (1991) *A History of Germany 1815–1990*, Hodder Murray.

Craig, G. A. (1999) *Germany 1866–1945*, Oxford University Press.

Evans, R. J. (1987) *Rethinking German History, Nineteenth century Germany and the origins of the Third Reich*, Harper Collins.

Fulbrook, M. (2004) *A Concise History of Germany*, 2nd edition, Cambridge University Press.

Geiss, I. (1997) *The Question of German Unification 1906–1906*, Routledge.

Kitchen, M. (2005) *A History of Modern Germany 1800–2000*, Blackwell.

Martel, G. (ed.) (1992) *Modern Germany reconsidered 1870–1945*, Routledge.

Rohl, J. C. G. (1970) *From Bismarck to Hitler*, Longman.

Seligmann, M. and McLean, R. (2002) *Germany from Reich to Republic, 1871–1918*, Palgrave.

Bismarck

Eyck, E. (1964) *Bismarck and the German Empire*, Norton.

Feuchtwanger, E. (2002) *Bismarck*, Routledge.

Lerman, K. (2000) *Bismarck*, Longman.

Stern, F. (1977) *Gold and Iron, Bismarck and the Building of the German Empire*, Allen and Unwin.

Taylor, A. J. P. (2003) *Bismarck: The Man and Statesman*, Sutton.

Waller, B. (1997) *Bismarck*, 2nd edition, Blackwell.

Williamson, D. G. (1997) *Bismarck and Germany 1862–1890*, Longman.

Kaiser Wilhelm II and the Second Reich

Berghahn, V. R. (2005) *Imperial Germany 1871–1914*, Berghahn Books.

Clark, C. (2000) *Kaiser Wilhelm II*, Longman.

Feuchtwangwe, E. J. (2001) *Imperial Germany 1850–1918*, Routledge.

MacDonogh, G. (2000) *The Last Kaiser*, Weidenfeld and Nicolson.

Mommsen, W. J. (1995) *Imperial Germany 1867–1918*, Hodder.

Palmer, A. (1978) *The Kaiser*, Weidenfeld and Nicholson.

Porter, I. and Armour, I. D. (1991) *Imperial Germany 1890–1918*, Longman.

Retallack, J. N. (2008) *Imperial Germany (Short Oxford History)*, Oxford University Press.

Retallack, J. N. (1996) *Germany in the Age of Kaiser Wilhelm II*. Palgrave Macmillan.

Rohl, J. C. G. (1996) *The Kaiser and His Court: Wilhelm II and the Government of Germany*, Cambridge University Press.

Rohl, J. G. and de Bellaigue, S. (2004) *Wilhelm II: The Kaiser's Personal Monarchy 1888–1900*, Cambridge University Press.

Simpson, W. (1995) *The Second Reich – Germany 1871–1918*, Cambridge University Press.

Wehler, H. U. and Traynor, K. (1997) *The German Empire 1871–1918*, 2nd edition, Berg Publishers.

The Weimar Republic

Balderston, T. (2002) *Economic and Politics in Weimar Germany*, Cambridge University Press.

Bookbinder, R. (1996) *Weimar Germany*, Manchester University Press.

Evans, R. J. (1990) *Proletarians and Politics: Socialism, Protest and the Working Class in Germany before the First World War*, Harvester Wheatsheaf.

Hiden, J. (1996) *The Weimar Republic*, Longman.

Kolb, E. (2004) *The Weimar Republic*, 2nd edition, Routledge.

Nicholls, A. J. (2000) *Weimar and the Rise of Hitler*, 4th edition, Macmillan.

Peukert, D. (1993) *The Weimar Republic*, Hill and Wang.

Acknowledgements

The author and publisher would also like to thank the following for permission to reproduce material:

p12 Quoted in Stern, F., *Gold and Iron: Bismarck, Bleichroder and the Building of the German Empire,* 1997; p17 Quoted in Lee, S., *Imperial Germany,* 1999; p19 Quoted in McKichan, F., *Germany 1815–1939: The Rise of Nationalism,* 1992; p22 Quoted in Mitchell, I. R., *Bismarck and the Development of Germany,* 1980; p26 Williamson, D., *Bismarck and Germany 1862–1890,* 1990; p28 Stiles, A., *The Unification of Germany,* 1990; p30 Mitchell, I. R., *Bismarck and the Development of Germany,* 1980; p31 Simpson, W., *The Second Reich,* 1995; p32 McKichan, F., *Germany 1815–1939: The Rise of Nationalism,* 1992; p33 Stiles, A., *The Unification of Germany,* 1989; p34 Simpson, W., *The Second Reich,* 1995; p36 Porter, I. and Armour, I., *Imperial Germany, 1890–1918,* 1991; p36 Table 4, taken from Stapleton, F., *The Kaiserreich – A Study Guide,* 2002; p36 Table 5, taken from Lee, S., *Imperial Germany,* 1999; p41 Simpson, W., *The Second Reich,* 1995; p43 Prince von Bülow, *Memoirs: Early Years and Diplomatic Service 1849–1897,* 1932; p45 McKichan, F., *Germany 1815–1939: The Rise of Nationalism,* 1992; p47 Palmer, A., *The Kaiser, Warlord of the Second Reich,* 1978; p47 McKichan, F., *Germany 1815–1939: The Rise of Nationalism,* 1992; p48 Röhl, J., Gaines, J., Wallach, R., *Young Wilhelm: The Kaiser's Early Life 1859–1888,* 1998; p53 Layton, G., *From Bismarck to Hitler: Germany 1890–1933,* 1995; p54 Simpson, W., *The Second Reich,* 1995; p55 Lee, S. J., *Aspects of European History 1789–1980,* 1988; p56 Craig, G., *Germany 1866–1945,* 1981; p56 Porter, I., and Armour, I., *Imperial Germany 1890–1918,* 1991; p56 Lee, S., *Imperial Germany,* 1999 p59 Traynor, J., *Europe, 1890–1990,* 1993; p60 Berghahn, V. R., *Imperial Germany 1871–1914: Economy, Society, Culture and Politics,* 1994; p61 Simpson, W., *The Second Reich,* 1995 p63 Lee, S., *Imperial Germany,* 1999; p72 Extracts from 'The Erfurt Programme'. McKichan, F., *Germany 1815– 1939: The Rise of Nationalism,* 1992; p75 Stackelberg, R. and Winkle, S. A., *The Nazi Germany Sourcebook,* 2002; p75 Stackelberg, R. and Winkle, S. A., *The Nazi Germany Sourcebook,* 2002; p77 Pinson, K. S., *Modern Germany: Its History and Civilisation,* 1966; p77 Fischer, H. W., *Private Lives of Kaiser William II and his Consort,* 1909; p77 Wolfson, R., *Years of Change: European History 1890–1945,* 1978; p79

Wolfson, R., *Years of Change: European History 1890–1945,* 1978; p79 McKichan, F., *Germany 1815–1939: The Rise of Nationalism,* 1992; p86 Asprey, R. B., *The German High Command at War,* 1991; p93 McKichan, F., *Germany 1815–1939: The Rise of Nationalism,* 1992; p94 Hite, J. and Hinton, C., *Weimar and Nazi Germany,* 2000; p96 Laver, J., *Imperial and Weimar Germany 1890–1933,* 1992; p100 Hugo Preuss, author of the Weimar constitution speaking in 1923. Quoted in McKichan, F., *Germany 1815–1939: The Rise of Nationalism,* 1992; p104 Adapted from Bracher, K. D., *The Nazi Take-over: History of the Twentieth Century No. 48,* 2000; p110 Adapted from Nicholls, A. J., *Weimar and the Rise of Hitler,* 2000; p115 The Reich Chancellor, Wolfgang Kapp, 13 March. From Laver, J., *Imperial and Weimar Germany 1890–1933,* 1992; p115 Lockenour, J., *Soldiers as Citizens,* 2001; p117 Hiden, J., *The Weimar Republic,* 1974; p117 Fritz Ernst, a German historian, recalls his own experience of the early years of the Weimar Republic. From Ernst, F., *The Germans and their Modern History,* 1966; p121 Quoted in Howarth, T., *Twentieth Century History: the world since 1900,* 1987; p123 Quoted in Howarth, T., *Twentieth Century History: the world since 1900,* 1987; p124 Quoted in Howarth, T., *Twentieth Century History: the world since 1900,* 1987; p128 Carr, W., *A History of Germany,* 1991; p130 Schacht, H., *Stabilizing the Mark,* 1927; p132 *The League of Nations Official Journal, Special Supplement No. 44, p.51, No. 22;* p140 Fulbrook, M. (ed) *German History Since 1800,* 1997

Photographs courtesy of:

Alinari/TopFoto p26; Ann Ronan Picture Library pp40, 56, 67; Edimedia Archive pp2, 12, 15, 35, 39, 55, 61, 73, 78, 89, 91, 105, 108 (top), 108 (right), 122, 124, 133; Getty p vi; The Literature Archive pp 21, 31 (left); Photo 12 pp17, 57, 63, 143 (right); James Staniforth p119; Topfoto pp18, 71, 112, 131, 140; World History Archive pp1, 23, 30, 31 (right), 34, 41, 45, 47, 49, 51, 59, 60, 76, 77, 79, 81, 84, 87, 88, 93, 94, 96, 100, 106, 113, 114, 118, 125, 127, 128, 138, 143 (left)

Cover photograph © Hayden Richard Verry/Alamy

With appreciation to Image Asset Management for Photo Research. Special thanks to Jason Newman and Ann Asquith

Index